THIRD WORLD EDUCATION

REFERENCE BOOKS IN INTERNATIONAL EDUCATION
VOLUME 44
GARLAND REFERENCE LIBRARY OF SOCIAL SCIENCE
VOLUME 911

THIRD WORLD
EDUCATION
QUALITY AND EQUALITY

EDITED BY
ANTHONY R. WELCH

GARLAND PUBLISHING, INC.
A MEMBER OF THE TAYLOR & FRANCIS GROUP
NEW YORK AND LONDON
2000

Published in 2000 by
Garland Publishing, Inc.
A member of the Taylor & Francis Group
19 Union Square West
New York, NY 10003

10 9 8 7 6 5 4 3 2 1

Library of Congress Cataloging-in-Publication Data

Third World education : quality and equality / edited by Anthony R.
   Welch.
       p.   cm. -- (Garland reference library of social science : v.
   911. Reference books in international education : v. 44)
     Includes bibliographical references and index.
     ISBN 0-8153-1394-2 (alk. paper)
       1. Education—Developing countries Cross cultural studies.
   2. Educational equalization—Developing countries Cross cultural
   studies.   3. Academic achievement—Developing countries Cross
   cultural studies.   I. Welch, Anthony R.   II. Series: Garland
   reference library of social science : v. 911.   III. Series: Garland
   reference library of social science. Reference books in
   international education : vol. 44.
   LC2607.T55   1999
   370'.9172'4—dc21   99-31491
                                                                    CIP

Cover photo: Courtesy of AusAid.

Printed on acid-free, 250-year-life paper.
Manufactured in the United States of America

Contents

v

Series Editor's Foreword

This series of scholarly works in comparative and international education has grown well beyond the initial conception of a collection of reference books. Although retaining its original purpose of providing a resource to scholars, students, and a variety of other professionals who need to understand the role played by education in various societies or world regions, it also strives to provide accurate, relevant, and up-to-date information on a wide variety of selected educational issues, problems, and experiments within an international context.

Contributors to this series are well-known scholars who have devoted their professional lives to the study of their specializations. Without exception these men and women possess an intimate understanding of the subject of their research and writing. Without exception they have not only studied their subject in dusty archives but have lived and traveled widely in their quest for knowledge. In short, they are "experts" in the best sense of that often overused word.

In our increasingly interdependent world, it is now widely understood that it is a matter of military, economic, and environmental survival that we understand better not only what makes other societies tick, but also how others, be they Japanese, Hungarian, South African, or Chilean, attempt to solve the same kinds of educational problems that we face in North America. As the late George Z. F. Bereday wrote more than three decades ago in *Comparative Methods in Education*: "[E]ducation is a mirror held against the face of a people. Nations may put on blustering shows of strength to conceal public weakness, erect grand façades to conceal shabby backyards, and profess peace while secretly arming for conquest, but how they take care of their children tells unerringly who they are" (New York: Holt, Rinehart and Winston, 1964, p. 5).

Perhaps equally important, however, is the valuable perspective that studying another education system (or its problems) provides us in understanding our own system (or its problems). When we step beyond our own limited experience and our commonly held assumptions about schools and learning in order to look back at our system in contrast to another, we see it in a very different light. To learn, for example, how China or Belgium handles the education of a multilingual society; how the French provide for the funding of public education; or how the Japanese control access to their universities enables us to better understand that there are reasonable alternatives to our own familiar way of doing things. Not that we can borrow directly from other societies. Indeed, educational arrangements are inevitably a reflection of deeply embedded political, economic, and cultural factors that are unique to a particular society. But a conscious recognition that there are other ways of doing things can serve to open our minds and provoke our imaginations in ways that can result in new experiments or approaches that we may not have otherwise considered.

Since this series is intended to be a useful research tool, the editor and contributors welcome suggestions for future volumes, as well as ways in which this series can be improved.

Edward R. Beauchamp
University of Hawaii

THIRD WORLD EDUCATION

CHAPTER 1

Quality and Equality in Third World Education

ANTHONY R. WELCH

> *Everyone has a right to education. Education shall be free, at least in the elementary stages. Elementary education shall be compulsory. Technical and professional education shall be made generally available, and higher education shall be equally accessible to all on the basis of merit.*
>
> *Education shall be directed to the full development of the human personality and to the strengthening of respect for human rights and fundamental freedoms.*
>
> —UNIVERSAL DECLARATION OF HUMAN RIGHTS (1948),
> ADOPTED BY THE UNITED NATIONS, ARTICLE 26

Starkly evident in this, and the following, chapters are some of the tensions of attempts to provide quality education for all—especially in a context of expanding populations and of heightened levels of aspiration, and at a time of significant global change and uncertainty—political, economic, and cultural.

The chapters in this volume are by specialists drawn from many parts of the world, and address issues of quality and equality in diverse settings: the Middle East, Africa, Latin America, the West Indies, Asia, and the Pacific Rim. For China watchers, the rewards are particularly rich: Price uses the "mirror of China" to examine relations of hierarchy and democracy in Chinese society and education, Epstein analyses questions of class and inequality in Chinese education, and Orton sets her analysis within the context of a theory of mutual intercultural relations, based, *inter alia,* on the work of Johann Galtung. Arnove's insightful analysis of Nicaraguan education examines tensions between quality and quantity, within the context of both the educational revolution introduced by the leftist Sandinistas (FSLN), and the succeeding, more conservative

UNO (National Opposition Union) regime, headed by Violeta Chamorro, which, after years of struggle, came to power at the elections of 1990. Just as one of the principal weapons used by the Sandinistas in Nicaragua was a mass literacy campaign, so too Frank Youngman analyses the Botswana literacy campaign of the 1980s, revealing, *inter alia,* some of the contradictions in the aspirations of the participants as against the language policies and economic objectives underlying the campaign. The effects on the social order in Botswana, including some of the contradictory effects for ethnic minorities, are also revealed. Tavassoli, Welch, and Houshyar also reveal the profound effect of social and economic influences upon the quality and equality of educational provision. Their analysis of Iran shows that, despite major efforts, the combined effects of the explosion of population in recent decades (which shows no sign of abating), severe financial constraints, literacy problems, persistent gender differences, uneven development (especially between rural and urban areas), and war prevailed against an increase in either quality or equality of education. Hickling-Hudson's powerful critique of educational reforms which do not at the same time attempt to equalise society is applied to two examples: the "Reform of Secondary Schools" project, the success of which was bedevilled by the extent of social stratification in Jamaica; and revolutionary and postrevolutionary educational reforms in Grenada, including the effects of foreign invasion in 1983. This analysis too, as with that of Tavassoli et al., reveals the extent of influence of factors well outside education, upon both quality and equality of education. Abu-Duhou further underlines the significance of independence in her analysis of the limits of reform in Palestine. Briefly, her study of educational reform in the Palestine Occupied Territory reveals a colonialist context (Wolpe 1975, Hassanpour 1993, Welch 1988, 1996) which sets narrow limits to prospects of improving educational quality and equality. Recent events have only underscored these concerns, despite the singular importance of education to Palestinians as a means of escape from landlessness and joblessness, at least for their children. Last but by no means least, Angela Little, whose work on the phenomenon known as the Diploma Disease is well known, examines the importance of educational qualifications for Sri Lanka over the past twenty years or so. She examines exit rather than entry criteria in determining the quality of educational experience, placing her analysis in the context of political and economic changes in Sri Lanka over the past two decades. The increasing mismatch between production of larger numbers of educated young people, and the inability of the labour market to absorb such numbers of skilled personnel, has led to significant escalation in the qualifications demanded for even basic labour market entry.

Quality of schooling is an issue of great urgency for all of the Third World settings that are treated in this volume. What is equally apparent, however, is that there is no overall definition for this key term. Is quality of education tied to cultural and political independence, as implied by several of the case studies which follow? Is it a matter of providing well-qualified teachers, good quality materials, and well-equipped schools, in an era when, for many Third World countries, expanding populations and heightened demand are set against a background of increasing fiscal restraint, making it increasingly difficult to cater in even a basic sense to popular aspirations for education? Is quality to be found in curricula which provide enhanced options and skills to all young people in society? Certainly, notions of quality are inextricable from the dominant set of values and form of culture in a society—which means that constructions of quality are socially indexed—they change over time, and vary according to political and cultural context. To give only two, rather obvious examples (each treated in the case studies which follow), what comprised good quality schooling under the regime of the Shah was deemed wholly inadequate and inappropriate in postrevolutionary Iran (Tavassoli, Welch, and Houshyar in this volume). What is thought to be good quality education by the Israeli authorities in Palestine is strongly resisted by Palestinians struggling to assert their own educational vision (Said 1994, Abu Duhou in this volume).

Even where efforts have been made to establish agreed indices of educational quality, such as by the World Bank, or among Organisation for Economic Cooperation and Development (OECD) countries, such products are often either contested, or unable to be applied universally due to technical difficulties. The World Bank's understanding of quality is often not shared by educational practitioners and politicians of the Third World, into which the bank wishes to extend its influence (see below). Equally, the recent development of an index of educational quality by the advanced industrialised nations of the OECD club does not extend easily, if at all, to many countries in the Third World, where, *inter alia,* basic statistics are all too often lacking. While the countries of the OECD have substantially extended the range of indicators of educational quality in recent years, to cover, for example, both expenditure (and sources of finances), participation rates at different levels of education, unemployment among youths and adults, progress in reading achievement, and university graduation rates, Heyneman illustrates that less than one half of of the OECD indicators are available for countries in the Middle East and North Africa (1996, 5–7), a phenomenon which is emblematic of the problems of data quality in many parts of the Third World, and which is both exemplified and addressed to some extent in this volume. Data are not always systematically collected, or complete, in all Third World states, and sometimes political considerations, national or international, ensure that it is difficult for scholars to gain access to that information that is available. In some cases too, teachers fail to cooperate with efforts to collect system data, on the grounds that, for example, compliance might lead to a the mandating of a new curriculum with which they were unfamiliar, or that compliance might take time away from the demands of an extra job, needed to supplement the teacher's meagre income. Head teachers, too, report false data at times: for example, inflated enrolments, where they have grounds to hope that this might result in extra textbooks, or a somewhat increased budget. In addition, failure to transfer data (accurately or at all) from schools to ministries, and lack of consensus about definitions and categories, all mean that data quality is at times very imperfect (Chapman and Boothroyd 1988, Abu-Duhou in this volume, Puryear 1995, World Bank 1995, 50–52), a situation which enhanced international economic competition, severe economic difficulties, and the heightened sense that education systems significantly underpin national economic success may have exacerbated, rather than mitigated.

Questions of quality in education can be (and all too often are) seen in terms of simple economic measures and formulae, or alternatively, in terms of educational indices that more closely approximate the real quality of classroom education that many of the people experience. In Burkina Faso, for example, in the mid 1990s, basic instructional materials are still absent from the majority of classrooms, while surveys of learning achievement revealed that some areas of the country now have lower levels of achievement than were found in 1991. Despite real efforts made over the last few years, a recent survey revealed that the ability to read simple texts with some understanding was present in only some 20 percent of pupils. Despite efforts to mass-produce cheap instructional materials for both teachers and pupils, the devaluation of the local currency meant that "few families can now afford to buy the books" (*Education for All* 1996, 29). In such a context, and with a curriculum which fails to relate to the lived experiences of the majority of children, "schools often succeed in little more than producing unemployed and poorly adapted young people" (*Education for All* 1996, 29). For this to change, it has been estimated that an increase of non-salary expenses of somewhere between 40 and 300 times the rate spent in many Third World contexts needs to occur (Heyneman 1996, 9). The chimerical quality of fulfilling anything like the demands that this statistic implies is underlined starkly by the increasing economic difficulties faced by many Third World states over the last decade (see below).

One of the issues such a bleak scenario raises is the extent to which indices of educational quality should embrace the relative status of the dispossessed and marginal in societies, that is, the most disadvantaged groups. To what extent should the schooling and opportunities available to girls be taken as a central index of educational quality, in contexts where their disadvantage has been so marked, historically? To what extent is the decision by Benin, for example, to exempt girls in rural areas from the payment of fees, or the move to allow pregnant girls to attend classes in Burkina Faso, a gain in quality of education, and not merely in equality?

From this same perspective, one can ask the extent to which conventional, economistic measures of educational quality include, much less mitigate, the experience of the substantial numbers of children and adults who never enter the formal schooling system. It has been estimated that the proportion of such students is around 15 percent in Brazil, for example, and as high as 35 percent in impoverished rural areas, a situation mirrored in many Latin American states (Arnove 1997), and in Africa, where "the number of children in the six to eleven age-group still unenrolled grew by some two million since 1990, totalling some 39.3 million" (*Education for All* 1996, 28). World Bank estimates are that some half of all school-age children in Africa are currently not enroled (World Bank 1995, 4). Worldwide, it is predicted that, largely as a result of demographic increases, the total of all unenroled children will rise from 129 million in 1990 to 162 million by 2015 (World Bank 1995, 38).

Adult illiteracy rates, too, which are recognised as being important both to national economic performance and to individual participation in society, also reflect gross disparities of class and gender, both in the Latin American region (Arnove 1997, 83 et passim) and elsewhere (*Education for All* 1996, 27–28). These, too, are predicted to rise over the next decade or so, especially among women (Watson 1996, 46). Surely such social distortions, which are worsening, in some instances, as a result of both demographic increases, and economic and social conditions which have been imposed at both national and international levels over the 1980s and 1990s (see below), must be included centrally in any attempt to assess educational quality. How is quality to be measured? Whatever one thinks of international tests of achievement such as the IEA and others (Purves and Levine 1975), it is undeniable that such tests consistently reveal a large gap between the achievement of classrooms in India (Kumar 1993), Latin America, and Africa and that in industrialised states, a situation which is often attributed to ongoing difficulties with teacher quality, curricula, and pedagogies (Kumar 1993), despite substantial efforts. Reservations about the methodological adequacy of such measures should not be allowed to obscure the stark disparities, not merely between more and less privileged groups within nations, but between countries of the Third World, and the industrialised nations:

> In 1994, the Educational Testing Service found that among a sample of 13 year olds who had completed fifth grade, only the Mozambican student population scored lower than Brazil on measures of mathematics and science achievement. The top five percent of mathematics students in Sâo Paolo, the most industrialised city in the country, achieved scores that were barely comparable to the average score of students in Taiwan, Korea, and Hungary. (Arnove 1997, 82)

Behind such difficulties lie deepening divisions in the international economic order. During the 1960s and at least much of the 1970s, despite difficulties imposed by the oil crisis of the mid 1970s, strong economic growth rates allowed increases in enrolments and demand to be catered to, in many developing countries. By the 1980s however, this long boom was well and truly over:

> In the 1960s, the average annual GNP growth rate for Latin American economies was 5.7%. In the 1970s, the growth rate was 5.6%, despite difficulties caused by the oil crisis. By the 1980s, the average annual GNP growth rate for Latin American countries dropped to 1.3%. As a result of this economic downturn, significant imporovements in education spending made during the 1960s and 1970s were effectively negated by drastic spending cuts in education. (Arnove 1997, 82)

Arnove cites the spectacular example of Bolivia where after a period when per capita expenditure on education increased at an annual rate of

3.62 percent (from 1975 to 1980), the rate of per capita expenditure actually declined by some 42 percent in the following five years (1980–1985). While the extent of reversal might be seen as singular, the pattern was common:

> On average, (unweighted) per capita expenditures in education in Latin America increased by 4.29% per year between 1975 and 1980, while they decreased by 6.14% between 1980 and 1985. The progress in educational finance made in the seventies was undone in the eighties. (Reimers 1991, 332)

And the pattern has continued into the 1990s where, in Africa for example, droughts, civil wars, and trade reversals meant that general economic growth rates slowed to around 2 percent per annum (but see Youngman, in this volume), while demographic increase averaged over 3 percent per annum. In the face of such ongoing disparities between economic and demographic growth rates, external debt for sub-Saharan Africa climbed to some US$130 billion, or 114 percent of aggregate GNP (*Education for All* 1996, 27). In Arab states, the effects of the Gulf War and economic recession of the early 1990s were aggravated by low oil prices, while demographic increase since 1990 averaged 2.6 percent for the region. Heyneman's recent survey of countries in the Middle East and North Africa (MENA) reveals a similar trend to that in Africa and Latin America: high economic growth rates between 1960 and 1985, followed by a precipitous decline in the subsequent decade. In the decade 1985–1994, Egypt's rate of increase in GDP per capita fell from 4.5 percent per year to 0.5 percent, while Algeria's fell from 2 percent to –2 percent over the same period (Heyneman 1996, 1). For this group of countries, GDP per worker fell by an average of around 4 percent in the period 1990–1993, after a period (1980–1990) in which it had already declined by 2 percent per annum (Heyneman 1996, 2–3). Real wage rates for public sector workers have fallen substantially over the last decade in a number of MENA states, while the ratio of public sector to private sector wages has also worsened considerably. In a number of Third World states, low and/or ineffective tax regimes exacerbate the difficulties of financing educational quality improvements, or indeed even difficulties of keeping pace with demographic increases.

The educational consequences of the increasing mismatch between low economic growth rates and high rates of demographic increase were predictable: while total school primary enrolment in sub-Saharan Africa, for example, increased by around 17 percent (or 10.4 million) between 1990 and 1995, reaching a total of 72.3 million pupils in 1995, the number of teachers increased by only 12 percent over the same period. Thus the pupil–teacher ratio worsened to a regional average of 45.4 per teacher (*Education for All* 1996, 27).

A 1995 combined UNESCO–UNICEF study of primary schooling in fourteen least-developed countries revealed that, although some half to three-quarters of children completed primary schooling, pupil–teacher ratios in at least half of the countries surveyed were higher than 40:1, while non-enrolments and drop-out rates were still high, especially in rural areas. Teacher morale was low and absenteeism was high, a phenomenon probably explicable in terms of the low status, wages, and levels of training of teachers in countries surveyed. "Nearly all children were taught in a language at school that was different from the one spoken at home . . . , lack of textbooks was a general problem, [and] in no country did every classroom have a usable chalkboard or sitting and writing places for all children" (*Education for All 1996,* 30). Arnove's study of the effects of neoliberalism in Latin American education further underlines these trends—his data show that, over the decade of the 1980s, teacher salaries fell by an average 35 percent, and in some countries by as much as 60 percent to 70 percent (Arnove 1997, 86, 94).

The continuing, widespread, and disfiguring pattern of children engaged in productive work also ensures that the poorest in society often continue to be denied the benefits of education. Although difficult to quantify, child labour was estimated to embrace between 30 million and 170 million individuals[1] worldwide who work either full or part time, in industries as diverse as mining, rug making, retail, farming, domestic service, and prostitution. The extent of the problem can also be partly guaged by statistics which show that in Brazil, for example, about 15 percent of all children never enter school (in northeastern Brazil this is as high as 35 percent), while, of those who do, less than 20 percent manage to complete eight years of schooling. Children are estimated to comprise around 18 percent of the workforce. In Iran, too, as the chapter in this book by Tavassoli, Welch, and Houshyar illustrates, child labour is both widespread and persistent, despite statutes which mandate eight years of compulsory schooling.

Although children are often very poorly paid, and in some instances unpaid, the impact of child labour is greatest on the poorest sections of society. In such families, child labour still contributes a significant part of household income. For example, research by the World Bank, UNICEF, and others indicate that child labour can often contribute 20 to 30 percent of family income (Myers 1991, Dewees and Klees 1995). In parts of Latin America, for example, child labour contributes approximately 25 percent of household income, and in Java can contribute as much as 40 percent (World Bank, 1995).

Projects such as those in Brazil can alleviate some of the worst excesses of the exploitation of children (which, according to Dewees and Klees (1995), included the murder of an estimated 4,600 children and adolescents in Brazil, by renegade police and vigilante groups, between 1988 and 1990). The comprehensive statutes passed in Brazil in 1990 vested full human rights in children and adolescents, including the right to at least eight years of basic education, with the promise that access to secondary education would be progressively expanded. Although implementation is imperfect, and still subject to considerable opposition, significant progress has been made, including with the assistance of many Brazilian nongovernment organizations (NGOs). Nonetheless, "even after a decade of advocacy and change, it was estimated that only about 500 programs for street children existed in 1990, when it would have required 40,000 such programs to reach all these children" (Dewees and Klees 1995, 93). Sadly, the phenomenon is probably growing, both in former socialist states, now in transition to a capitalist economy, where street children had largely been eradicated, and in newly industrialising states, where the interests of children are also often overwhelmed by the forces of economic deregulation and the abandonment of legislative and social protection:

> In socialist systems, the state organised work and excluded children. Now, free markets and private employers try to get the cheapest labor. With the state's role diminished, and no social protection or legislation in place, child labor is growing. . . . Children, now part of the productivity process, are treated as [short-run] economic goods, rather than society's future (Dewees and Klees 1995, 95).

EXTERNAL INFLUENCES: THE POLITICAL ECONOMY OF STRUCTURAL ADJUSTMENT

Increasing poverty and internal differentiation, as well as child labour, however, are not merely products of national policies and trends. Questions of quality and equality in Third World education also relate to the external context in important ways. The significance of sovereignty in the Third World is heightened by the fact that many states still occupy an uneasy postcolonial situation, in which formal independence from former colonial masters is undermined by continuing economic, cultural (Said, 1994), and political dependence upon First World polities and agencies. This dependence has indeed deepened among many Third World nations over the 1980s (Jones 1992, *Education for All* 1996, Tarp 1993), not merely by an international economic downturn (Carnoy 1986) and by poor economic vistas at home, but also by the increasing globalisation of international economics and ever more insistent, and monolithic, economic agendas by agencies such as the World Bank (see below), and the International Monetary Fund (IMF).

While the effects of such factors have not been uniform, and significant differences among nation states must be acknowledged, the decade of the 1980s has nonetheless been characterised as "disastrous for most of sub-Saharan Africa" (Tarp 1993, 11), and as a "lost decade" for much of Latin America, for example. At the same time, it is crucial to reiterate that the burden of economic hardship was by no means shared equally. Growing disparities in income were evident in Latin America, and elsewhere, whereby women heads of household, the retired, unemployed youth, and street children (the "new poor") were added to the traditional poor, while on the other hand, quite small sections of business and political elites profited substantially, from specific incentives and strategies, to become much wealthier still:

> It was also during this time that certain sectors of the Latin American financial and industrial bourgeoisie, especially those associated with the businesses and investments of the Latin American states, took substantial advantage of investment contracts and state protection through fiscal incentives or market protection. (Boron and Torres 1996, 113, n.2)

What Boron and Torres term the "stampede towards towards stabilization policies, structural adjustment, fiscal discipline, privatization, deregulation and commercial liberalization" (1996, 103) fuelled a trend whereby the wealth ratio between the richest 10 percent and the poorest 10 percent in Buenos Aires grew from 9.9:1 to 12.6:1 over the decade from the mid 1980s. Over the same period, the same ratio in São Paolo and Rio de Janiero rose from 21:1 to 26.6:1. It has been estimated that over 60 percent of the population of Latin America are living in poverty in the mid 1990s (that is, some 292 million persons), and that, unless the situation improves, this number will grow to some 312 million by the new

Table 1.1. Public Expenditure on Education as Percent of GNP: 1990–1993

Region	1990	1993
Sub-Saharan Africa	5.3	5.7
Arab States	5.2	5.8
Latin America/Caribbean	4.1	4.6
East Asia/Pacific	3.0	3.0
South Asia	3.9	3.7
All Developing Countries	4.0	4.1
Least Developed Countries	2.9	2.8

Source: Education for All (1996) 25.

millenium. The process of deepening divisions in the Third World has been termed "belindianisation"—some few individuals in Africa or Latin America live as though in Belgium, while the increasingly impoverished masses live as though in India.

Equally, over the period since 1990, and despite improving enrolment ratios, the group of least developed nations "fell further behind (in terms of their relative investment in education): as a group they devoted only 2.8 percent of GNP to education" (*Education for All* 1996, 25). Table 1.1 reveals some of the differentials among groups of nations over the 1990s.

Such developments often mean that newly industrialised countries (NICs) or, more usually, less-developed countries (LDCs) become more dependent, both economically and politically, "on external actors and events" (Tarp 1993, 146), in particular upon limited injections of foreign capital, either through bilateral agreements, or often through institutions such as the World Bank, which alone now accounts for more than 25 percent of of "all bilateral and multilateral assistance to education" or well over US$2 billion annually (Watson 1996, 43, World Bank 1995). Although the bank is certainly not the only lender for development, indeed it has been argued that

> The World Bank's role as a lender to developing countries has also been partly usurped by the markets. In 1993, the bank lent around $24 billion to them; net private capital flows to developing countries reached $88 billion. (*Economist* 1994b, 67)

It is also true to say that the bank's advice is very influential (Jones 1996), a fact of which it is very mindful, and that it has a reputation which it carefully guards.

The increasing dependence of Third World states upon ideologies of economic orthodoxy only highlights differences which exist between the World Bank and the IMF, on one side (and this should not be taken to imply that there are not differences between these two Bretton Woods institutions[2]), and the expressed development needs, priorities, and prescriptions of either individual Third World nations or of regional groupings of such states. This is not to say that there are no differences within the bank, for example, the cited tensions between US/UK goals of increased support of the private sector, and European support of the poor and the environment (*Economist* 1994b, 67). Nonetheless, Tarp, Jones, and others have underlined the extent to which programme lending by the World Bank was bound more and more tightly to the economic ideology of structural adjustment, over the decade of the 1980s:

> Agreement upon an IMF supported set of stabilization measures has normally been a pre-condition to entering into structural adjustment programmes supported by the World Bank. Similarly, bilateral donors and commercial banks (in the London and Paris club fora) insist that agreements be reached with the Bretton Woods institutions before they support inititiatives concerning balance of payments and development financing. (Tarp 1993, 1)

The public face of unity presented in official World Bank documents, and loans ideologies, should not be taken to imply an absence of dissent in the Third World, however. The UN Economic Commission for Africa (ECA 1989), for example, was one organisation which began from different principles (an emphasis on national self-determination, and the human costs of adjustment) and concluded that conventional programmes by the World Bank "are not only inadequate, but have in fact made matters worse, rather than better" (Tarp 1993, 143). Equally, the Economic Commission for Latin America (ECLA) pursues a broadly neostructuralist approach which rejects many of the principles of structural adjustment, while organs such as UNICEF propound a less strictly economistic agenda, sometimes called "adjustment with a human face."

The argument that pressure to conform to economic orthodoxies such as "structural adjustment"—used by agencies such as the World Bank as a yardstick against which to evaluate funding decisions—has only deepened the difficulties of development, has been made before, by structuralists and dependency theorists. In many parts of Latin America, as well as Africa, and elsewhere such as Papua New Guinea (PNG) (Ahai and Faraclas 1993), national self-determination is substantially undercut by the insistence of funding agencies such as the World Bank and the International Monetary Fund that specific structural economic reforms be undertaken as the price for receiving development loans. Such policies invariably entail "domestic austerity programmes and export promotion" (Carnoy 1986, 209).

In practice, the implementation of such programs denotes the introduction of more regressive taxation policies, sharply reduced public-sector spending in areas such as welfare, housing, public transport, food subsidies, and public schooling (but notably not other major areas of public-sector spending, such as defence) and policies to deregulate the labour market (a euphemism for anti-trade trade-union policies, lax health and safety standards for workers, and inadequate wages and conditions, including salary freezes, especially in the public sector). The tension between resources devoted to education and military spending was by no means an abstract policy choice; indeed, by around 1981, defence spending "had reached approximately 3% of GNP in developing countries, almost as large as a share of output as educational spending" (Carnoy 1986, 209).

As argued above, the impact of such austerity programs does not fall equally upon rich and poor, male and female, rural and urban. The removal of subsidies upon food and other staples has a much greater impact upon poor urban workers than upon their employers. The ending of health and welfare provisions has a greater effect upon poor women and their families than upon wealthier groups. The increasing privatisation of education in several Third World states in recent years has a much greater effect upon poorer families, rural and urban, who are often already struggling to sustain their children at school. Arnove's data on the impact of such policies in Latin America, for example, show that in metropolitan areas of some of the largest cities in Argentina and Brazil, the poorest sections of the community have lost income, while the top income earners have forged ahead (1997, 22):

> As a result, in Latin America, class structures have become more polarized, with the rich and poor sectors separated by an increasingly wider gap . . .

In countries like Brazil and Nicaragua, over 70 percent of the population is living in poverty, over a quarter of the population in situations of extreme destitution. In such conditions, charging even a nominal user fee of approximately one dollar a month for a family with three or four children (often the norm) presents a dilemma: to pay the fee or buy needed medicines, clothing, even food. The situation is so desperate for so many families that these fees are barring access to or driving poor children out of "public" school systems. At the same time, a free nutrition program that provides a daily glass of milk and a snack may induce a family to send a child to school.

One result of the dire economic situation and such educational policies and practices is that as many as twenty percent of school age children in a number of countries do not even enter the school system. This generation of youth will swell the number of totally or functionally illiterate adults whose needs have traditionally been neglected in Latin America.

. . . the number of illiterates in Nicaragua increased between 1980 and 1995, despite a widely acclaimed literacy campaign that taught over four hundred thousand youths and adults to read. In 1995, the illiteracy rate represented approximately one-half the population over the age of ten. Brazil, another country with a history of innovative literacy programs and large-scale national efforts in adult basic education, still has over eighteen million illiterate adults. (Arnove 1997, 91–92)

In addition to the poor, however, many of the middle class also experienced a substantial drop in their incomes, including in Mexico in recent years, under the influence of NAFTA.

Although the core neoliberal economic policies of privatisation and decentralisation have been defended on the basis of extending democracy at the local level, and lessening the inflexibility and corruption of the state, in practice communities are often poorly adapted to take advantage of the additional democratic rights that are supposed to accrue (Welch 1996, Smyth 1993) while neoliberal policies in education, such as introducing fees for secondary schooling and higher education, are often socially regressive and often contradict their stated aims:

Government policies designed to charge user fees for previously free services are likely to bar access to schooling on the part of poor children . . . or drive them out of the school system. Decreasing participation rate in schooling, combined with the lack of priority given to adult education in the current policies of the World Bank and many national governments, is contributing to rising rates of illiteracy throughout the hemisphere. Any responsiveness to local needs and concerns these policies are supposed to promote is countered by attempts to impose national curricular standards and assessment procedures in a number of countries. (Arnove 1997, 88)

Priorities and Strategies: Whose Priorities? What Strategies?

Despite evidence of increasing poverty and social differentiation, and an identified concern with the promotion of equity, it is interesting to note that the recent World Bank review of education (which needs to be understood in the context of previous specific bank policy papers on primary education, vocational and technical education, and higher education), nonetheless holds fast to a clearly economistic view of education, based squarely on human capital theory. The dominant rationale for education within the *Priorities and Strategies for Education* review is economic: "It is largely concerned with finance, economic returns, human resource development, efficiency, effectiveness, costings, private funding and the like" (Watson 1996, 49) which, although perhaps predictable for a bank, is evidently less willing to acknowledge noneconomic dimensions, or other forms of scholarship, than previous bank policies in education (World Bank 1980). In consequence, despite some admission of the inadequacies and unidimensional quality of the methodologies, most of the bank's recommendations and much of its rhetoric is based on rate-of-return analysis in education. This methodology, which seeks to estimate the benefits of education in terms of a complex mathematical calculus, usually takes little or no account of noneconomic factors and does not allow for regional or cultural differences and diversity. *Priorities and Strategies* adopts a banker's approach to education, seeing education in terms of human-capital theory: "primarily a form of investment in the development of knowledge and skills" (Samoff 1996, 8). This undervalues or parenthesises the role of wider benefits not included in earnings (so-called "externalities") which are often associated with more education (such as decreased fertility rates, improved health, and more active citizenship). And as Samoff shows, not only are the limitations of human-capital theory not acknowledged, but rate-of-return analysis is misused in order to justify a prior bank stance in favour of increased private spending on education, rather than public spending (Samoff 1996, 18). Samoff is not the only researcher to criticise the World Bank for failing to adopt a more reasoned and evaluative, rather than hortatory, approach to research findings and techniques that it favours. Moreover, the bank's views are presented with external, clinical detachment, ignoring the perspectives of participants such as teachers and pupils. As Samoff notes, "The medical metaphor casts learners as the objects rather than the subjects of their own learning" (1996, 20).

Another index of this insularity is the fact that no serious consideration is given to policy alternatives (Samoff 1996). The World Bank's *Priorities and Strategies* concentrates upon inputs and outputs and so on, but is silent upon the processes of education, the so-called black box of what goes on in classrooms each day (Samoff 1996, 6–7), despite the fact that some of its own research shows this to be a problem (Heneveld and Craig 1996, xv–xvi). There is no real discussion either of the learning process or of the wider social goals of education. In so doing it perpetuates disjunctions between, for example, African governments and educators, and bank priorities:

> There is little or no attention here, for example, to fostering an inquiring and critical orientation among learners, eliminating discrimination and reducing elitism, promoting national unity, preparing young people for the rights and obligations of citizenship, equipping them to work cooperatively and resolve conflicts non-violently, or developing among learners a strong sense of individual and collective competence, self reliance and self confidence. Yet these features have all featured prominently in statements of Third World leaders and ministers of education over the last three decades. (Samoff 1996, 7–8)

Lastly, and further compounding the narrow context upon which the bank's advice is based, little research completed by specialists outside the bank is considered:

> Of the several hundred research papers cited in *Priorities and Strategies* only a handful are from the very rich UK and Australian and Asian research base [or, one might add, from US scholars not connected with the bank. ARW] Contrary views are therefore not considered or recognised . . . The result is a self fulfilling prophecy. Research data supports the policy that the bank wishes to pursue because the research has already helped to shape that policy. (Watson 1996, 49; see also Samoff 1996)

Upon closer scrutiny, the insistence upon matters of "quality" throughout the document consists largely of concerns about the efficiency with which public funds are expended in education, rather than with the quality of the pedagogical relationship, or the quality of the knowledge gained in schools, despite, as indicated above, substantial evidence, including some by the bank's own researchers, underlining the importance of in-school quality issues.

The phenomenon of "wastage" is also analysed by the bank in ways that gloss over questions of equity and social differentiation. Samoff points to the methodologically suspect nature of lumping together all forms of "wastage," whether good or ill: "disaffected learners who drop out of school, pupils whose poor examination scores lead to their exclusion, and students who score well but who are precluded from continuing by the lack of available places" (Samoff 1996, 20). Once again, such economics overwhelms ethics here in that techniques which simply aggregate all forms of "wastage" actively hide the effects of social inequality, which is an important part of the phenomenon.

Finally, bank recommendations largely ignore the important role of nonformal and adult education,[3] which can be an effective medium both for community learning and for promoting equity (Stromquist 1992), while it argues in a series of grand generalisations (based on a small number of selective examples) that vocational education and training should be given over to employers (privatised), higher education should be made far more based on "user pays" principles, and parental choice and institutional competititon should be extended. The fact that these are the selfsame principles which have dominated educational reforms in a number of industrialised nations over the past decade (often with no more consideration of the role of regional or cultural differences than in *Priorities and Strageqies*), or that there is now a substantial critical literature which points to the divisiveness of such policies (Welch 1996, Smyth 1993, Weiler 1990) is not acknowledged. Nor is there any recognition that processes of structural adjustment are intensifying the processes of differentiation; are indeed impoverishing larger and larger sectors of national populations.

International trends towards a climate of accountability, choice, and efficiency of the last decade or so, influenced by tighter economic circumstances and a move away from the former notion of the welfare state, are reflected in the 1996 review. International mantras of educational reform such as privatisation, enhanced quality, greater responsiveness in education via local/family involvement in school governance, self-managing schools, and increased parental responsibility for (higher) education are all to be found in the latest bank review of education and, as Jones indicates, had been developing for some time.[4] There is little, if any, acknowledgement of cultural or geographic differences, however, in assessing the utility of such proposals, nor any recognition of other (non-economistic) traditions of analysis, which understand the role of education in development rather differently. In this respect, the bank's most recent document is significantly different from its earlier 1980 sector review (World Bank 1980). What is also evident is a clear enunciation of the principles that, while priorities may change, there is only one standard for the setting of priorities:

> While governments determine priorities for many reasons, economic analyses of education—in particular rate of return analysis— is a diagnostic tool with which to start the process of setting priorities. (World Bank 1995, 94)

As Samoff and others (Welch 1993) have argued, this reveals a clear, if underlying, technicist (Habermas 1971 (1978), Marcuse 1968) orientation to policy; that is, that a strategic means-ends orientation dominates the bank's consideration of setting policy goals in education (Jones 1996, 14). This is policy as technique, rather than the realisation of values which have first been openly determined and debated: "That is, not values, not goals, not societal debate, but a particular diagnostic tool should be the starting point for setting priorities in public policy" (Samoff 1996, 4). Educational policies, then, become subject to fundamentally economic considerations and techniques. "The starting point is human capital theory" (Samoff 1996, 5) which the bank wrongly assumes "has no genuine rival of equal breadth and rigor" (World Bank 1995, 21). At the least, this ignores (wilfully?) the substantial critiques of human capital theory which have been developed over the past decade or more (Marginson 1993, Maglen 1990), including some by economists once persuaded of its singular worth and utility (Blaug 1985).

CONCLUSION

The last decade or two of the twentieth century may well come to be seen by historians as one in which economic considerations came to dominate educational policy and practice internationally: "[The educationists] are largely on the sidelines. It is the economists who are still in the ascendancy" (Watson 1996, 59). Indeed, by the mid 1980s it was already being claimed that the "pressures for using the schools for reproduction of the work force have achieved primacy over those on the side of democratic and equalitarian reforms" (Carnoy 1986, 213). The decade to the mid 1990s only served to confirm the prescience of that analysis, and there is little sign of changing priorities. Internationally, education is caught up in a shift from the welfare to the competition state (Cerny 1990, Yeatman 1993, Welch 1996), whereby the state's primary, or only, justification for regulation or intervention is in order to enhance economic growth and national and international competitiveness. This reorientation has profound implications for both the kind and extent of educational provision, and places no inherent limit on the extent of privatisation in education, or on increasing inequities which are often a concomitant of hitching education more and more tightly to the national (and international) economic bandwagon.

What is known is that the era of postwar expansion in education has changed substantially. The first three to four decades after 1945 revealed "a rapid and large increase in the amount of education available to the world's young people . . . in every group of countries, primary, secondary and higher education expanded significantly" (Carnoy 1986, 206).

In the past decade or two, however, the context for educational expansion has changed: "What has changed are the economic constraints for educational planners, and the political-ideological context in which educational decisions are made" (Carnoy 1986, 205). Slower rates of economic growth in some parts of the world have been paralleled by spectacular growth rates among several of the NICs, in particular the so-called Asian tiger economies. This has only widened the gap between such states and others, often in Africa, which continue to languish at the base of the international economic pyramid and in which a combination of ethnic discord (most tragically displayed in central African states such as Rwanda, or in north African Somalia), an ongoing inability to sustain levels of agricultural production adequate to self-sufficiency, and at times ongoing corruption and lack of democracy, conspire to prevent internal development. Much the same factors also make it a less-attractive context to foreign investment, both by transnational corporations and via agencies such as the World Bank.

The increasingly international polarity between developed and developing nations has also arguably sharpened the distinction between those who hold that investment in education should be oriented towards enhancing economic growth, and those who hold that education is a significant source of social and economic mobility and equity.

Those who support the first view argue that an investment in education specifically for growth and in a way that allocates resources in a
growth-efficient way is a crucial contribution to the dynamic of capital
accumulation in any country and by gearing the school system to this
purpose, eventually everyone (even those who don't get schooling) will
be better off. Those who support educational expansion for social
participation in the development process argue that economic growth
without the full participation of all members of society is only partial
development. In addition they contend that by gearing the educational
system to full participation, society can mobilise social resources that
will reduce the costs of schooling and increase school yields. In a sense,
they argue that it is more "efficient" to stress participation rather than
economic efficiency for growth objectives. (Carnoy 1986, 206)

Carnoy pointed to the substantial tension between two divergent aims in
education: on the one hand, preparing pupils to enter a hierarchical world
of work, and on the other, preparing students for active citizenship in a
democratic society, where such exists. The actual contours of the struggle are played out in the context of the contest between more and less
powerful groups in particular societies, a much more internationalised
economic world order and cultural setting, and differing degrees of constitutional protection for dissent.

What is evident in the above dichotomy is different paths to development, each with different implications for the quality and equality
of educational provision. Of relevance too are political and religious
ideologies, which also imply differing models of development, and
conceptions of quality and equality of education. Arguably, as is evident from a number of chapters in this volume, one of the dilemmas
facing contemporary China is the attempt to marry a capitalist path to
economic development with a socialist political and social path. Where
does this leave education, which on the one hand is charged with the
transmission of socialist political ideology to the younger generation,
and which on the other is part of the increasing move towards economic liberalism in contemporary China. Privatisation of educational
provision in 1990s China (Mok 1997) is only sharpening this tension.
Which path should education follow? Equally in Iran, Islamic social
doctrine may conflict with the demands of sectors of the economy,
or of external economic and cultural forces. Education is not immune
from such tensions.

The resolution advanced here is clear: a preference for democracy over technocracy. Given a choice between the economists, wielding rate-of-return analyses as a universal recipe for educational reform, (which, as we have seen, ignores not merely the expressed wishes of those for whom the reforms are designed, but also the particular social and political contours of local contexts), or alternatively, a form of education which responds to the needs of the impoverished, the rural dwellers, the street children, and marginalised women, our clear preference is for an inclusive and democratic mode of reform, and education. Despite the severe economic constraints of the last decade or more, there are still educational choices which contribute to the democratisation of societies. Indeed, it is imperative that this is the case:

> The problems of the quality of education, access, retention, and relevance continue to be central and problematic issues for education, even with the deceleration of the growth and massification of educational systems. However it is inconceivable that the problems of education can be resolved without simultaneously dealing with the problem of poverty and the segmentation of the . . . societies which it is causing.
> (Boron and Torres 1996, 12)

This means that the state must assume central responsibility for providing the widest possible access to education, especially for the poor, whose needs are arguably greater now than ever. Certainly, a path which follows the dicates of neoliberal economics, with its ideology of reduced state activity, more individual contributions to education, and increased deregulation and privatisation of the economy, will only exacerbate the existing chasms between rich and poor, both within and between nations and regions of the world. Equally certainly, the private sector cannot be relied upon to attain equity and democacy in society.

Ultimately, education, as an important means for enhancing the quality of life of the dispossessed, and for providing some form of social emancipation leading to greater equality in society, is either part of the problem or part of the solution. Those regimes that ignore this, in the interests of technocratic recipes in education, whether internal or external in origin, will eventually fail: "in the medium run, democratic governments that remain indifferent to the urgent needs of the poor and to growing poverty may be digging their own graves" (Boron and Torres 1996, 107).

NOTES

1. Under the age of eighteen.

2. The two institutions, which recently celebrated their fiftieth birthdays, were originally established to fulfil different functions. Indeed, part of the reason that it is still suggested at times that these two Bretton Woods institutions should merge is because the IMF has outlived its original rationale—to oversee a monetary system based on fixed exchange rates. Another reason sometimes given is to cut down on bureaucracy (*Economist* 1994b, 16).

3. See, for example, Jones' (1996) Tables, where he reveals that not only does non-formal education (NFE) account for only about 1 percent of total bank expenditures in education, but that NFE literacy projects were not funded at all in the period from 1987–90. Does rate-of-return analysis fail to support its benefits, or is NFE not simply measured by such techniques?

4. "It assumed that, especially for low income countries, that significant levels of finance were available for transfer to the education system, and that privatisation, quality, economic relevance, and equity went hand in hand, whereas public education was marked by inefficiences, declining quality and waste" (Jones 1996, 14). Jones goes on to draw the obvious conclusion: "For low income countries in particular, Bank policies of privatisation and quality enhancement were incompatible and contradictory" (14).

REFERENCES

Ahai, N., and Faraclas, N. (1993) "Literacy and Integral Human Development in Papua New Guinea." In P. Freebody and A. Welch, *Knowledge, Culture and Power: International Perspectives on Literacy as Policy and Practice*. London, Falmer Press.

Arnove, R. (1997) "Neo-liberal Education Policies in Latin America: Arguments in Favour and Against." In C. Torres and A. Puiggros (eds.), *Latin American Education: Comparative Perspectives*. Boul♠r, Westview Press, 79–100.

Blaug, M. (1985) "Where Are We Now in the Economics of Education?" *Economics of Education Review* 4 (1): 17–28.

Boron, A., and Torres, C.A. (1996) "Education, Poverty and Citizenship in Latin America. Poverty and Democracy." *Alberta Journal of Educational Research* 17 (2): 102–14.

Carnoy, M. (1986) "Educational Reform and Planning in the Current Economic Crisis." *Prospects* 16 (2): 205–14.

Cerny, P. (1990) *The Changing Architecture of Politics: Structure, Agency and the State*. London, Sage.

Chapman, D., and Boothroyd, R. (1988) "Threats to Data Quality in Developing Country Settings." *Comparative Education Review* 32 (4): 416–29.

Dewees, A., and Klees, S. (1995) "Social Movements and the Transformation of National Policy: Street and Working Children in Brazil." *Comparative Education Review* 39 (1): 76–100.

Easton, P., Klees, S., et al. (1994) "Asserting the Educational Rights of Street and Working Children: Lessons from the Field." New York, UNICEF.

Economic Commision for Africa (ECA) (1989) *African Alternative Framework to Structural Adjustment Programmes for Socio-Economic Recovery and Transformation.* Addis Abbaba, ECA.

Economist (1994a) "Thoroughly Modern Sisters." 23–29 July: 14–16.

Economist (1994b) "Fit at Fifty?" 23–29 July: 67–68.

Education for All: Achieving the Goal (Working Document) (1996) Paris, UNESCO.

Habermas, J. (1971) "Science and Technology as Ideology." *Toward a Rational Society.* London, Heinemann.

Habermas, J. (1974) *Theory and Practice.* London, Heinemann.

Habermas, J. (1978) *Knowledge and Human Interests.* London, Heinemann.

Hassanpour, A. (1993) "The Pen and the Sword: Literacy Education and the Revolution in Kurdistan." In P. Freebody and A. Welch, *Knowledge, Culture and Power. International Perspectives on Literacy as Policy and Practice.* London, Falmer Press.

Heneveld, W., and Craig, H. (1996) *Schools Count: World Bank Project Designs and the Quality of Education in Sub-Saharan Africa.* World Bank Technical Paper No 303, Washington, D.C., The World Bank.

Heyneman, R. (1996) *The Quality of Education in the Middle East and North Africa.* EMT Working Papers No. 3, Washington, D.C., The World Bank.

Jones, P. (1992) *World Bank Financing of Education: Lending Learning and Development.* London, Routledge.

Jones, P. (1996) "World Bank Policy Objectives in Education." Paper. Ninth World Congress in Comparative Education, University of Sydney, Australia, July.

Kumar, K. (1993) "Literacy and Primary Education in India." In P. Freebody and A. Welch, *Knowledge, Culture and Power: International Perspectives on Literacy as Policy and Practice.* London, Falmer Press.

Maglen, L. (1990) " Challenging the Human Capital Orthodoxy: The Education–Productivity Link Re-examined." *The Economic Record,* December.

Marcuse, H. (1968) *One Dimensional Man.* London, Sphere Books.

Marginson, S. (1993) *Education and Public Policy in Australia.* Melbourne, Cambridge University Press.

Mok, Ka-Ho (1997) "Privatisation or Marketisation? Educational Development in Post Mao China." *International Review of Education* (Special Double Issue: Tradition, Modernity and Postmodernity) 43, 5–6, 547–567.

Myers, W. (ed.) (1991) *Protecting Working Children.* London, Zed Books.

Purves, D., and Levine, A. (1975) *Educational Policy and International Assessment: Implications of the IEA Surveys of Achievement.* Berkeley, McCutchan Publishing Corporation.

Puryear, J. (1995) "International Education Statistics and Research: Status and Problems." *International Journal of Educational Development* 15 (1): 79–91.

Reimers, F. (1991) "The Impact of Economic Stabilization and Adjustment on Education in Latin America." *Comparative Education Review* 35: 319–353.

Said, E. (1994) *Culture and Imperialism.* London, Vintage Books

Said, E. (1994) *The Politics of Dispossession: The Struggle for Palestinian Self Determination 1969–1994.* London, Chatto and Windus.

Samoff, J. (1996) "Limiting Horizons: The World Bank's Priorities and Strategies for Education 1995." Paper. Annual Conference of the Comparative and International Education Society, Williamsburg, Virginia.

Smyth, J. (1993) *A Socially Critical View of the Self Managing School.* London, Falmer Press.

Stromquist, N. (1992) "Empowering Women Through Knowledge: International Support for Nonformal Education." In R. Burns and A. Welch, *Contemporary Perspectives in Comparative Education.* New York, Garland Press, 265–94.

Tarp, F. (1993) *Stabilization and Structural Adjustment: Macroeconomic Frameworks for Analysing the Crisis in Sub-Saharan Africa.* London, Routledge.

Watson, K. (1996) "Banking on Key Reforms for Educational Development: A Critique of the World Bank Review." *Mediterranean Journal of Educational Studies 1* (1): 43–61.

Weiler, H. (1990) "Comparative Perspectives on Educational Decentralisation: An Exercise in Contradiction." *Educational Evaluation and Policy Analysis* 12 (4): 433–48.

Welch, A. (1988) "Aboriginal Education as Internal Colonialism. The Schooling of an Indigenous Minority in Australia." *Comparative Education* 24 (2).

Welch, A. (1993) "Class, Culture and the State in Comparative Education." *Comparative Education* 29 (1).

Welch, A. (1996) *Australian Education: Reform or Crisis?* Sydney, Allen and Unwin.

Wolpe, H., (1975) "The Theory of Internal Colonialism." In I. Oxaal et al. (eds.), *Beyond the Sociology of Development.* London, Routledge.

World Bank (1980) *Education.* Sector Policy Paper. Washington, D.C., The World Bank.

World Bank (1990) *Primary Education: A World Bank Policy Paper.* Washington, D.C., The World Bank.

World Bank (1991) *Skills for Productivity: Policies for Vocational and Technical Education in Developing Countries.* Washington, D.C., The World Bank.

World Bank (1994) *Higher Education: The Lessons of Experience.* Washington, D.C., The World Bank.

World Bank (1995) *Priorities and Strategies for Education.* Washington, D.C., The World Bank.

Yeatman, A. (1993) "Corporate Managers and the Shift from the Welfare to the Competition State." *Discourse* 13 (2): 3–9.

CHAPTER 2

The Tension Between Quantity and Quality in Nicaraguan Education*

ROBERT F. ARNOVE

The goal of balancing the imperatives of educational expansion and improvement has proven to be elusive in Nicaragua, as in other societies. Over the past thirteen years, two dramatically different political regimes have attempted to extend schooling to the mass of Nicaraguan society and gear education to the ends of political legitimation and national development. The intended educational reforms of these regimes, during the period 1979–1992, have reflected diametrically opposed models of development, views of democracy, and conceptions of the appropriate aims, content, and methods of schooling. Despite opposing views and approaches, both the government of the Sandinista National Liberation Front (July 1979–April 1990) and the National Opposition Union (post April 1990) have found transforming inherited education systems an almost intractable problem.

The difficulty of revamping education systems to meet the plans of political regimes is an all-too-familiar phenomenon. Nonetheless, Nicaragua represents an interesting case for purposes of comparative analysis: a dependent and underdeveloped society (see typology in Fägerlind and Saha 1989, 238) that, within a relatively brief period, underwent a revolution to replace a dynastic dictatorship that was almost feudal in nature; pursued a socialist path to development; experienced a counterrevolution organised and supported by the dominant superpower in the region; and, then, by means of national elections replaced the regime in power with a

*This paper is based on my previous publications (Arnove 1986, Arnove and Dewees 1991) and field research conducted in Nicaragua.

government committed to reintegrating the country into the capitalist world economy by following the neoliberal policies of the International Monetary Fund and the World Bank. As I have indicated elsewhere (Arnove and Dewees 1991, 109), studies that examine the unprecedented transitions and transformations in the societies and schools of Eastern Europe, the former Soviet Union, previously one-party states of Africa, and Nicaragua promise to contribute to theory building on the potential as well as limitations of schools to effect social change under radically different types of political regimes.

After contrasting the differing conceptions of the Sandinista National Liberation Front (FSLN) and the National Opposition Union (UNO) concerning the relationship between the quantity and quality of education and democracy, this chapter will examine the extent to which the two governments have been able to accomplish their goals for educational reform. The focus of the chapter will be on tensions, issues, and contradictions involved in balancing the imperatives of educational expansion and improvement. The chapter concludes with reflections on what lessons might be learned from the Nicaraguan case.

EDUCATIONAL GOALS OF THE FSLN

In 1979, a broad coalition of forces led by the Sandinista National Liberation Front (*Frente Sandinista de Liberación Nacional*) overthrew the repressive regime of the Somoza family that had governed the country as its personal fiefdom (see, for example, Carnoy and Torres 1990, 319–20), in combination with a praetorian National Guard, for over four decades. The new regime set out to transform the society, pursuing what might be generally described as a socialist path to development while adhering to the overarching principles of a mixed economy, political and cultural pluralism, and a nonaligned foreign policy.

The education system inherited by the Sandinistas was characteristic of the underdeveloped economy and undemocratic political system of the country over the past forty years. A mass system of public schooling that would foster the education of critical inquiring citizens made little sense in a society characterised by limited opportunity in the modern sector of the economy and constricted opportunity for political participation. Educational statistics in 1979 reflected this situation.

Half the nation was illiterate with more than three-fourths of rural populations unable to read or write. There were under 25,000 students enrolled in adult education programs, many of which were the responsibility of the private sector and church groups. Primary education reached only 65 percent of the relevant age groups; preprimary education was available to a mere 5 percent of children, mostly in private, fee-paying centers. Special education enrolled 355 students. Of those entering the school system, 22 percent completed the sixth grade—38 percent in urban areas and 6 percent in rural areas. Women and the indigenous populations of the Atlantic Coast region were the least schooled of all.

If Nicaragua under the Somoza family could be characterised as an underdeveloped and dependent capitalist society, the new regime quickly delineated a different path to development. As noted by Miller,

> Development and transformation, they [the FSLN] believed, depended in the short run on national reconstruction and in the long run on a transition to socialism. . . . According to this view attainment of such a society required economic growth, extensive redistribution of power and wealth, and broad-based citizen participation. (1985, 30)

Congruent with this model of development, the new guidelines for educational policy set forth these principles:

1. The emergence of the great majority of the people formerly dispossessed and socially excluded, as the active protagonists of their own education.
2. The elimination of illiteracy and the introduction of adult education as priority tasks of the revolution.
3. The linking of the education process with creative and productive work as an educational principle, leading to educational innovation and promoting the scientific and technical fields.
4. The transformation and realignment of the education system as a whole, to bring it into line with the new economic and social model. (UNESCO 1983, 35)

In shaping the education system to be an integral component of the revolution, the leadership of the Ministry of Education envisioned the expansion, improvement, and transformation of education as contributing, respectively, to the democratization of basic social services, the independence of the Nicaraguan economy from foreign domination, and the development of a new model of capital accumulation based on different social relations of production and forms of public and private ownership. The overriding goal of education in Nicaragua during the Sandinistas—as is typical of other revolutionary socialist societies such as Cuba—was "to contribute to the formation of the new man [and woman] and the new society" (Ministerio de Educación (MED) 1981, 139).

This goal was articulated in a national consultation, conducted by the Ministry of Education in January and February of 1981, that involved the participation of thirty mass organisations and 50,000 Nicaraguans participating in the discussion of a fifty-five-item questionnaire concerning the outcomes and shortcomings of the pre-1979 education system and the "Goals, Objectives, and Principles of the New Education System" (see Arnove 1986, 96–98, Barndt 1991, 47–52). One of the tasks of the national consultation was to define what democracy meant in the new society. The most common definition of democracy to emerge from the national consultation was that of "the active participation of the organised people in executive, legislative and judicial actions of the government, as well as participation in the tasks and achievements of the Revolution in the political-social and the economic-cultural [areas]" (see MED 1981, 79).

Although, over time, the FSLN came to define democracy also in terms of representative government,[1] the fundamental notion of what they termed "popular democracy" was broad-based participation in mass organisations to influence decision making in key areas of local and national life. According to junta member and later Vice-President Sergio Ramírez,

> democracy is not merely a formal model, but a continual process capable of giving the people that elect and participate in it the real possibility of transforming their living conditions, a democracy which establishes justice and ends exploitation. (Cited in Ruchwarger 1987, 4; also see Vanden Bem Den 1988)

Quantitative expansion of education in order to reach the mass of previously disenfranchised individuals (notably peasants, workers, women, and indigenous groups) to equip them to participate in the tasks of the revolution, thus, was integrally related to Sandinista notions of democracy. The single most impressive educational undertaking of the FSLN, the national literacy crusade of 1980, was described in these terms:

> To carry out a literacy project and consolidate it with a level of education equivalent to the first grades of primary school is to democratize a

society. It gives the popular masses the first instruments needed to develop awareness of their exploitation and to fight for liberation. (MED 1980, l, MED 1987, 2)

For these reasons, the FSLN, during the initial years of the revolution, gave great emphasis to literacy efforts, follow-up programs of adult basic education, and the expansion of preprimary, primary, and special education, while offering the hope that any student might be able to attend higher education at public expense.

Notions of quality, during the period 1979–1990, involved providing the necessary skills, knowledge, and values that would contribute to enhancing productivity and stimulating economic growth. Closely related to notions of overcoming the economically backward status of the country and its dependency on raw materials exports were efforts to develop curricula and publish textbooks that reflected the new Nicaraguan reality.

Overcoming the nation's dependent economic status was tied to a new model of capital accumulation that involved the state's playing a major role in directing development efforts and controlling certain key areas of the economy (banking, foreign commerce, mining, public utilities). The mixed economy envisioned by the Sandinistas consisted of a combination of publicly owned enterprises, together with a large cooperative sector, and a private sector of individually owned property and enterprises.[2] The educational implications of this new economic model of capital accumulation was an education system that helped bridge the traditional gaps between intellectual and manual work, school and community, and attempted to form a new type of individual who was more predisposed to altruistic and cooperative behaviour, and more willing to make sacrifices on behalf of the nation.

EDUCATIONAL GOALS OF UNO

The coalition of fourteen political parties and alliances that defeated the FSLN in the February 25, 1990, national election has set out to dismantle many of the Sandinista economic and social projects. Similarly, over the past two years, it has taken a number of measures to reverse and modify substantially the educational policies and practices of the Sandinistas. Three months after coming to power, the new government of Violeta Barrios de Chamorro issued in July of 1990 a set of guidelines *(lineamientos)* indicating new directions in education. The document does recognize a number of the educational achievements of the Sandinistas:

some meritorious efforts were made in certain areas of education; . . . coverage was not only extended to sectors of the population traditionally marginalized from education, but also, in spite of considerable economic limitations, former officials tried to accommodate teaching to the country's agrarian and occupational characteristics; . . . officials and technicians from the central MED offices and teachers at all levels made altruistic efforts and sacrifices in return for the lowest state salaries. (MED 1990, l, cited in Arríen 1991, 19)

The overall tone of the document, however, is critical of education during the Sandinista period. Indeed, the 1980 national literacy campaign, programs of adult popular education, and the entire system of state-financed and regulated schooling (primary through higher education) during the period of Sandinista rule, July 1979–February 1990, is viewed by the current government as attempts at state indoctrination to win youth to the revolutionary cause of the Sandinista regime. UNO educational policymakers view the undue emphasis on partisan ideology as polarizing the society, and setting back the overall quality of education and the development of the country.

As Juan B. Arríen, former head of the department of educational planning and development, noted in his prize-winning essay in the Central American history journal, *Envío,*

The new government's education project is built on two essential cornerstones: to erase the ideology that constituted the Sandinista project for 10 years and to uphold the neoliberal economic project, adapting components and elements of education to its consolidation and development. (1991, 24)

The neoliberal project which is being implemented throughout Latin America and other regions follows the austerity measures and structural readjustments recommended by the International Monetary Fund and the World Bank to reduce a country's external debt and fiscal deficits, control inflation, and promote economic growth. These measures involve drastically reducing the state administrative apparatus and social spending, selling off state enterprises, charging user-fees for social services, ending trade barriers, and opening the countries' markets to foreign investment (see Evans 1992).

This economic and political project provides a large part of the context for understanding the educational policies of the UNO government.

Another key element of this context is the strong influence of the Catholic Church hierarchy concerning the aims of education and what values will be taught. Although the UNO government seems to advocate policies in line with Sandinista concerns with educational equity and social justice— for example, giving priority attention to primary and preprimary education (grades 1–4), literacy and adult education, technical and vocational education—and raising critical consciousness, the interpretive frameworks of FSLN and UNO educational decision makers are diametrically opposed (see Quandt 1991). A more striking parallel and ideological affinity is found in the concepts and vocabulary of the U.S. conservative education agenda propounded by Diane Ravitch (1989, 1992) and Chester Finn (1992), whose writings on education and democracy are circulated within the MED—a vocabulary and notions of a longer school year, national standards, tightening-up of school-leaving exams, model schools, competition, choice, undercutting the power of organised teachers and giving a greater voice to parents, introducing user fees, and making university students pay the true costs of their education.

Education for democracy is linked to the goal of peace and is defined in the MED document in this way:

> The new education ought to form individuals capable of acting and deciding responsibly in a democratic context. It should be an education for liberty and peace, where students learn the virtue of dialogue and mutual respect. In essence . . . the new education should overcome political sectarianism and promote the development of a national framework based on consensus and . . . compromise. In the present circumstances, this implies strengthening patriotic values and symbols common to all, as well as democratic values and the rule of law. (1990, 8)

In another section, democratization of education is viewed in relationship to parents' being more actively involved in the education of their children. Democratization refers to the right of parents to choose the type of education they want their children to have. The guidelines further indicate that public and private school teachers, students, and diverse civic agencies, professional associations, and labor unions directly interested in the educational process should contribute to the reformulation of education for a New Nicaragua. To this end, the ministry proposed a national consultation to determine the criteria and resources that would define new directions for education (MED 1990, 11–12). (More about the UNO national consultation later.)

Although democracy is not directly defined in the guidelines, it generally is viewed in relationship to freedom of individuals *from* state political indoctrination and intervention in major spheres of life, such as the workings of the marketplace and, in the case of education, the primacy of the family and religious institutions in values education. By contrast, Sandinista notions of democracy and freedom are related to the rights of individuals to participate in societal decision making. There is no question that two competing ideologies are at play: the view of "the individual with social obligations but always mysterious, never reducible to a category, with a dignity gained from the son of God taking on human flesh" (a paraphrase of Sofonías Cisneros Leiva, first UNO Minister of Education),[3] versus the view of individuals as the subjects of history, who gain meaning and express self as participating members of mass organisations. Also there are significant differences between a Christianity based on liberation theology that is outward looking, collectively and social-change oriented; and a Christianity that is more inwardly directed and oriented toward personal and social redemption, with the family as the basic unit of society. According to former Minister of Education Padre Fernando Cardenal, the difference is between a Christianity oriented toward social justice, and one concerned with forgiveness.[4]

To return to the issue of quantity versus quality: it is obvious from remarks made by current high-level MED officials that the Sandinistas emphasized quantity to the point of seriously impairing quality. Basic primary and adult education should be emphasized, but greater attention, in their view, needs to be given to developing a skilled workforce that will enable Nicaragua to compete more successfully on the international market. According to the July 1990 statement of educational principles:

> in the decade of the nineties, Nicaragua enters a much more competitive and difficult world at a greater disadvantage than ten years ago. A world in continuous technological revolution, where past economic strategies, export of traditional agricultural products and protection of inefficient national industry, can no longer, even under best of conditions, assure national prosperity. In the coming years, Nicaragua, before this vital imperative, must produce for the world market . . . new and better products—manufactured goods and nontraditional exports—or remain in the backwaters, condemned to the relative and perhaps absolute impoverishment of its population. (MED 1990, 5)

The document then asks how Nicaragua can respond to this situation if its students lack technical and academic skills needed to compete on an international level, and if its youth does not learn new habits of responsibility, efficiency, and discipline.

TENSIONS AND CONTRADICTIONS DURING THE FSLN

During the period 1979–1989, the FSLN achieved a remarkable expansion of the education system (both formal and nonformal). The greatest growth took place during the first four years, when overall educational enrolments nearly doubled from 513,499 students in the prevolutionary year of 1978 to 979,580 in 1983. Altogether, over one-third of the Nicaraguan population was enrolled in some form of publicly supported systematic instruction in 1983. Between 1979 and 1984, the education budget quadrupled and spending on education increased from 1.9 percent (in 1979) to 4.9 percent of gross domestic product. The teaching force expanded from 12,706 in 1978 to 53,398 in 1984. This number includes some 20,000 volunteer teachers working as "popular educators" in a program of adult basic education that reached, at its height in 1983, approximately 187,000 students.

Despite extraordinarily adverse conditions, the education system continued to incorporate a sizeable proportion of the school-age population, especially from rural areas that previously had been neglected, and incorporate a greater number of preschool and special education populations (see Table 2.1).

These conditions included a U.S.-supported counterrevolution that resulted in over 50,000 casualties in a country of some 3.5 million, billions of dollars in direct and indirect costs/damages to the economy, and massive displacement of hundreds of thousands of rural inhabitants who either fled to neighbouring countries or were relocated in other regions of

Table 2.1. Number of Students

	Preprimary	Primary	Secondary	Special Education
1978	9,000	369,640	98,874	355
1980/81	30,524	472,167	139,743	1,430
1989	64,956	595,612	161,212	2,556

Source: Ministry of Education, Managua. It should be noted that there are slight discrepancies in the figures of different publications of the Ministry for the number of students enroled at different levels of education for the 1989 school year.

Nicaragua. These conditions also included direct and indirect economic warfare waged by the United States against the Sandinista regime and mismanagement of the economy by the Sandinistas themselves—all leading to a significant downturn in economic production, a deterioration of the GDP to pre-1950 levels, and rampant inflation that ran in the tens of thousands by the end of the 1980s. In the early 1980s, education and health accounted for over 50 percent of the national budget, while the military received approximately 18 percent. By 1987, because of the external aggression, over 50 percent of allocations went to the military, with education and health receiving only 25 percent.

In attempting to reach the so-called "popular sectors" of the society with various modalities of education, the FSLN was emphasizing the revolutionary goals of mass mobilization and participation, incorporating previously excluded populations into the nation-state building process. The provision of education as a social good helped win certain sectors of the population to the cause of the revolution, thereby consolidating its political legitimacy. But, as Carnoy and Torres point out, there are tensions in the conflicting demands for expansion as well as qualitative improvements in education:

> the demands of the revolution for rapid educational democratization (rapid educational expansion for youth and adults) tends to reduce the "quality" of education; second, the pressure to develop skills for economic growth tends to push the educational system into more "traditional" modes, sacrificing revolutionary socialization and more socially ideal curricula and educational methods. To the extent that the expansion of social services conflicts with capital accumulation, that expansion will be slowed . . . To the extent that democratizing formal education and the work process appears to retain capital accumulation, a tension also develops in the transformation of social relations. (1990, 334–35)

Carnoy and Torres (1990, 350–52) argue these tensions came to a head in 1983, when the Sandinista youth and popular educators, who thought that the Ministry of Education was too much in the hands of technocrats and traditional pedagogues, pressed for a major overhaul of educational policy and practice. I believe that Carnoy and Torres probably overstate the case of internal strife within the FSLN over educational policy. My own assessment is that throughout their decade of rule, the political and educational leadership within the FSLN attempted to maintain a balance, as best they could, between the imperatives of educational expansion and qualitative improvements. Nicaragua has never experienced the violent swings between national mobilizations aimed at radical egalitarianism or rapid modernization, between education for political socialization and education for expertness, that have characterised other socialist regimes such as that of the People's Republic of China.

The FSLN, moreover, had to achieve a balancing act between the demands of diverse, and potentially antagonistic, social sectors for different amounts and kinds of education. Because of the strategy of the FSLN leadership to maintain national unity in a war situation and to offer incentives to members of the capitalist class to stay in the country, higher education was virtually offered free of charge and expanded at rates twice that of primary and secondary education during the initial years of the revolution (see Carnoy and Torres 1990, 344). Although efforts were made to incorporate thousands of working-class and rural youths through a special preparatory faculty, generous scholarship assistance, and a system of regional quotas as part of admission policy, the majority of university students continued to come from favoured social classes. This occurred because of differential access and survival rates through successive levels of the education systems, based on residence (urban–rural, Pacific Coast–Atlantic Coast) as well as the differing ability of social classes to meet direct and indirect costs of education. So, despite the intentions of the FSLN to favour the popular sectors of society, the government ended up spending over ten times as much per university student as it did on primary school students.

The most obvious tensions between quantity and quality were found in the 1980 national literacy campaign and in the follow-up program of adult basic education (EPB, *Educación Popular Básica*) offered in educational "collectives" throughout the country. The literacy campaign has been described in great detail elsewhere (see, for example, Miller 1985; Arnove 1987; Lankshear 1993). Although the five-month campaign was primarily viewed by the FSLN leadership as a political act with educational implications—with the goals of integrating the countryside and the city, winning youth to the cause of the revolution, incorporating greater numbers of women and other previously neglected populations into public life, and strengthening mass organisations—the basic literacy skills that were supposed to have been imparted should not be minimized. Hundreds of thousands learned to read and write or had incipient literacy skills strengthened. However, it is also the case that FSLN claims that the campaign reduced the illiteracy rate from 50 to 13 percent of the population over 10 years of age are exaggerated.[5] A 1992 study conducted by the School of Medicine of the National Autonomous University of Nicaragua–Managua and the School of Tropical Medicine of the University of Liverpool in the department of Masaya, adjacent to the capital of Managua, found that approximately one-third of a sample of 500 women, declared to be literate by the MED, were unable to read or write the most basic sentence from an adult education primer; some could not even write their name. Contrary to claims that these women had participated in the campaign and had become literate as a result of it, many indicated that they had participated in the campaign only a few days or weeks; and several reported that they had not even participated in the campaign one day. These findings must be contrasted with dramatic cases of previously illiterate peasants who, for example, went on to complete various levels of education and ended up in the national assembly of the country and high-level positions in the FSLN party, government, and mass organisations; or the thousands of individuals who were able to use their literacy skills to run agricultural cooperatives, obtain bank credit, and, generally, participate in various spheres of private and public life more effectively (see Lankshear 1993).

The reasons for the low-level literacy skills of a substantial number of those who participated in the campaign are many. Less than half of them continued with any form of adult education. The lack of reading materials in rural areas combined with the struggle for everyday survival, and the constant disruptions wrought by the war raging in the countryside for a seven-year period, made it very difficult to build on the minimal skills acquired during the campaign.

For those who did enter the follow-up problem of adult basic education there also were innumerable problems. What was supposed to have been a political strength of this programme—thousands of minimally schooled volunteers serving as teachers—also may have constituted a serious shortcoming. Many instructors, in fact, were only one step ahead of their student neighbours and friends. Moreover, despite claims of using participatory teaching–learning methods, most teachers without adequate preparation simply resorted to traditional methods of instruction.

Drop-out rates were high, with less than half the students completing the third of six levels of EPB. The knowledge and skill levels of these students was therefore very low.

The content of the various educational materials was heavily politicized, especially the language and social studies readers, to the point that many of the adult learners, even those heavily sympathetic to the Sandinista cause, began to complain about excessive indoctrination. By 1987, the adult education division within the MED had initiated efforts to decentralise literacy efforts and develop more technically oriented curricula related to problems of the workplace. MED educators, together with representatives of the Rural Workers Associations (ATC, *Asociación de Trabajadores del Campo*) and the Farmers and Ranchers Union (UNAG, *Unión Nacional de Agricultores y Ganaderos*) over the next two years designed easy-to-read and practical pamphlets addressing specific problems such as how to increase the productivity of cattle raising or improve rural health. The thrust of adult education efforts during the final years of the Sandinista government was away from consciousness raising to skill provision. But by this point, enrolments were under 75,000.

Efforts to increase the number of students studying in technical institutes or work–study agricultural schools at the secondary education level did not result in major improvements. Enrolments in programs specifically related to increasing industrial and agricultural production reached only about 5 percent of high-school-level students. For the most part, secondary education consisted of traditional, preuniversity academic curricula (Arnove 1986, 85–86).

At the university level, however, there were significant shifts to priority fields related to development. The fields of agricultural sciences, medical sciences, education sciences, and technology, which comprised less than half (42 percent) of enrolments in 1980, represented 70 percent of enrolments five years later. Moreover, the number of higher education career offerings increased from 83 to 116 by 1988. These offerings included 16 medical specializations and 5 master's degree programs (including one in environmental science.)

Other accomplishments included graduating a substantial number of professionals despite extremely difficult working conditions due to the war situation and the poverty of the country, and increasing the number of full-time faculty. During the period 1980–1988, the universities graduated an average of 2,200 high-level professionals each year. The number of full-time instructors increased from 44 percent of a total of 1,474 faculty in 1980–1981, to 70 percent of 1,750 faculty in 1984. The percentage, however, fell to 62 percent in 1988.

The military draft and the constant mobilizations of university students and faculty around various production and defence tasks, which may have contributed substantially to political socialization, also had its deleterious consequences on enrolments and quality of instruction. Higher education enrolments, which had expanded to over 39,000 in 1984, had declined to some 25,000 in 1988.[6] Annual drop-out rates at the end of 1980s averaged between 20 and 25 percent. Fifty percent or less of any student cohort failed to graduate. Sandinista educational authorities candidly admitted that the shortage of educational materials, unstimulating curricula, and uninspiring pedagogy contributed to high attrition rates, together with the difficulties the society was undergoing.

Heavy politicization and indoctrination in certain faculties like philosophy and economics, where essentially dialectical and historical materialism constituted the crux of the curriculum, also are heavily criticized not only by opponents of the Sandinistas but by former Sandinista university officials, who admit that other current currents of thought and various technical skills should have been taught. The practice of giving credit for participation in the national literacy crusade, or production brigades to harvest cotton and coffee, by university academic units, such as the School of Engineering—in lieu of courses in resistance of materials or thermodynamics—also led to professional associations such as the national engineering society refusing to recognize university graduates with these credentials.

The creation of a National Higher Education Council (CNES, *Concejo Nacional de Educación Superior*) responsible for specific detailed curricular plans that were to be followed by all university departments may have led to closer integration of higher education with national development plans, but the constant intervention of CNES into areas viewed as being within the authority of university faculty contributed to many talented faculty members leaving or simply surviving by mechanically going through the motions of repeating a standardized, lockstep curriculum.

The bureaucratic and technocratic model of higher education, heavily influenced by the Cuban system, most likely stifled, rather than contributed to, the stated goal of the universities' playing a key role in the generation of knowledge and the raising of critical consciousness.

The issue of quality at all levels of education hinges on the competence and commitment of teachers. At the primary and secondary education the low level of teacher preparation and the high level of teacher turnover were never satisfactorily resolved. Increasing the number of teacher training institutes from five to fourteen and doubling the salaries of teachers in 1984 (while reducing their workload) still did not result in sufficient numbers of adequately prepared teachers. From 1987, rampant inflation rates so seriously eroded teacher salaries that they were not making enough to live on. Street vendors of uncontrolled items like cold water often made in several days what a teacher made in a month. By the end of the 1980s, the annual turnover rate was more than one-third (35 percent) of the teaching force. Under these conditions, it is not surprising that approximately two-thirds of teachers were uncertified. In-service efforts to certify and upgrade teachers was compared to pouring water into a container without a bottom.

Against these setbacks and constant challenges, there were notable efforts to revise curricula in such areas as the sciences, introduce innovative approaches to language instruction, and enhance the capacity of the country to design and produce textbooks (Arnove 1986: esp. Chapter 4). For the 1987 school year, despite a chronic shortage of paper goods, 3.7 million texts were produced. Furthermore, the reformed school system encouraged students to apply their knowledge to the solution of everyday problems. National science fairs with prizes awarded by top government leaders further stimulated students to solve real-world problems (although the war also, by 1988, had diminished the possibility of holding national-level fairs as transporation and related costs became prohibitive).

In concluding this section on quantity and quality, it is necessary to point out that in many respects Sandinista definitions of quality education were often as simple as providing a minimum of four years of basic education to its entire population and ensuring that no school child had to sit on a mud floor and that every child had a textbook.

Yet, in the end, even these goals proved elusive. When the new UNO government of Violeta Barrios de Chamorro assumed the reins of power on April 25, 1990, the educational situation in the country, both quantitatively and qualitatively, presented major challenges and deficiencies not unlike those faced by the FSLN, when it first took power.

TENSIONS AND CONTRADICTIONS IN UNO EDUCATION

These challenges included approximately one-fifth of school-age children's not being reached by the education system; a dropout rate of approximately 50 percent in the first grades; high desertion rates throughout primary education with less than 25 percent of a student cohort completing sixth grade, and less than 10 percent of rural populations completing this level; and a largely uncertified teaching force with high turnover. Moreover, hundreds of schools were in need of serious repair or unusable, and textbooks and school supplies were either nonexistent or in short supply in rural areas. The war years and economic hardships had clearly frustrated the best of Sandinista intentions and efforts.

With the support of international and national technical assistance agencies (principally UNESCO and USAID—the U.S. Agency for International Development), the new team of MED policymakers conducted a survey of the state of education in the country and designated priority areas for action. Initial assessment efforts were geared towards preparing the national delegation that would attend the "World Congress on Education for All" in Jomtien, Thailand, in March 1990. Congruent with the priorities of that congress, the UNO government highlighted the importance of attention's being given to basic education (grades 1–4) and preschool and adult education.

The national consultation conducted by UNO (supposedly inspired by Jomtien, but most likely also as a response to the 1981 FSLN *Consulta Nacional*) took place in September and October of 1991, and further affirmed these priorities. Designated the First National Educational Congress: "By and for All" (*El Primer Congreso Nacional de Educación*: "*Con Todos y Para Todos*"), the consultation involved some 6,300 participants by various means, including the following: 281 school-level consultations; 80 municipal and 9 regional consultations; and a culminating national congress. According to UNO, it was "an example of participatory and pluralistic democracy, where all of Civil Society offered opinions related to key themes . . ." (Barreto Arias 1992, 12).[7] In addition to giving priority attention to adult and basic education, which would favour the poorest sectors of the society (especially rural populations), the congress called for improvements in teacher salaries, improving the quality of education with the assistance of friendly countries and international technical assistance agencies (specifically mentioned in this order were the Agency for International Development—AID, UNESCO, UNICEF, Van Leer—a Dutch foundation, the Organizacion de Estados Americanos [or Organisation of American States]—OEA, and the European Community—EC), involving parents and communities in educational reform efforts, revising curricula to reflect local needs, decentralising education to the municipal level, and establishing a National Education Council (with representation of diverse interests) to further the democratic process (1992).

In the first issue of the MED publication *Maestro* (Teacher), which also contains the summary of the 1990 national consultation, UNO educational leaders list the achievements of the 1991 school year. School enrolments increased from 784,841 in 1990 to 851,589 in 1991, while the annual retention rate increased from 80 to 87 percent, and the dropout rate declined from 19.6 percent to 12.5 percent. UNO officials also report that 120,305 school desks were constructed, benefiting 240,610 of the 400,000 children without desks. One of the most touted, as well as controversial, achievements of the 1991 school year was the distribution of over 6.9 million primary and secondary education textbooks and workbooks, at a cost of US$12.2 million, to almost every corner of the country. USAID picked up the costs of designing, printing, and distributing the texts.

The examples of textbooks, and several other policies instituted for the 1992 school year, in particular school user fees, will now be used the focus of discussion concerning tensions between quantity and quality in Nicaraguan education, in particular how these tensions/contradictions relate to differing notions of democracy.

Perhaps the most tangible example of sweeping changes in education was the almost immediate replacement of all textbooks. The Chamorro administration was inaugurated on April 25, 1990; by the beginning of the March 1991 school year, over 110 new titles had been purchased, the vast majority from other Latin American countries (notably Colombia, Venezuela, Mexico, Costa Rica). The existing Sandinista texts in a few symbolic cases were burned in public; the majority were sent to shredding machines and turned into pulp, much to the disgust of donor countries such as Norway, which had underwritten the expenses of these texts.

Although the texts were adopted with only slight modifications from other Latin American countries, there were several notable exemptions. The texts for a new subject—civics and morality (taught at both the primary and secondary levels), and the texts on the history and geography of Nicaragua were written by nationals.[8]

While there are objections to the non-national and inappropriate images, language, and content of these texts (often portraying middle-class life styles and material possessions beyond the range of most Nicaraguans), as also to the methodology of many of the texts, and their lack of correspondence to any curricular framework, it is the civics-and-morality and the Nicaraguan history texts which have provoked the most negative response. The civics texts are heavily imbued with Christian messages that are objected to by those who believe the content violates the constitutional mandate that education be secular (the separation of church and state was established as early as the presidency of José Santos Zelaya, 1893–1909), and by members of evangelical sects that believe that the religious message is too closely tied to Catholic doctrine and interpretation of the Old and New Testaments. In the sixth-grade text, *Aprendamos a Convivir* (Let's Learn to Live Together), the first unit of study concerns individual morality. This concept is presented within

the framework of the Ten Commandments of the Bible.[9] Some examples
of the text are the following:

> God shows us that sexual relations outside of marriage are illicit. In mar-
> riage sex is pure and is a gift from God. Young people should save sex for
> the person with whom they will unite their lives in matrimony . . .

and

> Modesty and chastity are great qualities. The lack of modesty causes
> temptation, sin, and scandal. We should be modest in the form that we
> dress, avoiding clothing or possessions that stimulate sexual desire in
> others.

MED officials with whom I spoke admitted that including the Ten Commandments in the textbooks was a mistake. They believe that the principles could have been introduced as universal values. They also admit
that Christian principles can be introduced without specifically mention-
ing Christ. But what they call "Christian-inspired values" will continue
to permeate the curriculum.

Thus, despite the stated objectives of UNO officials to depoliticize
curricula and avoid attempts at indoctrinating youth, what is occurring in
Nicaragua is the substitution of one set of values ("Christian-inspired"
beliefs) for another set ("socialist-inspired"). Moreover, all vestiges of
Sandinista symbols have been exorcised from curricula and replaced
with more traditional patriotic symbols (particularly the blue and white
national flag) and less commonly known patriotic figures in lieu of the
Sandinista heroes and martyrs that abounded in school texts. This process
of inculcating youth with the values firmly held by MED top-ranking officials closely allied with charismatic Christian movements is understand-
able—but also at odds with their notions of democracy that are related
to freedom from imposition of state values and the rights of families to
choose an education that respects their values.

The inappropriateness of the texts is further highlighted by their use
with the indigenous and minority populations of the Atlantic Coast
region of the country. A 1987 autonomy law and the 1987 national constitution grant substantial authority to the region in matters of education
and culture. Yet, despite substantial opposition to these texts on the part
of indigenous educational leaders holding key positions with both MED
and the regional governments, the primary school language textbooks

series *Azul y Blanco* (Blue and White) were adopted and translated into Miskitu and English with very few major changes. To add insult to injury the Miskitu texts were not even translated by nationals of Nicaragua, but by Miskitus of Honduras, where a different version of the language is spoken (for further discussion, see Arnove and Ovando, 1993).

A striking example of the inappropriate content of the texts is the following: In the third grade Miskitu reader (*Siakni Bara Pihni,* 118), children are asked to imagine being left home alone with a robot that watches over them while their parents are away. When the robot speaks gibberish the children in the textbook conclude that it must be talking "Indian." This equation of gibberish with Indian talk reflects the mainstream Nicaraguan attitude toward indigenous Atlantic Coast culture as being inferior (see Bulloven 1991; and Arnove and Ovando 1993).

Another major issue is that of privatisation. By privatisation I do not necessarily mean a dramatic expansion of the number of private schools, which account for approximately 13 percent of primary educational enrolments, and 19 percent of secondary education.[10] I am referring principally to the practices of subjecting the educational system to market forces, competition for clients, the introduction of user fees, and a lessening of state regulation over the chartering of private schools and their internal operations, even though half of these schools are subsidized by the state.

The most controversial issue is the introduction of matriculation and monthly fees for both primary and secondary education students, as well as charging purchase or rental fees for the textbooks that were obtained and distributed with USAID funding. The fees would appear to be nominal: for primary schools students, a 5-córdobas (one dollar) matriculation charge and 5 córdobas per month over a nine-month period; for secondary students, 10 córdobas (two dollars) matriculation charges, and 10 córdobas monthly fees. To many, however, these fees are prohibitive. Given the dire poverty of most Nicaraguans and the 60 percent unemployment and underemployment throughout the country, the fees represent an obstacle to many Nicaraguans. For example, high-school textbook and school-supply fees (which may average anywhere from 34 to 160 córdobas a year), plus the cost of the obligatory blue-and-white uniform and school insignias—added to matriculation and monthly fees—could cost families up to several weeks' wages, when most Nicaraguans do not earn enough to purchase the basic commodities needed to sustain themselves nutritionally. (It is estimated that 16 percent of children suffer from malnutrition and 70 percent are at risk.) Even though primary school fees are supposed to be voluntary, many primary schools which are facing a situation of inadequate space for the increased demand for schooling require parents to prove their insolvency or contribute voluntary labor to improve school facilities—measures which bar a number of parents from placing their children in school. Some schools even charged parents fees, at the beginning of the 1992 school year, to preregister their children in order to assure space for them in overcrowded schools.

The fees are supposed to be used to supplement teacher salaries, which are woefully low. Depending on qualifications and other merit considerations, teacher wages usually average between $65 and $80 monthly, clearly not enough to live on and support a family.

By making teacher supplemental income contingent upon user fees, the MED potentially has pitted parents against teachers. In some cases, parents are willing and able to pay the fees. In others, they resent the fees or take stances that the income raised by user fees should not go to some central Ministry fund to be divided equitably among all schools, rich and poor, but remain only in their local school. Teachers themselves, as well as their unions, are divided over these fees.

One of the most interesting potential conflicts concerns private education. Although the MED, under the current UNO government, is viewed as strongly supportive of private education and certainly less intrusive with regard to supervising the internal operations of private schools, there is the distinct possibility that, beginning in 1993, the MED will limit the fees that will be charged in these schools. Under discussion at the moment is the prospect that, in exchange for government support, private schools may not levy fees greater than those currently being charged in public schools. This policy may or may not generate opposition by the private sector. Free of state subsidies, private schools may have greater autonomy to charge whatever fees their clients are willing to pay. Some schools, however, may not be able to attract sufficient clients and therefore will be forced to close.

To date, the most significant conflict over funding of education and the prospect of charging tuition has been at the higher education level. In a frequently cited set of articles in the newspaper *La Prensa* (October 26, 1991, part 2 of 3), Minister of Education Humberto Belli observed the unfairness of a situation where 30,000 university students receive almost the same budgetary allocation as 700,000 primary school students; in fact, higher education represented approximately 4 percent of all students, and received the equivalent of 30 percent of the MED budget for all preuniversity and adult education. He went on to note that in 1991, only 2,461 students graduated from the universities at the cost of $10,000 to $20,000 per graduate, 18 times more per capita than what was spent on a primary school student. Among other arguments used against free higher education were that of 2,442 students enroled in the law school, only 89 graduated; and that in a number of fields, there would be no job for graduates. It was unfair, he claimed, for tax payers to have to pay for an "individual's educational whims."

To these argument also must be added the undeniable situation that the university is presently a major source of opposition to Minister Belli and the UNO government. In the final months of its administration, the Sandinista-dominated national assembly passed a university autonomy law that granted higher education institutions a degree of internal freedom that the Sandinistas claimed was unnecessary during its period of rule. The university, in many respects, has become a refuge, an asylum for Sandinista militants, many of them government functionaries who returned to their previous careers in academia after the FSLN lost the February 1990 national election.

It is ironic that the university, which did not enjoy autonomy or faculty academic freedom throughout the 1979–1990 period, now enjoys these conditions in the post-Sandinista period. But it enjoys them in a situation in which it is being starved for funding.

In July and August of 1992, the nation was convulsed by a fifty-day university student and faculty strike protesting inadequate funding. Specifically, the strike was over differing interpretations of the 1990 university autonomy law decreeing that the state shall allocate 6 percent of the national budget to higher education institutions: the universities claimed that the 6 percent should include international as well as national revenues, while the government argued that only national revenues should be considered. The difference amounted to US$7.6 million,[11] which the universities asserted they needed in order to meet expenses for the remainder of the academic year. On August 18, the National Assembly supported the position taken by the universities. As of mid-December 1992, however, the government still had not been able to locate and disburse all of the US$7.6 million the national legislature decreed it owed the universities. This situation further has the potential of pitting faculty and students not only against the central government but against one another, as decisions have to be made concerning whether funding—once it materializes—will go towards improvements in facilities and materials that favour students or for increments in faculty salaries.

The government's objective appears to be to force the universities into charging tuition as a way to increase available funds. Although the universities have resisted such moves to date, it is likely that the Jesuit-run

Central American University will charge some fees for the 1993 academic year, which begins in March. As noted earlier, the FSLN held open the promise that all students could eventually study at the higher-education level free of charge. Moreover, they defined basic education as comprising the first nine years of schooling. In contrast, the UNO government has defined basic education as consisting only of the first four years of schooling.

The preceding discussion suggests, however, that the introduction of user fees may limit the provision of education to those sectors the government has declared it most wishes to serve. In addition to primary education, literacy and adult education were to be priorities for the UNO government. In a country where unofficial estimates of illiteracy run over 35 percent, and there are over 700,000 illiterates (which also was the case in 1979), the current budget for literacy efforts is under US $5,000. In 1992, the MED planned to reach no more than 15,000 to 25,000 adults with literacy instruction and another 10,000 with postliteracy courses. The two largest items in the adult education budget are for (1) the accelerated primary education program that confers a degree in three years and is essentially the same curriculum as for children, and (2) night-time secondary education. Whatever funding literacy and postliteracy instruction will receive will have to come from external sources.

CONCLUSIONS

Thus, in 1992, Nicaraguan educational policymakers faced a set of educational problems that are strikingly similar in some respects to those confronting the Sandinistas when they assumed power in 1979. In addressing the issue of quantity versus quality, the FSLN tended to give greater weight to expansion and extension of the education system (both formal and nonformal) as an integral part of the democratization of the society. Significant efforts also were initiated to improve quality. Overall, however, quality and quantity suffered by virtue of the great emphasis placed on the role of education for the purposes of political socialization and legitimation—the creation of a qualitatively different citizen in a transformed society. The constant mobilizations of youth for production activities and other tasks of the revolution—particularly the defence of the country, with a military draft instituted in 1983—may have been powerful socializing experiences, but they also had their costs in decreasing the time and opportunities available for systematic instruction in the essential knowledge and skills needed for economic development. Political socialization, characterised by a vanguard party dictating the correct political line at any particular time, further ran counter to Sandinista notions of a participatory democracy with mass organisations playing a key role in articulating grassroots demands and contributing to policy formation and implementation. The extent to which the social experiment envisioned by the FSLN may have succeeded will never be known because of opposition by the United States and the surrogate counterrevolutionary army it organised and funded. After nearly a decade of incessant warfare and economic hardships, the Nicaraguan electorate voted the Sandinistas out of power—perhaps the greatest testimony to the commitment of the FSLN to democratize Nicaraguan society (Ramírez 1991).

The coalition government headed by Violeta Barrios de Chamorro that took power on April 25, 1990, set out on a diametrically opposed path to development. It favoured a diminished role for the state in capital accumulation, giving priority to market forces as the motor that would propel the Nicaraguan economy forward, and in values education, promoting the private sphere of family and religious institutions to remedy social ills such as divorce, abandoned children, drug addiction, and prostitution. Unlike the Sandinistas, the subsequent educational policymakers favoured quality over quantity, emphasizing skills that would prepare the Nicaraguan labor force to compete successfully in international markets. However, significant tensions and contradictions in UNO policies have emerged over the past two years. A case can be made that excessive attention has been given to moral socialization, to imparting "Christian-inspired" values that may lead to polarization rather than reconciliation—running counter to the UNO government's stated goals of education for democracy and peace. Moreover, UNO policies favouring introduction of user fees, and the low level of funding provided for literacy and adult education, belied the government's stated objectives of favouring the most disadvantaged sectors of society, preparing them to participate as thinking, critical citizens in national life. The economic policies introduced by the UNO government helped stabilize the Nicaraguan currency and dramatically reduced the inflation rate to a very satisfactory level, but they also have generated extraordinarily high and unacceptable levels of unemployment and underemployment that leave a majority of Nicaraguans destitute. Under such circumstances, it is unlikely that foreign capital would want to invest in the country.

The tensions and contradictions that have been noted in education reflect problems inherent in the models of development pursued by both the Sandinistas and UNO. Whether or not an alternative model can be developed that allows for both greater private initiative as well as a vital role for the state in guaranteeing national sovereignty and providing for the basic (social, cultural, economic, and political) rights of all citizens remains problematic. My study of education and social change in Nicaragua these past years has led me to be cautious in reaching any conclusions about the power of education systems to miraculously contribute to the formation of a new person, a transformed political culture, or model of capital accumulation. Instead, the demands made on education systems must be more modest, and the claims of success viewed with some skepticism. Nonetheless, the goal of education for democracy, for critical, participatory citizenship must remain an ideal to strive for—just as the elusive goal of achieving both quantity and quality must be attempted, no matter how difficult the balancing act may be.

NOTES

1. The FSLN held national elections for the presidency, vice presidency, and a constitutive national assembly in November 1984, and again in February 1990, when it lost power.

2. Over time, the Sandinistas favoured greater distribution of land to individual peasants as a way of gaining the loyalty of the rural sector to a revolution under siege.

3. Interview with Sofonías Cisneros Leiva, Managua, March 1992.

4. Interview with Fernando Cardenal, Managua, April 1992. For further discussion of the church in Nicaragua, during the Sandinista period, see Conor Cruise O'Brien (1988, 80–121).

5. The Ministry of Education claims that the illiteracy rate was reduced to 12.96 percent, but it should be noted that this figure is based on the decision to subtract from the target population of illiterate adult approximately 130,000 individuals who were considered unteachable or learning impaired. If this population is included in literacy statistics, then the illiteracy rate was reduced to approximately 23 percent by the end of the campaign.

6. The number of secondary students also declined by more than 5,000, most likely because of the draft and the displacement of populations by the war.

7. Even though executive officers of the Sandinista national teachers association (ANDEN, *Asociación Nacional de Educadores Nicaraguenses*) participated in the final national congress in October 1991, they refused to recognize it as being a sufficiently representative and democratic consultation, compared with that conducted by the FSLN in 1981, the principal reason being that ANDEN officials believe that mass organisations, the true representatives of the popular

will, were not the basic units being consulted—even though UNO claims that 67 organisations were involved in the process.

8. In some cases, nationals who had been residing abroad during the Sandinista years and continue to reside abroad.

9. In the fourth-grade text, the Ten Commandments are presented outright.

10. However, a number of critics of UNO educational policies, particularly the Sandinista teacher union ANDEN, believe that the current government does have the intention of expanding private education to the detriment of public schooling.

11. The initial allocation to the universities was 117 million córdobas; the universities claimed they should have received 155 million córodobas, which eventually the National Assembly awarded to them. The discrepancy of 55 million córdobas amounts to US$7.6 million based on the then-official exchange rate of 5 córdobas to one U.S. dollar.

REFERENCES

Arnove, Robert (1986) *Education and Revolution in Nicaragua.* New York, Praeger.

Arnove, Robert (1987) "The 1980 Nicaraguan National Literacy Crusade." In Robert F. Arnove, and Harvey J. Graff (eds.), *National Literacy Campaigns,* 269–92. New York, Plenum.

Arnove, Robert, and Dewees, Anthony (1991) "Education and Revolutionary Transformation in Nicaragua, 1979–90." *Comparative Education Review* 35 (l) (February): 92–109.

Arnove, Robert and Ovando, Carlos (1993) "Contested Ideological, Linguistic and Pedagogical Values in Nicaragua: The Case of the Atlantic Coast." *WCCI Forum* (Journal of the World Council for Curriculum and Instruction).

Arríen, Juan B. (1991) "The Transformation of Education: UNO's Political Project." *Envío* (Managua) 10 (122) (September): 17–27.

Arríen, Juan B., and Lazo, Roger Matus (1989) (eds.) *Nicaragua: Diez años de educación en la Revolución.* Managua, Ministry of Education.

Barreto Arias, Violeta (1992) "El Primer Congreso Nacional de Educación: 'Con Todos y Para Todos'." *Maestro* (Managua, MED) l (l): 12.

Barndt, Deborah. (1991) *To Change This House.* Toronto, Between the Lines.

Bulloven, Hans Petter (1991) "*Siakni Bara Pihni*," *Barricada* (Managua), 5 June: 3.

Carnoy, Martin, and Torres, Carlos Alberto (1990) "Education and Social Transformation in Nicaragua 1979–1989." In Martin Carnoy and Joel Samoff (eds.), *Education and Social Transition in the Third World.* Princeton, Princeton University Press, 315–57.

Cruise O'Brien, Conor (1988) *Passion and Cunning: Essays on Nationalism, Terrorism, and Revolution.* New York, Simon & Schuster.

Evans, Trevor (1992) "The Impact of Adjustment Programmes on the Public Sector in Central America and the Caribbean: Preliminary Report." Paper prepared for the Public Services International 4th Interamerican Regional Conference Montego Bay, Jamaica 26–28 April. Address of author: Coordinadora Regional de Investigaciones Economicas y Sociales (CRIES), Managua, Nicaragua, mimeographed.

Fägerlind, Ingemar, and Saha, Lawrence (1989) *Education and National Development.* New York, Pergamon.

Finn, Chester (1992) *Education Reform in the 90s.* New York, Macmillan.

Lankshear, Colin (1993) "Adult Literacy in Nicaragua 1979–90." In Peter Freebody and Anthony R. Welch (eds.), *Knowledge, Culture and Power: International Perspectives on Literacy as Policy and Practice.* London, Falmer Press, 114–41.

Miller, Valerie (1985) *Between Struggle and Hope: The Nicaraguan Literacy Crusade.* Boulder, CO, Westview.

Ministerio de Educación (MED) (1980) "The Great National Literacy Campaign: Heroes and Martyrs for the Creation of Nicaragua," report trans. and ed. National Network in Solidarity with the Nicaraguan People. Managua, Ministry of Education, January, mimeographed.

Ministerio de Educación (MED) (1981) *Consulta nacional para obtener, criterios que ayuden a definir los fines y objetivos de la educación Nicaragüense, informe preliminar.* Managua, Ministry of Education.

Ministerio de Educación (MED) (1987) "Estratégia nacional de alfabetización en el marco de la educación popular de adultos." Managua, Ministry of Education, mimeographed.

Ministerio de Educación (MED) (1990) "Lineamientos del Ministerio de Educación en el Nuevo Gobierno de Salvacion Nacional." Managua, Ministry of Education, July.

Quandt, Midge (1991) "U.S. Aid to Nicaragua: Funding the Right." *Z Magazine* (November), 47–51.

Ramírez, Sergio (1991) *Confesion de Amor.* Managua, Nicarao.

Ravitch, Diane (1989) "Que es la democracia y como debe enseñarse en las escuelas." Paper. Polish National Ministry of Education and Teacher Solidarity, November. Distributed by the Nicaraguan Ministry of Education.

Ravitch, Diane (1992) *Democracy Reader: Classic and Modern Speeches, Essays, Poems, Declarations, and Documents and Freedom and Human Rights Worldwide.* New York, Harper.

Ruchwarger, Gary (1987) *People in Power: Forging a Grassroots Democracy.* South Hadley, MA, Bergin and Garvey.

UNESCO (1983) *Educational Cultural Development Project Nicaragua.* Paris: UNESCO.

Vanden Bem Den, Harry E. (1988) "Democracy and Socialism in the New Nicaragua." Paper. Forty-sixth International Congress of Americanists. Amsterdam, 4–8 July. Address of author: Department of Political Science, University of South Florida, Tampa, FL 33620.

CHAPTER 3

The Struggle to Achieve Quality
A Case Study of Palestinian Education

IBTISAM ABU-DUHOU

On the thirteenth of September 1993, a historical document was signed between the Palestinian Liberation Organization and the State of Israel. Known as the "The Declaration of Principles," the document aimed, among other things, to "put an end to decades of confrontation and conflict" and to "establish a Palestinian Interim Self-Government Authority . . . for the Palestinian people in the West Bank and Gaza Strip" (The Declaration of Principles Document).

This declaration was a particularly significant historical moment in the year of Indigenous Peoples. From an educational point of view, it was important, for it was to lead the way for the Palestinians—a colonized people—to have for the first time control over their education. On August 28, 1994, the responsibility for education in the Occupied Territories was transferred from the Israeli hands (an occupying authority) to the Palestinian National Authorities (PNA). The task of the PNA in delivering educational services to the Palestinians is fraught with many obstacles, the most significant of which is overcoming the problems created by the process of educational expansion in past decades. The PNA inherited a system that suffered from the total absence of any developments since 1976, at a time of expanding population and world development.

This chapter examines the expansion of the educational system in the West Bank and Gaza Strip (hereafter WBGS), and the effect of this expansion on educational quality in the territories. The analysis will show that, since education is a system which has always been controlled by a "foreign power," the greatest impediments to educational quality were the many political factors which have been at play for decades. The prime factor was the lack of an indigenous national government which could develop a vision of a system to serve the Palestinians. It is thus argued that the lack of national sovereignty and the machinery of national government led to severe problems in education, leaving the PNA with an exceptionally difficult task of restoring the system's quality.

After an overview of the history of education in Palestine, the chapter first explores the Jordanian and Egyptian policies of expansion in the 1950s and 1960s and the impacts of these policies on educational quality in the WBGS. This is followed by an exploration of the Israeli policies during the decades of occupation and an exploration of Palestinians' educational aspirations in relation to the Israeli Occupation. The analysis reveals that the first attempts at rapid expansion were achieved at the expense of quality, while the Israeli Occupation has inhibited, and at times prohibited, the delivery of education as the term is used in ordinary language. The latter part of the chapter examines recent attempts to overcome the political constraints over education.

AN OVERVIEW OF EDUCATIONAL
DEVELOPMENT IN PALESTINE

Throughout this century, Palestine has undergone several historical changes. Four hundred years of Ottoman Turkish rule came to an end during World War I, followed by thirty years of British Mandate (1917–1948). On May 15, 1948, the British Mandate ended and a new regime was declared for 78 percent of Palestine. For centuries, Palestine was inhabited by Palestinian Arabs. Their presence as a cohesive national group in their homeland was forcibly terminated when Israel proclaimed itself a state, driving the Palestine Arabs into forced exile between 1947 and 1949. Approximately 780,000 Palestinians were made homeless as a result of the creation of Israel. In 1950, Egypt established a military administration in the Gaza Strip and Jordan annexed eastern Palestine and changed its name to the West Bank (i.e., west of the Jordan River). After the 1967 war, Israel managed to occupy the rest of Palestine and to expel some 186,000 additional Palestinians. The Palestinians, accordingly, "suffered a kind of political extermination as their ancestral homeland was transformed into a Jewish colonial settler society during the past [four] decades" (Aruri 1984, 5).

While Palestine ceased to exist as a political community, it continued to exist in the collective consciousness of its own people. And, for the 5.5 million Palestinians dispersed all over the world, education has become an important end: "both as an individual escape route from the refugee camps and as a means of keeping alive a national identity" (Graham-Brown 1984, 5). This is an important fact to keep in mind when considering the demands for rapid expansion in the system.

The development of education in Palestine coincided with the following political history (Graham-Brown 1984). During the Ottoman period, four types of schools appeared: (1) state schools run by the Ottoman government where education was limited to the training of administrative and military personnel or to religious instruction; (2) schools established by Christian missionaries of various denominations who were eager to set up schools in the "Holy Land" as European influence grew in the second half of the nineteenth century; (3) Muslim schools, a number of which were also established in the later part of the nineteenth century; and (4) private schools (Christian and Muslim), numbers of which were established by those landowners who wished to advance their children within the Ottoman administration. By 1917, the end of the Ottoman era, there were 379 private schools and 95 state schools. At the same time, a new Arab nationalist consciousness was beginning to take root in reaction to Turkish political and cultural domination. This led to the revival of interest in Arabic language and liberation, and to the establishment of Arab newspapers and "communal" schools (Graham-Brown 1984, 16).

The years of British rule up to 1948 witnessed a growing struggle between the Arab Palestinians and successive waves of Jewish immigrants. According to Graham-Brown (1984), the immigration aimed at colonizing the land. In practice, this meant the development of an enclave economy and society which had its own dynamic and goals and which, under the terms of the Mandate, was afforded a measure of autonomy not offered to the Palestinian Arab community (Graham-Brown 1984, 14). On the education front, there was a growing demand for education in both the rural and the urban areas. Two systems of education were created by the British: a Jewish and an Arab system. The Jewish education system, including public schools with teaching in Hebrew, was only indirectly controlled by the British government. It was administered by a Zionist organization, Vaad Leumi, and financed by the Jewish Agency and the Jewish community. The Arab public system, by contrast, was directly controlled by the government and funded mainly from general government revenues, with limited contributions from municipal and local council funds (Graham-Brown, 1984). The two education systems were separate but certainly not equal in quality and the Arab system did not keep pace with the growing demand for education. A report by the 1937 Royal Commission, which was set up to examine the causes of the 1936 General Strike, stated that "it is most regrettable that after 17 years of mandatory rule, the government system is able to satisfy no more than half the Arab demand for education" (Graham-Brown 1984, 20). Further, the curriculum was predominantly oriented to colonial needs along the pattern set up by the British in India and Egypt. The curriculum displayed a "blandness of approach to political and cultural issues which amounted to a form of disinformation" (Graham-Brown 1984, 20). Dr Khalil Totah, an educator and former principal of the Men's Training College in Jerusalem, stated in a testimony before the Commission:

> The major grievance of the Arabs as regards education is that they have no control over it . . . It would seem that Arab education is either designed to reconcile the Arabs to this policy [of establishing a Jewish National Home in Palestine] or make that education so colorless as to make it harmless and not endanger the carrying out of that policy. (Cited in Graham-Brown 1984, 19–20)

The end of the British Mandate, however, was also effectively the end of Palestinian society as it had existed. Yet, by 1946, there were a total of 795 schools in Palestine with 118,335 Arab students: 478 were government schools, 134 were private Muslim schools, and 183 were private Christian schools. Although the British attempted to suppress and discourage any nationalist ideas, the discouragement and suppression merely kindled aspirations for indigenous control. Despite teachers' strikes, school closures, inadequate financing, and British heavy-handiness, Palestinians may have been better educated than most of their Arab neighbors when the Mandate ended. Most importantly, with a growing nationalist consciousness among the Palestinians, the "idea became implanted of education as a universal solution, a means of individual advancement and cultural modernization" (Graham-Brown 1984, 24).

Following the 1948 war, Jordan assumed responsibility for the West Bank and Egypt for the Gaza Strip. In the field of education, both states created a government school system in the Palestinian territories under their control, with elementary (grades 1–6), preparatory (grades 7–9), and secondary (grades 10–12) levels. Both governments also institutionalized a matriculation examination at the end of the twelfth grade for the General Secondary School Certificate, commonly known as the Tawjihi, which was used to assess applicants for postsecondary education. A number of teacher education and vocational education programs were established. Both governments also established a salary and benefit system for teachers and administrators. All textbooks, classroom materials, and student-teacher certification procedures originated in Amman or Cairo. At the same time, both governments incorporated into the textbooks materials concerning Arab history and culture. Like the British, however, both governments "assiduously avoided references to Palestinian history, society or culture" (Graham-Brown 1984, 49).

Among the refugees, education was often the only way for families to climb out of their landless, and often jobless, situation and to regain some kind of independent status—by helping their children to do so. Since 1950, Palestinian refugees have also had access to education through the programs of the United Nations Relief and Works Agency for Palestine Refugees in the Near East (UNRWA). Currently, UNRWA provides nine years of education for the children of the majority of registered refugees, and has a large-scale operation in health, welfare, and community services in Lebanon, Jordan, Syria, and the West Bank and Gaza Strip. UNRWA is still a major provider of schooling up to the preparatory level, both in the West Bank and Gaza Strip.

This aforementioned "amalgam of local, Turkish, British, and Egyptian-Jordanian systems of education" (Mahshi and Bush 1989, 472) continued after the Israeli occupation of the West Bank and Gaza Strip in 1967. The occupation was assumed by most people, including many Israelis, to be a temporary phenomenon. Thus, while leaving the basic structure of education intact, the Israeli military government took over the functions of the Egyptian and Jordanian governments with respect to the government-operated schools, and did its best to significantly alter the content of education in Palestinian schools. While the implementation of the Jordanian-Egyptian system and curricula continued, the Israeli authorities added further to the alienation within the system by banning and suppressing any reference to Palestinian history and culture. The three systems of education (UNRWA, private, and government schools) all were forced to adhere to "essentially alien curricula, in which Palestinian culture and history have been ignored or actively suppressed by the Israelis" (Mahshi and Bush 1989, 472).

EDUCATIONAL QUALITY (1950–1967)

What were the impacts of both Jordan's and Egypt's policies of educational expansion on education quality? After 1948 Jordan assumed responsibility for schools in the West Bank, and Egypt in Gaza, just as the worldwide demand for universal schooling exploded. In Gaza, and on the West Bank, one significant factor in this rapid expansion differed from factors operating in other regions in the world. Educated Palestinians in 1948 carried their education in their heads, and school certificates in their hands. Those rich individuals without education left houses, lands, and wealth behind to become destitute when cash ran out. Their fellow Palestinians observed and deduced—hence the survival value of education, exemplified in a certificate, deeply embedded itself in Palestinian consciousness.

Jordan and Egypt faced extraordinary demands for expansion of schooling. To their credit, and that of UNRWA, virtually universal schooling was achieved by 1965 (i.e., in only fifteen years). Inevitably, however, standards fell, and they fell from a level found inadequate in Europe and America in the post-World War II era. While the scale of the education system was enlarged beyond that which was described earlier by Totah, both the Egyptian and the Jordanian government schools continued the outdated Mandate practices: rote method, external examinations, and an exam-based curriculum; nontechnical training and a career-oriented education.

A decline in the quality of teachers was another significant outcome of this rapid expansion. Between 1948 and 1965 some of those with traditional nonformal education remained influential in the Palestinian territories. Some fine "natural" teachers (energetic, dedicated, and broadly educated) remained in the schools. As schools expanded, however, the prestige of teachers fell, comparative values of salaries dropped, and recruitment standards for teachers were compromised. To put teachers in every new classroom in the West Bank and Gaza prior to 1967, administrators resorted to short-term "training" with very narrow scope (for example, how to teach third grade, or maths for fifth and sixth grades). They trained people with little breadth of general education—often without energy and uninterested in teaching, but interested only in a "job." In Palestine, this occurred over a dozen years or more, but most profoundly in the years 1965–1967.

In the West Bank especially, and in Gaza to a lesser extent, three other factors drastically affected teacher standards. Firstly, every year from 1950–1966 the broadest-educated, best-trained, and most experienced teachers were recruited away by the oil-rich Arab states (that is, the Arab states of the Gulf region including Saudi Arabia and Kuwait). Some good teachers would not leave for family reasons or could not get out, for political reasons, especially in Gaza. Secondly, those teachers who remained were often only narrowly trained to teach at one level, but were nonetheless promoted to levels they had not the slightest idea how to teach—due merely to seniority. Moving teachers to the higher grades proved to be very destructive of educational quality. Finally, inflation drove teachers' real income down to poverty levels, forcing most teachers to accept additional jobs or to leave teaching. By 1965 the teaching profession had largely lost its status, whereas in 1950 teaching had been highly prestigious.

EDUCATION UNDER THE ISRAELI OCCUPATION (1967–1997)

After 1967, the Israeli Occupation authorities (first military, then civil administration within the Ministry of Defense) exercised control over all three systems of Palestinian education (UNRWA, government, and public), while directly controlling both the finances, and the hiring and firing, in government schools. Government schools, in addition, were placed under the responsibility of the Ministry of Defense, rather than the Ministry of Education. In 1996–1997, schools were providing services for a total of 712,820 students enroling in three systems of education: government schools, which are under the supervision of the Palestinian Ministry of Education and had an enrolment of 481,678 students; UNRWA schools, which have an enrolment of 187,518 students; and the private sector, which has 43,624 students. Table 3.1 shows the distribution of students by type of school, both in the West Bank and the Gaza Strip.

During the thirty years of occupation, the Israeli authorities employed restrictive orders and drastic measures against the educational institutions,

Table 3.1. Distribution of Students by School Type in the West Bank and Gaza Strip, 1996–1997

Type of School	In the West Bank	In Gaza Strip
Government Schools	343,775	137,903
UNRWA Schools	47,735	139,783
Private Schools	40,055	3,569
Total Enrolments	431,565 students	281,255 students

and in particular the government schools, which hampered their growth and development. The Occupation authorities largely ignored curriculum development and external exams. Perhaps it was considered more important that existing curricula would serve the authorities' needs rather than develop the inhabitants of Gaza and the West Bank. Interference in the schools took three main forms: "security" matters, alleged political activities of teachers and/or students, and the censorship of textbooks.

From the Palestinian perspective, one important continuity was evident: "Just as the Palestinians created popular institutions to preserve and transmit their culture during Turkish rule and British rule, they have also resisted integration under the Israelis" (Mahshi and Bush 1989, 472). They developed educational, cultural, and grassroots organizations to preserve their culture and to nurture self-reliance and resist dependence on the Israeli authorities. These attempts gave a more appropriate, active definition to alternative quality education. To understand the meaning of *quality* as it is used in this chapter, it is appropriate to use the words of the Palestinian spokesperson Hanan Mikhail-Ashrawi:

> Unequivocally, in our dictionary there is no "quality" under occupation except in the quality of our resistance to it and active rejection of all its imperatives and implications. (Mikhail-Ashrawi 1989, 9)

That is, the Palestinians sense of "quality," as expressed effectively in their own transformation of social realities and priorities, is entirely oppositional. As the popular committees emerged in the years of the Intifada from each neighborhood, village, and camp, a new structure and "quality" materialized to replace those which had been artificially and externally imposed by the Occupation. In this context, the term *Occupation* takes on a special meaning as explored below.

THE MEANINGS AND IMPLICATIONS OF OCCUPATION

The term *Occupation* has many meanings. One meaning refers to the possession, use, or settlement of land in the sense of occupancy. It means that "act or process of taking possession of a place or an area," "the holding and control of an area by a foreign military force," "the military force occupying a country or the policies carried out by it" (*Webster's* 1967). Here the term is construed as taking possession of the land by the Israeli military; holding and controlling it; settling and carrying out policies of its own and for itself without regard to the right to education of the

Palestinian inhabitants. Thus, the relationship of the Israeli Occupation to the Palestinian educational aspiration, as described in the previous section, is at best a colonial one. The colonized context has been characterized by Paulo Freire as the "culture of silence" (1970, 38). According to Clignet (1984), this refers to the "colonizer's attempts to prevent the colonized from understanding his [*sic*] position in time and space, and hence from maintaining contact with his [*sic*] own past or with alien cultures" (84). As for the Palestinians, the preceding analysis has shown that development of the system has been constrained by political powers which have been working either from outside its boundaries, or are "foreign" to the needs and aspirations of the people it served. System expansion took place under different state authorities, none of which was an authentic Palestinian body. From this point of view, the Palestinian people have been forced to deal over the years with an education system and curriculum which were mainly alien (colonialist or an extension of colonialist education). At the time of this writing, it was still the Occupation which principally prohibited educational development.

From this perspective, the relationship of Palestinians to the education with which they were provided for much of the period since the 1920s, and even more so after 1967, is best described as that of the "colonized" to the "colonizer," while the current relations between them and the Israelis mirror that of the "occupied" to the "occupier." This latter relationship has been described as the "asymmetry" of occupier and occupied, "an unequal relationship which is difficult to envision being rectified without being recognized" (Mikhail-Ashrawi, in various media appearances). In reality, the Israeli Occupation endeavors to sustain practices of "internal colonization" over the lives of the Palestinians in general and over their education in particular. Clearly, the concept of "internal colonization" offers an adequate theoretical framework for locating the history of Palestinian educational aspirations in relation to the Israeli Occupation. Here, internal colonialism extends beyond the "domination of one nation by another" to a domination of one group which "occupies the same territory as the colonized people" (Hartwig 1978, 120; see also Welch 1988, 1996; Welch and Gientzotis 1996; Altbach and Kelly 1984).

In spite of the absence of either a national government, or Palestinian control over education for the past few decades, Palestinians, as noted earlier, have always placed high emphasis on formal educational attainment. They have always regarded education as a primary means of survival, of national struggle and a way to secure jobs and a decent living. Shaath in

1971 estimated that the number of Palestinians studying in universities in proportion to their population as a whole was among the highest in the world (92–94). Palestinians have since achieved a high educational rank in the Arab World (Abu-Duhou 1987, 1993, Mahshi and Bush 1989, Fasheh 1990). However, the types of degrees sought by Palestinians were "determined by the professions, areas of specialization, and types of jobs that were available" (Fasheh 1990, 26). While local Palestinians are well educated and well read in a classical sense, they have been denied access to many crucial skills related to economic development of the community and late twentieth-century developments in computer technology, management skills, communication, and the financial world. In addition, they have been denied access to knowledge of government, public finance and financial accountability; about the intellectual, social, and creative development of children; the development of relevant research paradigms; and women's issues.

Moreover, as indicated, Palestinian educators have been struggling to overcome the profound problems created by the Israeli occupying force after 1967. They have had to contend with continuous and prolonged closures of schools and universities, academic restrictions, banning of textbooks and materials, and onslaughts by the military (Abu-Duhou 1993). Schools and other educational institutions were less able to function because of military harassment and closure orders (Abu-Duhou 1993, Fasheh 1990). Even when they were functioning, as noted by Fasheh, "conditions are not conducive to teaching or studying because of increasing class size, shrinking salaries and budgets, escalating fear and harassment of teachers and students, lack of proper facilities, and so forth" (26). The effects of such an educational environment and policy on the quality of education have been severe, and are still being felt.

In the early 1980s, many Palestinian educators became critical of the present system of education and its applicability to their society. They began to introduce relevance into the curriculum and into the education system. However, their work has been limited to a very small number of private schools in the West Bank. The majority of schools, which were under direct Israeli control, remained outside the sphere of influence of these educators and experimentation. It was the Palestinian Intifada and the Israelis' response to it, including the collective closure of schools, that triggered the challenge within the educational community to reexamine the present system and to look for short- and long-term alternatives to it. The Intifada challenged the Israeli Occupation and its institutions. The Intifada has not only served as a catalyst for creating alternatives to closed schools but it has also pressed the need for a national curriculum which is more suited and relevant to Palestinian needs and aspirations. The discussion which follows will examine the impact of the Israeli Occupation on educational quality and then examine the educational challenges and responses created by the Intifada.

EDUCATIONAL QUALITY UNDER THE ISRAELI OCCUPATION

The quality of education has declined drastically after 1967, in government schools more than others. No new schools were built during the first ten years of the Occupation, and very few were built thereafter. The expansion of school facilities and the hiring of additional teachers did not kept pace with the dramatic growth in the student population. Classrooms became more and more overcrowded. The average class size in a government school reached forty. Some classes reached as high as sixty students. Most government schools lacked basic facilities, such as science laboratories, libraries, vocational education workshops, and audiovisual teaching aids. Meagre funding and the high number of banned books limited the schools' capacity to provide adequate libraries for their students. Similarly, where science laboratories did exist, they lacked sufficient equipment necessary for carrying out practical experiments. Many schools lacked essential facilities such as proper toilets, healthy classrooms, and playgrounds. Extracurricular activities, essential for the academic, social, and cultural development of the students and for preparation for adult life, including science clubs and cultural lectures, were banned by the authorities, although (as indicated below) they continued to exist in private schools.

Moreover, the continuation of restrictive measures taken by the authorities against government school teachers made it difficult for these schools to reach sound educational standards. Hiring practices, such as refusing to hire graduates of West Bank universities, also added to the problem of maintaining quality education—in practice this meant that most government school teachers lacked the proper qualifications specified by Jordanian educational law (Abu-Duhou 1993). Teacher training was also inadequate. The Israeli authorities in the Occupied West Bank and Gaza Strip have held very few in-service teachers' training courses over their thirty years of occupation. Furthermore, these courses reached very few teachers and were held mostly in universities in Israel. The Israeli authorities, as their employer, prohibited government school teachers from attending courses organized by local Palestinian universities and other private Palestinian educational institutions. Furthermore, the low salaries paid to government school teachers, compared to those paid in Jordan and Israel and to those in UNRWA and private schools, made it difficult for these schools to maintain teacher quality—specifically the capacity to keep good teachers or attract new ones of ability. Low salaries compelled many teachers to seek a second job to supplement their family income.

The severity of the education situation in the WBGS reached an acute level during the early years of the Intifada, which started in December 1987. The extended and repeated closure of schools by the Israeli authorities constrained the schools' ability to run the structured learning–teaching processes in a normal way. Israeli authorities were driven largely by security concerns; thus they were more concerned with building high fences around the schools than with improving the schools' facilities. For example, in July 1990, the authorities informed many private and UNRWA schools that unless they raised their fences higher around their perimeter, they would not be allowed to open in September. This directive strained the already marginal budgets of these schools. Private schools, especially, were forced to raise large sums of money to pay for labor and materials.

In this context, it was most difficult to assess the quality of instruction or levels of achievement. Unfortunately, there were no objective data or studies to inform judgment on the matter. In 1990, however, an attempt was made to address this vacuum, and an initiative was taken to assess the skill levels of about 3,000 elementary school children in the central region of the West Bank (Tamer Institute for Community Education 1991). This unprecedented study found that elementary school children were experiencing great difficulties acquiring even basic skills in Arabic and mathematics. A number of randomly selected results showed that: (1) only 24 percent of the fourth graders tested could accurately measure with a ruler a given line segment that was 5 centimeters long; (2) 73 percent of the fourth graders tested could not add $\frac{1}{2} + \frac{1}{4}$; (3) only 2.3 percent of the fourth graders tested and 22.8 percent of the sixth graders tested were able to produce the required number of sentences specified in the test. Further, the sentences they wrote lacked correct grammatical structure, relevant ideas, and appropriate vocabulary; and (4) sixth-grade responses in the reading comprehension section were fully correct no more than 30 percent of the time. Overall, the study documented the fact that the current situation in education is far worse than generally recognized.

Further along the education ladder, secondary education, too, was always a concern to Palestinian educators. As noted earlier, at the end of twelve years of schooling, all students have to sit for the General Secondary School Certificate Examination (known as the Tawjihi examination), which is based on the twelfth-grade curriculum only. Prior to 1967, students prepared for a Jordanian-based examination in the West Bank, and an Egyptian-based examination in the Gaza Strip. For the Gaza schools, which have to follow the Egyptian curriculum, the Egyptian Ministry of Education continued to administer the exam. After 1967, a local examination board was set up in Nablus for West Bank students. The West Bank exam was based on the Jordanian curriculum which all West Bank schools had to follow. The Board in Nablus worked in close cooperation with the Jordanian Ministry of Education. Registering students for the exam and selecting examiners and graders were among the duties of the Board. At the conclusion of the examination, the board issued certificates to the candidates with their results, which were later exchanged in Jordan for Jordanian certificates. While the local board was to a degree affiliated to the Jordanian Minister of Education, it nevertheless had to report to the Israeli Education Officer responsible for the West Bank.

The Tawjihi examination presented a real example of the quality of education, or perhaps more accurately lack of quality, in the WBGS. The exam depended heavily on rote learning, did not measure critical or independent thinking, and was based on the final year of schooling, which limits its scope and content. Neither did the exam test the students' ability to apply in practice the knowledge they gained in the sciences and vocational education courses. Palestinians, however, have always placed great emphasis on the Tawjihi examination because students' admission to all Palestinian universities and most universities abroad depends on Tawjihi scores. The utility of the exam as a yardstick for admission into universities has always been questioned by Palestinian educators and universities in the WBGS. First, there was an immediate discontinuity in that school curricula are controlled directly by the Israelis and indirectly by the Jordanians, while the Tawjihi examination itself was directly controlled by Jordan and Egypt. Second, the severity of the exam, the average pass rates, and the grading levels were set each year by the Jordanian-Egyptian education ministries in relation to their own educational plans and their own universities' needs. Yet this affected the results of the WBGS as well, even though the student population in the territories did not necessarily fit into Jordan's and Egypt's educational planning.

Many educators, including the author (Abu-Duhou 1987), doubt the suitability of the Tawjihi as a measure of student ability and argue that students arrive at university poorly prepared. Fasheh was another to have questioned the validity of the exam:

> Starting in 1978, general questions on every subject were distributed by the departments of education at least four months before the exam, both in Jordan and in the West Bank. The writers of the questions on the exams were instructed to choose half of the questions exactly as they had appeared in those general questions, and in the other half to make only minor changes. At most one question could be different from the set of questions distributed to students. Rote and meaningless learning has never been treated better anywhere in the world! (1984, 302–303)

This phenomenon created serious problems for the Palestinian universities under Occupation. The universities found it necessary to provide courses designed to bridge the transition from secondary schools, and administered locally designed aptitude exams in mathematics, English, and general science. While the Tawjihi exam has not changed much in content and style for the last two decades, it nevertheless has lost much of its significance during the Intifada. The repeated and prolonged school closures by the Israeli military during the first two years of the Intifada did not allow secondary students adequate time to prepare properly for the exam. For example, in 1988–1989, such students attended approximately 120 school days instead of the minimum 210 required by Jordanian law. Thus, many students felt compelled to cheat in order to get a passing grade. A meeting of thirty educators in July 1990 saw the Tawjihi as one of the major issues troubling the Palestinian community, especially during the years of the Intifada (*Educational Network Newsletter* 1990). For the first time, students engaged in openly unethical behavior, cheating during the exam. The cumulative effects of the repeated and prolonged school closures and harassment of students by the Israeli military were taking their toll. The detrimental impact of these Israeli actions on the moral conduct of students was never more evident.

In such an environment, it was little wonder that the term *quality* had little purchase, though the need for quality was always keenly felt. Hardly a day passed without one's hearing people in the West Bank and Gaza expressing concern about their children's education. People's worries revolved around the gradual deterioration of students' acquisition of the skills and knowledge necessary for contemporary life. The prolonged school closures imposed by the military authorities, curfews, and general strikes had cut regular school time by more than half. Moreover, there was little to indicate that there was to be any improvement as long as the Israeli Occupation continued. Results from one study, which tested some 3,000 students, indicated that the deterioration of Palestinian education reached emergency proportions. As demonstrated so far, many factors contributed to that state of affairs. The formal education sector was hampered by overcrowded classrooms, inadequate budgets, ill-trained teachers, and a traditional curriculum that was grossly out of date as well as censored by Israeli authorities. In the classroom, much emphasis was given to the memorization of information instead of skills related to problem solving or critical thinking. The prolonged school closures had only exacerbated the general situation. For example, government schools in the districts in which the student achievement testing took place lost as much as 67 percent of their school days in 1988–1989 and 54 percent in 1989/90. Statistics from the UNRWA indicate that, on the average, students in the UNRWA schools missed 48 percent of their school days in the West Bank and 51 percent in the Gaza Strip in those two academic years. Further, political restrictions, low pay, and difficult conditions of work were affecting teachers' morale, while avenues of extracurricular nonformal education were largely closed.

The decline in teacher quality, the lowering of school standards, and the restrictive measures of the Israeli authorities combined to present a picture of crisis in education on the West Bank and in Gaza. On the eve of the Intifada, Palestinian educators saw this educational regression accelerating further under Occupation, and the events during the Intifada heightened interests in education. As Mahshi and Bush (1989) rightly claim, the Intifada had been a "catalyst" for educational change, by creating "a giant educational laboratory, which challenges conservative educators to start afresh" (470–483). This challenge was also posed to those educators who live in the West Bank and Gaza. By taking a new look at the overall educational practices within the Palestinian community, these educators worked against tremendous odds to offer alternative forms of schooling.

THE INTIFADA: EDUCATIONAL
CHALLENGES AND RESPONSES

Carnoy (1974) claims that such situations of colonialism, as described here, can give rise to substantial movements that have nationalistic characteristics (for examples African Americans, Mexican Americans, Puerto Ricans, and Native Americans within the United States). He maintains that

liberation from colonial rule requires a redevelopment of humanness
and self-esteem; a *redefinition* of what it means to be independent.
When people are colonized, they are *dependent* and do not even know
how to behave in a liberated condition. Decolonization, or liberation,
demands personal and societal struggles which go far beyond lowering
one flag and raising another. (19–20)

For the Palestinians, this drive was manifested in the Intifada, which had
challenged the Israeli Occupation and its institutions. But, what was the
Intifada and what were its unique characteristics? As asserted by a leading Palestinian, the Intifada was the product of many decades of oppression and suffering. It was a

> simultaneously active statement of rejection and affirmation, an unequiv-
> ocal rejection of the Israeli occupation with all its implications, norms,
> and realities; and the affirmation of the inalienable rights of the Pales-
> tinian people including . . . the right of freedom, self-determination, and
> statehood. (Mikhail-Ashrawi 1989, 15)

The Intifada was thus a movement against the Israeli Occupation. It was
considered as the "coming of age of the Palestinians" in the WBGS, a

> culmination of a gradual process of organization and resistance which
> has taken the form of a spontaneous eruption, an upheaval that has
> shaken the very foundations of the occupation, and brought into ques-
> tion all the compliant assumptions which underlie its short-sighted
> policies and expansionist dreams. (Mikhail-Ashrawi 1989, 16)

What really happened in the Occupied West Bank and Gaza Strip was a
contest between the will of the indigenous people in asserting their rights,
and the desire of the colonial power to affirm its capacity to control. One
would expect that the means the occupied people employ in the struggle
would correlate with the degree of injustice inflicted upon them. Equally,
one might predict that the occupier would utilize all the resources at its
disposal to defeat the challenge. This was the asymmetrical relation mentioned earlier.

The Intifada's democratic process was clearly demonstrated at every
level and stage of its development with a dynamic that was singularly
appropriate to its perspective and objectives. Comprehensive and deep
rooted, "the Intifada emanated from the grassroots and cut across all lines
such as region, sex, religion, and political/factional affiliation. It unified

all classes and sectors of society in an active pursuit of clear objectives and goals" (Mikhail-Ashrawi 1989, 16, Abu-Duhou 1989).

In education, a revolution was created under the Intifada and took the form of grassroots institutions and programs. Most of these started before the outbreak of the Intifada, but the Intifada reinforced their vision and educational philosophy. Mahshi and Bush claimed that

> All of these programs have a common desire to create genuine alterna-
> tives to the existing educational system: All of them seek to develop a
> new system relevant to Palestinian society and focusing on the devel-
> opment of well-rounded human beings. (1989, 479)

These innovative programs covered a wide spectrum of educational levels: from preschool through high school to university education. At the school level, the list included: neighborhood or popular education movement, alternative modes of instruction designed to bypass school closures but still using the existing system and textbooks, informal community-based education programs, education for awareness and involvement, and long-term planning as part of the nation-building process.

The remainder of this chapter will focus on some of these programs and will show how they have impacted on education. These programs "advocate comprehensive curriculum change, as well as a major trans-formation in teaching methodology on all levels" (Mahshi and Bush 1989, 480). They also stress the need for the integration of school and community, and insist on education that is relevant to the needs of the community. The premise of these programs is that quality education in general should be an education that will not impose obsolete, ready, fixed, or irrelevant mental maps of reality on people, but rather an education that will help people clarify and develop maps that reflect, as accurately as possible, the world around them and that can assist in transforming their conditions (Fasheh 1990, Mahshi and Bush 1989). To these educators, quality education is that which focuses on the world of practice, with the goal of producing knowledge in the context of action.

GRASSROOTS ATTEMPTS TO IMPROVE EDUCATION

Events during the years of the Intifada were revealing that, as Fasheh, a prominent Palestinian educator, claimed, " Fundamental changes in edu-cation are usually not generated from within education itself, and do not happen as a result of preaching, conferences, or resolutions, or by grand designs or expertise on the subject." Rather, he asserted,

> such changes are usually generated in response to drastic changes, events, or crises in the environment, by people who are ready to seize the opportunity created by the new conditions and who are competent in recognizing and dealing with the accompanying challenges and needs. (1990, 21)

One expression of this development was the widespread growth of organisations at the grassroots level. Most significantly, many neighborhood committees were formed to deal with basic problems and needs in the community.[1] Given that schools were closed indefinitely at the outbreak of the Intifada, these committees assumed responsibility for education by organizing schools and offering alternative modes of instruction. Classes were held in houses, gardens, clubs, mosques, and churches and were taught by anyone in the neighborhood who was educated and willing to volunteer time. But these neighborhood committees were dealt a severe blow by the Israeli military order of August 18, 1988, which made it a crime for anyone to be involved in popular committees, including those concerned with gardening and teaching children in homes. The penalty for engaging in such activities was up to ten years' imprisonment. This order significantly curtailed the activities of the neighborhood committees. As noted by Fasheh, it was "actually ironic when one considers the role of home teaching in the survival of the Jews in Europe for many centuries" (1990, 21).

SELF-STUDY PROGRAMS

Despite this, in September 1988, in response to the prolonged closure of all West Bank Palestinian schools, some private schools and UNRWA schools initiated a home-study program for their students. Teachers in these schools prepared and distributed study packets for their students to use at home. In October 1988, just after this initiative was launched, and after the first set of these packets had been distributed, the military outlawed this activity. It was made a criminal act for Palestinians to try to educate their children in their own home. (It is an interesting irony that during the Gulf War in 1991, the Israeli educational authorities implemented the very method of home-study as described above which they had outlawed in October 1988.) It is also important to note that the Israeli authorities, who were bound by international law to "facilitate the proper working of all institutions devoted to the care and education of children" (Article 50 of the Fourth Geneva Convention, to which Israel is a signatory), did not act to guarantee the normal functioning of Palestinian institutions of formal education.

Following the ban on home schooling, Palestinian educators started a new tactic of training themselves in individualized instruction methods and preparing materials for school children in the WBGS. As described in the *Education Network Newsletter* (June 1990), the project, established in 1989, intended to develop curriculum materials which require students to take an active role in their education. Its philosophical premise was that motivation and learning increase when students are actively engaged with their learning material, and that learning takes place when students mentally or manually work through the problems or situations they encounter in life. By 1991, the program expanded to include seventeen teachers from several schools, representing all three sectors of education. These included teachers of social studies, science, Arabic, English, or mathematics.

To maximize the effectiveness of these initiatives, teachers were trained, by a professor from a local university, in the philosophy and methods of individualized teaching and learning, and trained to write their own teaching materials, which would meet the diverse needs of their students in the classroom and at home. Again, a consultant from the International Extension College (UK) was brought in 1991 to lead an eight-day intensive training seminar on "individualized instruction methods." Participants were encouraged to start developing their own self-study materials, which were applied for the school year 1991–1992. The material was evaluated and revised in 1992 and proved to be very effective. A manual for teachers on how to write and use self-study materials was produced, and additional teachers, with help from the original core group, were being trained. This was seen as the first step towards curriculum development in Palestine, a vital and unprecedented experience for the Palestinians. Under the PNA, groups involved with these initiatives have been invited to expand their activities beyond the limited boundaries of private schools.

DEVELOPMENTS IN COMMUNITY EDUCATION

In different parts of the world, community education offers local citizens the opportunity to actively address the needs they themselves have identified as necessary for the improvement of the quality of their life.

The main idea is to involve citizens in solving their own problems. In the WBGS, community education was nonexistent prior to the Intifada. In 1989, a pioneering initiative in education was established by the Tamer Institute for Community Education. Its work revolved around creating settings where projects taken on by the community help each individual increase his/her ability to express experiences, construct knowledge and thought, and make sense of the social environment. The goal was a changed human being, more capable of getting information, of identifying and solving problems, of addressing needs, and of producing something useful.

The Institute's philosophy was to view education as a process which involves the interplay of action, thought, and dialogue. The institute, through a small, centralized staff, cooperated with a countrywide network of organizations, schools, and individuals to foster the exchange of information, ideas, and experiences and to promote projects that have practical applications in the community. These projects included

raising general community issues through, for example, a reading campaign to develop people's habit of reading; reflecting with local "managers" on the effectiveness of Palestinian social organizations by looking at how institutions are built and how they function; and involving youth in community work;

promoting cultural expressions by, for example, setting up creative writing workshops; developing a Palestinian character who can voice in a candid way experiences Palestinians are going through; creating toys and games with Palestinian cultural traits;

producing books, songs, slides, and a video based on discovery trips through the "small continent" to make it better known;

enriching school subjects and methods of teaching by, for example, organizing workshops to support and stimulate the work of teachers; producing materials for teachers; producing educational materials for children to study at home; collecting stories from Palestinians, young and old, to write a Palestinian history of Palestine;

developing communication networks, by systematically making efforts to reach out to institutions and individuals working in the community with the purpose of identifying educational needs and implementing projects to meet them. (Tamer Institute for Community Education 1991)

By 1995, the impact of the institute was being felt at all levels in Gaza and the West Bank and in areas of Israel where there is a majority of Arab population, like Akka. The work of the institute is best appreciated by detailing one of its projects noted above: the small continent. The Small Continent for children is a comprehensive project where youth and adults join in a common venture to explore their relationship with their common geographical, historical, sociological, spiritual, and cultural environment. The project not only emphasizes harmony between human beings and their environment, but also establishes communication among people by connecting various disciplines (archaeology, botany, history, geography, and education) and various forms of expression (writing, story-telling, illustration, slides, video, drama, music, singing, and dancing). There are few places as rich as Palestine with historical events that took place throughout the ages. However, Palestinian children usually are not aware of this wealth surrounding them. In school they study the history and geography of neighboring countries but not their own. The same applies to television programs, which are never about their immediate environment.

This was one of the most creative projects, for it opened up new horizons about what it was possible to do in those circumstances, by extending the children's imagination. Strategies such as travel helped to create alternatives to what was presented to them. For example, a group of children and adults would go on a trip to one of the valleys with two archaeologists leading the way along the valley to prehistoric caves. This achieved two purposes: first, the children gain a feeling for what life was like thousands of years ago, and secondly they discovered how the space was used today. To record their impressions, children would be expected on each trip to produce an essay, a drawing, or a song keeping in mind that they would be talking to other children who were not able to join them on the trip. Each adult would also contribute his/her special skills during and following each trip, in order to produce a series of discovery books, cassettes, and videotapes.

EDUCATION FOR AWARENESS AND INVOLVEMENT

At the school level, the most significant attempt to make education more meaningful was the program entitled "Education for Awareness and Involvement" (EAI). The purpose of this innovative program, according to its pamphlets (1989), was to make school education in the WBGS more relevant. Its goal was to develop a model program of education capable of transferring the educational process in the area from a "traditional," noninteractive, and nonmeaningful approach to an approach that was based upon active participation, internal motivation, individual problem solving, and personal and national relevance. In short, it aimed at helping students become more aware of themselves and their community and, at the same time, preparing them for involvement in the solution of the problems of their society and its development.

The central issue of EAI was to provide education for awareness about self, society, and career as well as, for involvement in the development of society, with a focus on the following broad objectives:

> To transfer teaching methods from one that stresses rote-learning to that which stresses learning by doing and active participation of the student while helping students develop positive self-esteems by becoming aware of their physical, intellectual and emotional abilities.

> To introduce courses which make school education more relevant to the world of work and production, including vocational education which is intended to develop the productive manual skills of the students.

> To introduce career counseling and a work experience program for secondary school students to help them in making realistic decisions in the choice of their future professions.

> To develop courses and activities for students to make them think about development-related issues and make them aware about the situation of their society and the need to preserve their physical and socio-cultural environment.

> To create better two-way links between schools and their communities. Special stress is put here on making EAI a means to re-educate the educated by giving the chance to educators from local universities to take part in relevant educational innovation. (EAI pamphlets 1989)

The implementation of EAI started in 1986 in five Evangelical Lutheran Schools in the West Bank, and other schools followed suit the following years. The program was motivated by both the reported high levels of graduate unemployment and the dissatisfaction with school education (Abu-Duhou 1987, 20–29). As in other Third World countries, education in the WBGS became infected with the "diploma disease," and academic higher degree awarding became the most important function of school education while the needs of about 90 percent of the students who never make it to university were not met (Abu-Duhou 1987, 29, Mahshi and Bush 1989). Thus, the value of schooling becomes highly questionable when its highest priority is to prepare students for academic higher education at a time when thousands of university graduates are unemployed.

One also needs to remember that the WBGS not only shared the problems of unemployment of the educated and underdevelopment with the rest of the Third World countries, but it also had to face the problems caused by the lack of independence and its subjugation to military occupation.

In such an atmosphere, educators who initiated the EAI project doubted the benefits of conventional schooling to the individual and to society, for it was evident that school education became dissociated from employment opportunities and irrelevant to the specificity, present needs, and future aspirations of society. The program objectives were designed accordingly to overcome these concerns. Activities to fulfil these objectives were implemented.

To transform the teaching practices from rote learning to active learning on the part of the student meant that students became the center of the teaching–learning process. Equally, the content of material taught at the schools was changed, to be more relevant to the surroundings of the students and the needs of their community. Several courses and practical workshops were held for teachers of all subjects in order to put into practice all the theories presented in the given courses. Local experts, as well as experts from several countries with similar educational conditions, were invited to supervise these workshops and enrich teachers with their different experiences in education. All these courses and workshops were attended by the teachers of the EAI schools, in addition to a number of teachers from other private and public schools in the WBGS.

The second objective of EAI stressed the importance of vocational education and the building within the student of respect for productive manual work. In order to better qualify the teachers of vocational education, workshops in electricity, carpentry, and metalwork were held for teachers who were intended to teach the subject. Vocational education workshops at some private schools were established and equipped to meet the needs of the students. A committee of teachers was also formed to help in the development of the workshops and assist the instructors of the vocational education training courses. Exhibitions are held to encourage students to exhibit and sell their products.

To help students become "career mature," potential career counselors at the EAI schools were trained, and career counseling centers were established in each school and equipped with the appropriate occupational tools. The purpose of these centers was to help students identify and clarify their personal abilities and interests, in order to be able to make a realistic career choice.

Skills, readiness, and vocational orientation of students covered several areas. Vocational education for the compulsory cycles was the most successful of EAI. Students at the preparatory cycle were trained in the various skills of carpentry, electricity, and metal work. The performance of the trained students was very impressive and their interaction was very encouraging. Several students decided to further their education in this field.

While vocational education was always a part of the official curricula offered in West Bank schools, very few schools have had either the proper vocational workshops or the trained teachers required for the proper teaching of the subjects. In order to be better acquainted with the world of work and to be able to choose a future career in a healthy and realistic way, grade 9 students were taken to visit different work sites in the country. Work experience programs were organized by career counselors, school principals, and parents' councils for the secondary-cycle students (grade 10 and 11). This program involved the placement of students for two weeks in a work site of their choice.

To enhance the importance of ecological awareness, science teachers at the EAI schools took training in the various specificities of the environment, in general, and the Palestinian environment in particular. This training started in February 1989 and continued for two years. During this workshop, participants made visits to some reserves, and went on several field trips taking pictures and video films.

A major component of the EAI was to teach students awareness about their society and their readiness to participate in its development. Voluntary work was one such activity, either within school boundaries or outside the school boundaries. Students' committees were also formed for voluntary work and environment preservation.

The final aim of EAI was to establish close cooperation between the school and the community. This aim was based on the philosophy that the education of children was the responsibility not of the school alone, but, of the whole community. The organizers believed that education shaped the social structure as much as it was shaped by it. Therefore, involvement of students' parents was essential for the success of the program. Parents' Councils were formed at the EAI schools and briefed about EAI and its implementation. They were encouraged to help in the implementation of some of the components of the program, particularly the work experience and the vocational orientation programs.

Schools participating in the EAI were reporting high success with the different aspects of the program. Given that the PNA is now responsible for all schools in the territories, it remains to see how much of these initiatives will be translated into actions within the whole school system!

CONCLUSIONS

This chapter principally dealt with the process of educational expansion in the West Bank and Gaza while the area was under Israeli Occupation since 1967 until the time of the transfer of responsibility of education to the Palestinians in 1994. The chapter presented factors which have impacted on the quality of education. From the many obstacles listed as facing education at that time, the Israeli Occupation was identified as the prime impediment to education, for it prohibited aspects which were essential to the pursuit of education. The Israeli Occupation had clearly inhibited the main purpose of education: sustaining and enhancing the quality of life of the people. So long as one group makes and enforces the rules for another, so long as there is a "culture of silence" (Freire 1970, 38), the status quo exists. Freire argues that literacy and education change individuals from merely being "in" the world to being "with" the world and that with this new awareness they become conscious of their situation and can no longer accept domination. This seems to be the case in several developing areas of the world, and the Occupied Palestinian Territories fitted into this paradigm.

Palestinians were determined to preserve their peoplehood, to obtain an education, and to be free. As such, they realized that the major cause of the problem in their education, as argued here, was the fact that school education and its curricula were imposed by outsiders without any regard to the specificity of the local Palestinian situation, as is the case in most Third World countries. At the outbreak of the Intifada, Palestinian educators felt the need to develop confidence in their ability to innovate in education in order to make school education relevant. This case study and the efforts made at the grassroots level provide an important illustration of the struggle for identity for those educators concerned with the quality of education in Third World countries. This chapter demonstrated that, like many others, Palestinians were forced to deal with an education which models the learner to a preconceived concept of education. The circumstances at that time and the Intifada made it appropriate to reverse the process and to set the stage for the PNA to build an education that fits the learner. Such an education not only holds a special conception of quality but aims at achieving equity and justice in educational provision.

As these lines were revised in early 1998, the major parts of the West Bank were still under the Israeli Occupation. However, the education system was in the hands of the PNA. Surely, the PNA inherited a system which suffered from "a deliberate and carefully thought out neglect" by the Occupation—a system which suffered from all kinds of ills, of which perhaps the most significant was the total absence of quality and equity, and the total absence of experienced administrative, policy-making, and planning personnel. This was so because the Palestinians had been deliberately excluded from the governing process of education, resulting in its being left in the hands of an inexperienced administration. Despite all of these obstacles, there were initiatives within the educated community which were seen as the first steps towards educational development and improvement in the territories. If these initiatives are nurtured and developed further, as a minimal condition, Palestinian education may revive from its "death bed." Still, the task of the PNA is tremendous and the road is very long.

NOTES

1. Grassroots groups actually started forming in the early 1980s. They included women's committees, medical and agricultural relief committees, and groups working in education and economic development. The activities of these committees included storing and distributing food, responding to health needs, taking care of the wounded and the needy, communal gardening, teaching children in homes, mosques, and churches, and alerting the community to army raids and settlers' attacks. Popular education dealing with these issues, as well as with school subjects, flourished for a few months after the beginning of the Intifada. See Fasheh (1990), Mahshi and Bush (1989), and Abu-Duhou (1989).

REFERENCES

Abu-Duhou, Ibtisam (1987) "An Analytical Model for Cost-Effectiveness Analysis in Higher Education with Application to University Education in the West Bank." Unpublished Ph.D. dissertation, University of Pittsburgh, Pittsburgh.

Abu-Duhou, Ibtisam (1989) "Solidarity in Oppression: Palestinian Women and the Intifada." Paper presented at the International Women's Day Meeting, Adelaide.

Abu-Duhou, Ibtisam (1993) "Educational Challenges in Institutions Under Siege." *Journal of Arabic, Islamic and Middle Eastern Studies* 1 (1): 26–38.

Al-Fajr Newspaper (1987) Interview with Dr. Gabi Baramki, Vice-President of Birzeit University, 20 February, 16.

Altbach, Philip G., and Kelly, Gail P. (eds.) (1978) *Education and Colonialism.* New York, Longman.

Altbach, Philip G., and Kelly, Gail P. (eds.) (1984) *Education and the Colonial Experience* (2nd rev. ed.). New Brunswick, Transaction Books.

Aruri, Nasser (ed.) (1984) *Occupation: Israel Over Palestine.* London, Zed Books.

Carnoy, Martin (1974) *Education as Cultural Imperialism.* New York, David McKay Company, Inc.

Carnoy, Martin (1984) *The State and Political Theory.* Princeton, Princeton University Press.

Clignet, Remi (1984) "Damned If You Do, Damned If You Don't: The Dilemmas of Colonizer-Colonized Relations." In Philip G. Altbach and Gail P. Kelly (eds.), *Education and the Colonial Experience* (2nd rev. ed.), 77–95. New Brunswick, Transaction Books.

"Education for Awareness and Involvement" Newsletter and pamphlets, n.d.

Education Network Newsletter (1990) 6:July.

Education Network Newsletter (1992) 9:July.

Fasheh, Munir (1984) "Education Under Occupation." In Nasser Aruri (ed.), *Occupation: Israel Over Palestine,* 302–323. London, Zed Books.

Fasheh, Munir (1990) "Community Education: To Reclaim and Transform What Has Been Made Invisible." *Harvard Educational Review* 60 (1): 19–35.

Freire, Paulo (1972) *Cultural Action for Freedom.* Harmondsworth, Penguin

Graham-Brown, Sarah (1984) *Education, Repression and Liberation: Palestinians.* London, World University Services.

Hartwig, Mervyn (1978) "Capitalism and Aborigines: The Theory of Internal Colonialism and Its Rivals." In E. L. Wheelwright and Ken Buckley (eds.), *Essays in the Political Economy of Australian Capitalism.* Sydney, Australia and New Zealand Book Company Vol. 3: 119–41.

Mahshi, Khalil and Bush, Kim (1989) "The Palestinian Uprising and Education for the Future." *Harvard Educational Review,* 59 (4): 470–83.

Middle East International (1993) September.

Mikhail-Ashrawi, Hanan (1989) *From Intifada to Independence.* Netherlands, The Arab League Office.

Shaath, Nabil (1971) "High Level Palestinian Manpower." *Journal of Palestinian Studies* 1 (2): 90–106.

Tamer Institute for Community Education (1991) *Assessment of Achievement in Arabic and Math of Fourth and Sixth Grade Students in the Central*

Region of the West Bank. East Jerusalem, Tamer Institute for Community Education.

Tamer Institute for Community Education Newsletter, No. 1, 1991.

Webster's New Collegiate Dictionary (7th ed.) 1967.

Welch, Anthony R. (1988) "Aboriginal Education as Internal Colonialism: the Schooling of an Indigenous Minority in Australia." *Comparative Education,* 24 (2): 203–15.

Welch, Anthony R. (1996) *Australian Education: Reform or Crisis?* Sydney, Allen and Unwin.

Welch, Anthony R., and Gientzotis, Jill (1996) "Something to Show for Years of Work? Employment Education and Training for Aboriginal Australians." *Journal of Indigenous Studies* 4 (1).

Whitehead, Clive (1981) "Education in British Colonial Dependencies, 1991–39: A Re-appraisal." *Comparative Education Review,* 17 (1): 71–80.

CHAPTER 4

The Mirror of China
Questions of Quality and Equality

R.F. PRICE

INTRODUCTION

The themes of quality and equality in education, whether in the Third World or any other "world," need to be related to more fundamental structures of society as a whole if they are to be of any help in overcoming the problems of the 1990s and the twenty-first century. In the face of a breakdown of the "world order" we have known since World War II, with yet new wars, mass unemployment, and greater consciousness of the frailty of the physical and biological environment on which human society depends, our approach to education has more than academic significance. China, as a mirror into which we can look in order to see our own problems more clearly, is of particular value because of its revolutionary history, an ancient culture which continues to influence people far beyond its own borders, and its history of relations (including a long history of comparative educational relations)[1] with other countries. An evaluation of what constitutes, and should constitute, quality is important if statements about education are to be other than purely descriptive and backward looking. What is needed is understanding which will suggest ways of harnessing education (learning) to achieve socially desirable goals. What qualities this would involve and what meaning needs to be given to "equality" is the underlying theme of this chapter. But, to begin, the term "education" itself needs to be examined.

The model of education I shall be employing is one which takes as central a learning–teaching process which is not limited to schooling, but includes all those other social situations in which humankind learns its place in the world and, perhaps, a vision of a better life. The model requires identification of the major agents of education. In the case of the People's Republic of China, the Communist Party has clearly been one of these, influencing people through a variety of other agents including the schools. Finally, the model considers the content of the education process, the information and ideas whether called knowledge or ideology, and a variety of skills of a social and technical nature. In a country like China, where until recently a high proportion of the population did not attend school for more than a short and often irregular period, it is particularly important to consider the agents other than school. But it is true everywhere that when one is considering the moral–political ideas which form our world view and shape how we behave with our fellow humans, the school is only one of the teachers, and probably seldom the most significant one.

The purpose of educational theory, like other theory, is either to describe and explain or to formulate recipes (know-how) for making and doing. The latter kind of theory has interested reformers in China at least since the middle of the nineteenth century, beginning with the "self-strengtheners"[2] with their concern for wealth and power, through the Nationalists (KMT or Guomindang) to members of the currently ruling Communist Party. The difficult theoretical problem is to relate the explanations to the know-how for change, to know which kind of explanation will be of use in formulating a recipe which will bring about the desired effect. It is also a question of "wealth and power" for whom. This is a different kind of theoretical question: the distinguishing of ideology (the representation of the conditions and interests of a minority group in society as the interests of the whole), of the rhetoric of the ruling class, from the reality experienced by different classes and groups.

A major failing of educational discourse is to confine it to schooling and to neglect the lifelong learning in society at large where the important learnings about "quality and equality" take place. Such a restricted conception neither explains important learnings nor enables one to formulate adequate recipes to achieve a stable "wealth and power," and certainly not for the majority of the population. Capitalism (in China today euphemistically described as "modernisation") is unequal and constantly produces and reproduces inequalities. To talk of inequalities of schooling as if eradicating them would change the inequalities in society as a whole is gross self-deception. Current Chinese leaders, at least, do not indulge in such rhetoric.

Posing of questions in terms of quality and equality of education, inequalities of educational opportunity and of treatment and outcome, sets us within the liberal democratic conceptual framework, a framework which I would argue has proved inadequate to the needs of this century and threatens disaster for the next. It also confines itself to education conceived narrowly in schooling terms, terms which I again would argue make it impossible to achieve the objectives of liberal democrats, let alone the aspirations of those who would go further. In this chapter I shall begin from the inequalities in society and the changes which have been and are taking place there, and I shall ask both what people are learning from living among these changes and what they might learn about a desirable future.[3] Space dictates that I can only sketch out what I see as important areas of questions and make a few assertions, leaving it to interested readers to take the argument further. While one needs constantly to question the meaning of quality if it is to be a tool of analysis and change, I shall structure this chapter around a number of gross inequalities, asking what lessons these are teaching people and what learnings would be needed for their removal. My assumption is that schooling contributes to the continuance of most of these inequalities and that there is little likelihood that changes in schooling alone can make any difference to them.

I shall begin with a consideration of hierarchy, an inequality which runs through Chinese, and other, history and which "modernisation"[4] has done nothing other than alter. The old hierarchies of imperial China died out with the abolition of the civil service examination system around 1905 and the monarchy itself in 1911. The hierarchies of a capitalist republic began to be established in the intervening period, but were in the main reshaped during the People's Republic period after 1949. Soviet-style hierarchies were introduced in the fifties when it was the fashion to "learn from our Soviet brother." In the current efforts at "modernisation," Euro-American hierarchies are to some extent being relearnt. My treatment of the topic assumes that most hierarchies are undesirable and that an ideal model of democracy would involve all of us in much more than occasional voting for what Marx called "misrepresentatives" (CW.22; 333), one which would more truly reflect Marx's conception of a self-conscious and self-determining community. I believe that only such a model can overcome the problems humanity faces today, both in and outside China, and that history repeatedly confirms this. I also believe it is important to distinguish between democracy, the question of power, and freedoms, such as freedom of information, of press and publishing, and the freedom to organise political parties and other social groups and organisations. Much discussion of democracy is vitiated by a failure to make this distinction.

EDUCATION AND HIERARCHY

In a recent discussion of hierarchy in the political culture of China, Oskar Weggel refers to Louis Dumont's study of the caste system in India where he speaks of *homo hierarchicus*. Weggel goes on to assert that the hierarchical principle is no less a feature of Chinese (and Japanese) society, an assertion he supports with historical example and from a description of the current structure of town and village (1992, 531–55).

In China the ideological weight of Confucian principles remains and has been reinforced by the Communist experience. The *Analects* of Confucius contains many passages on filial behaviour, for example, "A youth, when at home should be filial, and, abroad, respectful to his elders" (cited in Price 1970). *The Doctrine of the Mean* contains the five "duties of obligation": "between sovereign and minister, between father and son, between husband and wife, between elder brother and younger, and those belonging to the intercourse of friends" (1970), all relations in which paternalistic hierarchy held sway. Kahn-Ackermann is one foreigner who has witnessed the working of these principles of hierarchy in daily life in China in recent decades. At one place he writes:

> In the eyes of many Chinese, the power that a person wields is still seen as legitimised directly by the position he holds. If he is sufficiently far up the hierarchy, then he is virtually impregnable. Our Chinese fellow-students were always irritated when they saw caricatures of leading politicians in the Western newspapers. . . . A member of the party leadership can be criticised or removed from office only by his equals or superiors; open criticism from below is confined to exceptional situations. (1982, 107–08)

The "exceptional situations" are presumably those mentioned in the *Mencius* where, invoking the principle of the rectification of names, the "right to rebel" depended on the Emperor's behaviour being such that he could no longer be called Emperor (Price, 1970, 50). While suited to the factional struggles within the Communist Party during the Cultural Revolution, this is a far cry from Marx's conception of democracy.

The model of "Mr. Democracy" which was brought into China in the May 4th Movement in the teens of this century (Chow 1967, 59) was, of course, that which Marx had already characterised as "misrepresenta-tive," a form which has added a new class to the hierarchy of "experts" and "betters" with which the Chinese people were already so familiar. The professional politician, confused at times with the role of "revolu-tionary," was a far cry from the vision of a self-determining democratic society and delegate authority of which Marx wrote. But there were no mechanisms to bring these last ideas to the notice of the mass of Chinese, and no models outside fringe (and foreign) communities which might have given them credence. Instead, under the influence of the Soviet Communist Party, the Chinese Communist Party introduced the princi-ples of *democratic centralism* to govern politics in the People's Repub-lic. While these included phrases like "the subordination of the minority to the majority" this was countered in theory and practice by the rule that "the decisions of higher bodies are obligatory for lower bodies" (Price 1977a, 35). Modifications in the 1970s to include phraseology of a Maoist flavour (the mass line; serve the people) did nothing to alter the top-down practice. Leadership was almost universally in the bureaucrat-manager style, with its "excessive concern for status and hierarchy," rather than in that of the cadre, who was supposed to be both leader *and* participant in work (Brugger and Seldon cited in Price 1977a, 36).

The tradition of a benevolent dictatorship carried out by an all-pervasive bureaucracy of self-selected guardians of the official ideology has no place for the kind of grassroots democracy which Marx saw as the alternative to class exploitation. While it no doubt at times produces ideas of revolt, especially when the dictatorship is not benevolent or times are hard, this is of the kind criticised by Marx as "crude commu-nism" (CW 3: 294–96] in which "general envy constitut[es] itself as a power" and we can expect the kinds of atrocities which occurred during the Great Proletarian Cultural Revolution of 1966–1969, one of the few periods when the Chinese people had a considerable amount of freedom from central control.

LEARNING AND THE ECONOMY

It is widely recognised that the hierarchical structures discussed in the last section largely derive from and are supported by the nature of the econ-omy, the way in which people produce and distribute the food, clothing, and other things which they need, and also the many things which in class-divided societies down the ages they have been forced to produce but which they do not need. That is, the division of labour determines the division of wealth and power. Which is not to say that this is a simple relationship or one which is fixed and unalterable. But it does mean that any consideration of education as a process of social learning must look carefully at the nature of the economy and the social relations, the classes and social groups determined by it at different times. China, having within living memory changed from an almost entirely agricultural society of a precapitalist kind, through a "state socialist" stage, to a society which appears again to be in transition to a form of capitalism, is therefore particularly interesting to observe. The economy needs to be studied in terms of learnings. We need to know what skills significant groups (classes) learn; how people's social position influences their world views, their view of how it *is*, and, equally important, their vision of how it *might* be. There is reason to believe that what is educationally important may be the mismatch between how it is supposed to be and how it is experienced, between the propaganda and the realities of life. Unfortunately all this, other than vocational schooling, which is a different, if overlapping question, is ill explored, and I can here attempt only some pointers to further reading.

As I have just said, China was until recently primarily an agricultural country and still today some 80 percent of the population are rural, if not all still engaged in agriculture. Perkins notes that until the 1940s and 1950s, industry "involved little more than the processing of cotton, grain, and other products of the land" and "commerce was occupied primarily with the distribution of food and clothing" (1969, 5). While there is some evidence of cooperation in agriculture before the founding of the People's Republic in 1949 (Myers, cited in Perkins 1975, 261–77), this probably did little to counter the learning of hierarchical forms and dominance–subservience behaviour. But learnings would have been different in gentry and peasant families, as is well described by Stover (1974), especially in his chapter on "the Cult of Poverty." Across China, particularly from south to north, the nature of farming, the size of landholdings, and the stability of the class system varied, further complicating the learnings which took place. Migrations, leading to families having widely dispersed connections, including overseas, have also been an important factor in the learning processes and especially in the provision of knowledge and contacts required for commercial success.[5]

In the period from the middle 1950s to the death of Mao Zedong in 1976 China underwent a massive industrialisation programme, agriculture was collectivised in the People's Commune system, and small enterprise was forced into cooperatives.[6] Intense propaganda for the virtues of state and cooperative enterprise, however, failed for a complex of reasons yet to be satisfactorily explained. Certainly, the oppressive nature of the regime and the continued general poverty were important factors. In the last decade, beginning in agriculture and spreading into industry and commerce, various forms of private (capitalist) enterprises have been allowed and even encouraged. This has resulted in great wealth for some and, through higher prices, greater hardship for others. The balance of learnings from these developments has yet to reveal itself. One recent paper to touch on these is that by Findlay and Jiang (in Watson 1992), who discuss various "interest groups" which they see as "defined by the shared attitudes of their members" (20).

The groups and/or classes whose learnings one might expect to be significantly different have undergone a number of changes in the period outlined. Whole classes have disappeared and new ones have developed. Under the late Qing imperial system the scholar–bureaucrats, self-selected through the famous Examination System, occupied the administrative and high-status positions. They were drawn largely from the landlord–gentry class. It is interesting to compare them with the cadres of the Communist Party who have occupied nearly all state administrative positions in the People's Republic period, another self-selected group with "sacred" texts and entry by a different form of "examination." Learnings among the peasantry is a difficult question. Chinese Communist Party thinking has tried to distinguish subclasses within the peasantry, emphasising the revolutionary nature of the "poor and lower middle peasants," but as others have shown such subclasses may have been transitory, both within and between generations. Then there are diverse groups engaged in merchandising, ranging from the wealthy merchant families of imperial times through to small peddlers and traders. Their success certainly has not depended on anything (other than, perhaps, literacy) they might have learnt from school and, until recently, few would have attended.

The confused state of the present social structure is brought out in a number of contributions to Andrew Watson's *Economic Reform and Social Change in China* (1992). Watson himself speaks of "groups which had lost some of their privileges," including "the centralised bureaucracy, the political cadres of the party and the urban-based state enterprises" (247). It is not clear whether he includes the workers in the last category or simply the cadres in charge of the enterprises. In their chapter on "interest groups" in the same book Findlay and Jiang concentrate on "one of the key social divisions of interest," that separating "urban wage earners and the peasants." In doing that Findlay and Jiang divide "urban residents" into four subgroups: production workers, cadres, intellectuals and workers in the tertiary sector" (25). The inadequacy of "intellectuals" I will comment on below. What is helpful for our purposes is the delineating of interests. Attitudes are assumed rather than discovered. Behaviour is better described in such articles as that by David Goodman on "China's New Rich" (1992).

Another group whose quality of life is significantly different is that described by Dutton as the "floating population" of China. He cites a Chinese source to suggest a figure of some 1.15 million people in 1988 who were living and working away from home. This figure includes people from the rural areas who have migrated into the towns. Beijing alone, he estimates, may have 660,000 "immigrants" (Dutton, in Watson 1992, 212). O'Leary, writing of the labour market, discusses the related problem of the rural labour surplus and cites one estimate, a figure of 240 million to 260 million for the year 2000 (cited in Watson 1992, 50). All of this makes talk about equality of education, particularly equality of schooling, almost irrelevant.

SCHOOLING AND DEMOCRACY

There are three aspects of schools which are significant for the learning of democracy.[7] The first is that schools form a "ladder to the clouds" (compare Stover 1974, Chapter 14), selecting out the "successful," who will occupy the top jobs in society. While there have been other routes to the top in China in the recent past which may again be important with the increasing development of capitalist enterprises, increasing school attendance has made the route through school dominant. In contrast to many capitalist countries, where it is the law faculties which lead into politics, in the USSR and to a lesser degree but increasingly in China, it has been engineering.[8] Also as in other countries, not all schools provide a long enough ladder. Those in the rural areas, even if extending through the full twelve years of primary, junior, and senior secondary school, seldom rank sufficiently to admit their graduates to the right tertiary colleges and thence the "top jobs." In the period after 1978 the selective, discriminatory nature of the schools was exacerbated by the designation of schools at all three levels as priority schools (*zhongdian xuexiao*) (Price 1979, 298–99, Henze 1982). Such schools were provided with extra funding, either from central, provincial, or local government, and teachers and students were specially selected. Now it would seem that, as the nine-year universal school is achieved, these will be phased out, at least at the primary and junior high school level (*China aktuell* 1991: 751(16)). Another development in the post-1978 period has been the attempt to convert a high proportion of general secondary schools into vocational schools, a development which appears not to have been popular and which introduces another inequality. In the past, vocational schools have been seen as of lower status, leading to lower status jobs, and there is no reason to believe this will not continue.

Turning to the internal organisation of schools, while Chinese schools do not all exhibit the disciplined conformity which has been so attractive to many foreign visitors and teachers of English as a Foreign Language, frustrated by "reluctant learners" at home, they are organised to reinforce the general societal teaching on hierarchy. In addition to such things as sitting up straight and standing to answer the teacher, each class has a hierarchy of duty monitors to whom the other students have to defer. In addition there are the hierarchies of the youth organisations, the Young Pioneers and the Communist Youth League, though membership in these and therefore their effect has varied greatly over time and place. Complex rules governing the preservation of "face" which, for example, preclude the student from questioning the teacher during the lesson, but not in the interval between lessons, also reinforce awareness of hierarchy.

The curriculum of the schools also contributes to the learning of undemocratic ways. Still grounded on the European model, it provides a comprehensive introduction to the main fields of academic knowledge, varied at times with concessions to the Maoist interpretation of the principle of "combining education with productive [sometimes "socially useful"] labour." Moral–political topics feature in all subjects and as a separate subject, consisting of idealised situations and abstractions such as "the five loves" or stories of heroes such as Lei Feng. In all schools there is considerable memorising of texts and the materials are presented as a "rhetoric of conclusions," to use that apposite phrase of Schwab's (1963, 39). Theory is presented as fact and there is little encouragement for the student either to understand the social production of knowledge or to take control of his or her own learning.

John Dewey is the name which must spring to mind in any discussion of democracy and schooling. When living in China from May 1919 to July 1921 he said in a lecture:

> school life *is* social life. . . . School can gradually develop the potentialities and the interests of the individual students, and do it in such a way that the individual, in the process of realising his own potentialities, develops social knowledge and becomes aware of the needs of

his society and of the many interrelationships between and among the different segments of that society. He learns, also, that associated living requires that at times the individual must sacrifice his own interests, or subordinate them to broader social interests. . . . (cited in Clopton and Ou, 1973, 299–300)

Dewey's Chinese student, Tao Xingzhi, was more realistic in recognising that the society *outside* the school "had to provide the live lessons for learning" (Keenan 1977, 105); the school, even if it could be radically changed, could not do the required job alone. Then, within the school and considering only the curriculum, there remain unsolved (even unconsidered) problems of just what should be taught and how, in order to provide a knowledge and skills basis for genuine democracy.[9] For a large percentage of students, school remains alien and what is taught irrelevant, and reading and other skill levels make the kind of materials needed for the exercise of democracy out of reach of a high proportion of the population.

THE GRADUATES

While those in the Enlightenment tradition believed that education (in the sense of increased knowledge and understanding) would promote democracy and equality, one must today qualify that optimism, particularly when one examines the behaviour of graduates of the school system. While it is true that knowledge and understanding are necessary for democracy they are clearly not sufficient. Moreover, I would argue that the schools not only do not provide the knowledge and understanding necessary for democracy; they train a high proportion of their graduates in antidemocratic attitudes and beliefs of various kinds. Coupled with a hierarchical society in which the top graduates go into jobs which serve elite interests and which rely on a pool of lower ranked "hands" to support them, it is not surprising that a significant proportion of the "new middle classes" neither believes in the possibility of, nor desires, genuine democracy. Let us briefly examine this class in today's China.

There is both terminological and conceptual confusion over those I have so far referred to as "the graduates." Sylvia Chan, in her recent essay, refers to "Intellectuals and Reform" (Watson 1992, 88–116).[10] A more neutral term with broader reference is *intelligentsia*. More important than the term used is the concept. Just who belongs to the intelligentsia and what their relations are to the major social classes is not just an academic question, but one essential to the theme of this chapter. Significant differences exist between those in bureaucratic-administrative positions and those concerned with the production of knowledge, to mention only one distinction.[11] There are also problems with Chan's claim that the intelligentsia

> have risen to social prominence and political independence in modern times, owing to their possession of the knowledge and skills essential to the development of a modern economy and to the management of a modern society. (Watson 1992, 90)

The distinction made by Ronald Dore, between knowledge to *get* a job and knowledge to *do* a job, is part of the problem (Dore 1976, 8). Political *in*dependence is also highly questionable since a significant part of the intelligentsia is concerned with rationalising political action, whether as "consultants," journalists, or as seemingly independent academics.

The lower ranks of the intelligentsia draw on secondary as well as tertiary school graduates. Numbers have increased dramatically since the Communist Party came to power in 1949, but they are still very unevenly distributed geographically. The Fourth Census, conducted in July 1990 (*China aktuell* 1990, 837–43), gives the following figures for school graduates in the population: tertiary, 1.4 percent; secondary and above, 32.8 percent; and primary and above, 69.9 percent. The more highly schooled are concentrated, being particularly high in the three major cities, Beijing, Shanghai, and Tianjin, where the numbers of tertiary graduates in the population reaches 9.3 percent, 6.5 percent, and 4.7 percent respectively. At the other end come provinces where reported rates of illiteracy are very high: Tibet, 44.43 percent, Gansu, 27.93 percent, Qinghai, 27.70 percent, Yunnan, 25.44 percent. These are also provinces with very high non-Han populations, but seven predominantly Han provinces range between 16.15 percent and 17.62 percent illiteracy.

Increasingly there has been an overlap between the tertiary graduates and the cadres, those persons occupying leadership positions in Communist Party, government, and other organisations. In 1987 cadres were distributed as shown in Table 4.1.

Cadres have all along been strictly ranked, and the proposed new regulations discussed by Burns strengthen this ranking in favour of certification criteria (Burns 1989, 739–70). My point in drawing attention to the cadre system is that here is a large and influential number of people taught by training and position to be undemocratic. The system has been

Table 4.1. Distribution of Cadres in 1987

Government Departments	4,000,000
Legislative/Judicial Personnel	350,000
Service Units: Education, Public Health, Scientific and Technical Personnel	10,800,000
Economic Enterprises	10,300,000
Others (Parties, Mass Organisations, etc.)	1,550,000
Total	27,000,000

Source: Burns 1989, 740.

described many times.[12] Had the much-cited slogan "red and expert" ever been more than an example of the traditional Chinese propensity to prefer exhortation to analysis,[13] it would still not have made the system democratic.

While the cadres have governed, the remainder of the population, denied access to information (the level of secrecy in China has been, if anything, higher than in most other countries) and the practice of power, is also taught to be undemocratic. That many Chinese among the schooled are quite conscious of this situation and consider it desirable is borne out by such remarks as those of Fang Lizhi, the well-known physicist and dissident, who is reported as saying that "Chinese intellectuals should become the leading force in society" (Cheng and White 1990, 13). Cheng and White comment that "while he is widely considered a great advocate for democracy, Fang has a clearly elitist outlook" (1990, 13). One final example of the attitude of many of "the educated" to the less schooled, working people is described in a recent article on the part played by workers in the Tiananmen protests of 1989. The authors, Andrew Walder and Gong Xiaoxia, describe how the student leaders resented any initiatives by workers and tried to keep them subservient to their own activities. As the workers concerned saw it:

> All of the elite were privileged; none of them had the workers' interests in mind. Despite the students' struggle against the bureaucrats, which the workers supported wholeheartedly, the workers found that the students exhibited the same lack of concern and condescension toward the ordinary folk, and the same seeking after power and privilege, as the Party leaders. (1993, 28)

Since the students concerned came from the elite universities of Beijing, this puts yet another question to definitions of "quality education."

REGIONAL INEQUALITIES

The regional inequalities which have received the most attention, both within and outside China, have been those distinguished as urban and rural. Much has been written about the distribution of schools, the quality of schools, both in regard to buildings and equipment and to the qualifications of the teachers, and the retention and promotion rates of students. The 1985 Central Committee decision on reform of the education system[14] divided China into three categories for the purpose of implementing the decision on nine-year universal schooling. The first comprised "cities, economically developed areas in coastal provinces and a small number of developed areas in the hinterland, accounting for about a quarter of the total population of our country." The second category consisted of "towns and villages with medium level development, accounting for about half the total population of our country," while the third comprised "economically backward areas, which account for about a quarter of the total population of our country." While the document predicted universal schooling in the second category by 1995, in the third no prediction was made, but state aid was promised and the hope expressed that "various forms to popularise basic education" would be adopted.

While certain parts of the country are less economically developed than others—for example, Xinjiang or Qinghai are poorer than Jiangsu or Guangdong—differences may be quite local. A small mountainous area may be only some 15 km. from a town, but because of poor communications it may be impossible for children to attend school. Hence the development of *xunhui xiaoxue,* or circulating schools, where a teacher would walk round from hamlet to hamlet and teach the children. Another inequality exists between people with different regional background, but living and working in the same place. An example of this, Subei people working in Shanghai, was described by Emily Honig (1990). Subei people are concentrated in the unskilled jobs and also suffer discrimination in such things as the finding of marriage partners. Honig gives examples of popular prejudices, ranging from belief that Subei people were collaborators with the Japanese in the 1930s to their being dirty and uncouth of speech and behaviour today, prejudices which are spread by common expressions and terms of abuse (282). Such prejudices are powerful teaching which formal teaching appears to be able to do little to combat.[15]

Anita Chan and Jonathan Unger have given a depressing account of the migrant workers being used in Chen Village in Guangdong, the village they studied when it was under the commune system (1992). Living in poor housing, the migrants earn low wages, pay a special residence tax, and are often threatened with violence from local youth gangs. They are prime suspects for all crimes and, while doing all the hard work, have none of the rights of residence. Furthermore, migrants are themselves hierarchised according to work conditions, which range from female Hunan textile factory workers at the top to Sichuanese workers on the Hong Kong capitalist-owned vegetable farms at the bottom. The lessons that both locals and migrants learn in such conditions are not the desirability of democracy or equality, but rather the resentments of the kind that fed the Great Proletarian Cultural Revolution of the mid-1960s and early 1970s.

GENDER INEQUALITIES

Another of the major inequalities in China, as elsewhere, is that of gender. Though there is no doubt that the situation is considerably better than it was when the Chinese Communist Party came to power in 1949, it is far from one where one could speak of genuine equality, much less democracy. The single most spectacular "liberation" is that from foot-binding, the most painful and enduring of many "mechanisms of subordination" which Elizabeth Croll described in *Feminism and Socialism in China* (1978). Women have been allowed into many jobs which were previously reserved for men, and marriage laws have been passed which, where they have been adhered to, have greatly improved the life of women (Davin 1976). But old attitudes persist and new measures introduce new, often unanticipated difficulties (Croll 1983). As elsewhere, women who work outside the house only add another burden to that of child rearing and household work. That many of the young university-trained males are beginning to take some share in household and child-rearing tasks does not do much to alter the general picture, and it is questionable whether this situation should be regarded as "a start."

There is little doubt about old attitudes persisting. Suzanne Pepper, in her study of universities in the late 1970s and early 1980s, noted a number of assumptions among academic staff members "about the physical and intellectual inferiority of women," including the incredible statement by one schoolteacher that "girls' brains stop developing earlier than do those of boys"! (Pepper 1984, 113). At the same time, there were numerous reports about female infanticide in the rural areas following

Table 4.2. Proportion of Females in Levels of Schooling

School Level and Type	1951	1988
Primary School	28.0%	45.6%
General Secondary School	25.6%	41.0%
Agricultural and Vocational Schools	—	43.8%
General Tertiary Schools	22.5%	33.4%

Source: From Lu Xin and Shi Jingxuan 1991, 73.

attempts to limit the size of families, a practice which reflects the relative valuing of male and female children in the village economy.[16]

In spite of such attitudes, as a recent article in *Jiaoyu Yanjiu* showed, the proportion of females attending different levels of schooling over the whole country between 1951 and 1988 rose. Table 4.2 gives the percentages.

However, the situation has varied considerably in time and place. Another article in the same journal compares participation rates of schooling of girls compared with boys, in one of the poorer provinces, Gansu. For the whole province, the number of girls entering school, as a proportion of the female school-age cohort, rose from 8 percent in 1950 to 89.2 percent in 1989. This was equivalent to a rise in the proportion of girls among primary school students from 24.3 percent to 42.82 percent. In the years 1986–1989 the number of boys and girls *not* attending school ranged from 8 percent of the age cohort in 1986 to 6 percent in 1989. But the proportion of girls among those *not* attending school ranged from 80 percent to 85 percent (Li Hanrong 1991, 39). It will be important to watch the relative fate of girls and boys, as more families have an incentive to make use of child labour as private employment increases.

CONCLUSION: A QUESTION OF QUALITY

I have argued the need to recognise education essentially as a social learning process with schools as only one of the teaching agents. Quality of education must be distinguished from quality schooling, and the latter must not be considered separately from the quality of life outside the school. Equality of schooling as we have known it worldwide is a liberal dream turned nightmare as its failure is demonstrated around the world, just as Mao's eminently reasonable slogan "red and expert" became a means for certain people to be excluded from positions and power.

China's experience with mass schooling mirrors that of the industrialised world on which it has been modelled. Moving towards universality, a form of equality of entry and, in its centrally directed form, of provision, it has certified the growing class of *zhishifenzi* (intelligentsia) whose short-term interests are at variance with those of the majority of Chinese people. The inequalities of the society at large which I have sketched would make a mockery of any attempt, were it to be made, to provide equality of schooling, and the present Chinese government has no such aim in the short term. Rather, it is attempting to construct a system of vocationally oriented schools which will train people for the existing slots in society and stem the flood of ambition which has made the university the unreal goal of so many.

"Quality" education has been, and still is, seen in narrow class terms, in the privileging of particular subjects: in Europe, until recently, the languages and (reconstructed) cultures of ancient Greece and Rome. In imperial China a quality education was shown by the ability to recall classical texts, the ancient poets, to write poetry in their style, and to have a good calligraphy. In addition an interest in and ability to practise something of the traditional medicine (herbal and acupuncture) was an admired skill. Much of this is retained today, as was demonstrated even in the calligraphy of the wall posters (*dazibao*) of the Great Proletarian Cultural Revolution. But questions of quality have been pushed into the background by the realities of the competitive struggle. "Success" is today increasingly measured in Beijing as it is in Tokyo or New York. A "quality" schooling is one that will lead to such "success." But if our goal is a peaceful, ecologically sustainable, and genuinely democratic world, a quality education, whether learnt in school or from other educating agencies in the society (mass media, the work situation), must provide *everyone* with the information and skills necessary to make judgements about the social issues which confront them.

If we look into the mirror of China today we must be pessimistic and admit that in the short term at least there is little sign that such an education is on the agenda. The weight of traditional hierarchy, combined with the continuing inequalities which I have outlined, promise only further inequalities and privileges for the few at the expense of the many. The recent history of China gives us useful negative examples if we can learn from them: the effect of imposed mass campaigns; the horrors of scapegoating and of the pillorying of persons rather than the pursuit of different policies. But in our pessimism we should be warned by the misreading of past events by both conservative "China watchers" and left-wing enthusiasts alike. Perhaps our hope lies in the unpredictability of events which the last few years have again shown us.

NOTES

1. Knowledge of China's classical civil service examinations, reaching Europe in the eighteenth century, influenced civil service and school examinations there. In the nineteenth century, Christian missionaries took European-type schooling to China, while in this century Chinese students have gone to many countries to be schooled. (See Wang 1966 and Price 1970, 96–106.)

2. Term given to various reformers in China, active already in the late nineteenth century. See, for example, Teng and Fairbank 1967, Chapter 5 and Part 4.

3. This last would require several volumes to explore. Wolfgang Bauer takes 704 pages. to explore *China & the Hopes of Happiness* over a period of some three thousand years (1971). I am indebted to Jürgen Henze for this reference and also for that of van der Loo and van Reijen in note 4.

4. The concept of *modernisation*, with its subconcepts of *differentiation, individualisation, rationalisation,* and *domestication* (van der Loo and van Reijen 1992) leaves out of consideration precisely the concept which holds the key to solving today's problems.

5. The importance of family and personal contacts for Chinese business is emphasised by Lever-Tracy and Tracy (1993) and by Young in Watson (1992, 76).

6. In Price (1970) I considered these developments as "obstacles to educational reform," while in Price (1977b) I compared economic policies with moral–political teachings and possible learnings. One of the best overall accounts is Prybyla (1970).

7. Space forbids my taking up the equally interesting and marginally relevant question of schooling for development. Zhang (in Watson 1992, 147) reruns the factor analysis arguments which purport to show that schooling accounts for so much of "total economic growth," arguments which I had taken and long ago rejected as unsound. Wang and Bai (1991), in the course of an argument which the translator, in her introduction, admits "gets uncomfortably close to Han chauvinism," claim that schooling was the third most important factor in their survey of entrepreneurship (50).

8. Data from the Politbureau of the Thirteenth Central Committee, 1987, indicates that 7/16 members studied either engineering or science at tertiary college

(*China aktuell* November 1987:871–86). Random sampling of the Personnel Change column of the same journal supports my assertion.

9. Roger Cross and I have discussed this in relation to *Teaching Science for Social Responsibility* (Cross and Price 1992). As these concerns affect the teaching of science in Chinese schools see Price and Cross (1992).

10. The Chinese term is *zhishifenzi,* which Chan translates literally as "elements with knowledge" (91). The 1951 edition of the Chinese etymological dictionary, the *Ci Yuan,* gives in English the word *intelligentsia,* which the *Shorter Oxford English Dictionary* links with Russian usage of 1920, giving a definition: "the class consisting of the educated portion of the population and regarded as capable of forming public opinion."

11. Chan cites a number of writers on this subject (in Watson 1992, 111–12). Draper is the best source for Marx's writings on this diverse social group, not a class in the strict Marxian sense (1978, 481–572). I have discussed this question in (1986, 135–39) and (1977a, 173–83). Merle Goldman writes on *China's Intellectuals Advise and Dissent* (1981).

12. References can be found in Price (1970, 79–82) and (1977a, 334–37 and 341–44).

13. See my comment in Brugger (1980, 205). For the meaning to be attributed to the slogan see Mao Zedong, 1969, "Sixty Work Methods," *Current Background* 892: 6–7, Mao Zedong (1977, 47 and 135), and Brugger (1981, especially 235).

14. Chinese text in Guojia Jiaoyu Weiyuanhui, 1985, translated in *FBIS Daily Report*, 30 May 1985, 1:104.

15. A Jewish colleague of mine described how he dreaded ethnic days in his school near Boston. Although the subject was ignored most of the year, teacher-talk about ethnic equality led to painful discrimination by his fellow students in the playground afterwards.

16. A significant factor is that the female leaves the family home when she marries and the "burden" of upbringing is not repaid.

REFERENCES

Bauer, Wolfgang (1971) *China und die Hoffnung auf Glück.* München, Carl Hanser Verlag, reprinted 1989.

Brugger, Bill (ed.) (1980) *China Since the "Gang of Four."* London, Croom Helm.

Brugger, Bill (1981) *China: Liberation and Transformation, 1942–1962.* London, Croom Helm.

Burns, John (1989) "Chinese Civil Service Reform: the 13th Party Congress Proposals." *The China Quarterly* 120 (December): 739–70.

Chan, Anita, and Unger, Jonathan (1992) *Access China* 1 (March): 22–25.

Cheng, Li, and White, Lynn (1990) "Elite Transformation and Modern Change in Mainland China and Taiwan." *The China Quarterly* 121 (March): 1–35.

Chow Tse-tsung (1967) *The May Fourth Movement: Intellectual Revolution in Modern China.* Stanford, Stanford University Press, first published 1960.

Clopton, Robert W., and Ou, Tsuin-Chen (trans. and ed.) (1973) *John Dewey: Lectures in China, 1919–1920.* Honolulu, East-West Center, University Press of Hawaii.

Croll, Elizabeth (1978) *Feminism and Socialism in China.* London, Routledge & Kegan Paul.

Croll, Elizabeth (1983) *Chinese Women Since Mao.* London, Zed Books.

Cross, R.T. and R.F. Price (1992) *Teaching Science for Social Responsibility.* Sydney, St. Louis Press.

Davin, Delia (1976) *Woman-Work: Women and the Party in Revolutionary China.* Oxford, Clarendon Press.

Dore, Ronald (1976) *The Diploma Disease: Education, Qualification and Development.* London, Allen & Unwin.

Draper, Hal (1978) *Karl Marx's Theory of Revolution: Vol. 2, The Politics of Social Classes.* New York, Monthly Review Press.

Goldman, Merle (1981) *China's Intellectuals Advise and Dissent.* Cambridge, Mass., Harvard University Press.

Goodman, David S.G. (1992) "China's New Rich: Wealth, Power and Status." *Access China,* 8 (November): 18–21.

Guojia Jiaoyu Weiyuanhui Zhengce Yanjiushi (ed.) (1985) *Jiaoyu Tizhi Gaige Wenxian Zuanbian.* Beijing, Jiaoyu Kexue Chubanshe.

Henze, Jürgen (1982) "Begabtenförderung im Bildungswesen der VR China: das System der 'schwerpunkt-Schulen.'" *Asien* 4: 29–58.

Honig, Emily (1990) "Invisible Inequalities: The Status of Subei People in Contemporary Shanghai." *The China Quarterly* 122 (June): 273–92.

Kahn-Ackermann, Michael (1982) *China within the Outer Gate.* London, Marco Polo Press.

Keenan, Barry (1977) *The Dewey Experiment in China: Educational Reform and Political Power in the Early Republic.* Cambridge, Mass., Harvard University Press.

Lever-Tracy, Constance, and Noel Tracy (1993) "The Dragon and the Rising Sun: Market Integration and Economic Rivalry in East and Southeast Asia." *Policy Organisation and Society* 6 (Summer): 3–24.

Li Hanrong (1991) "Jingji wenhua bu fada diqu de nütong jiaoyu wenti." *Jiaoyu Yanjiu* 6: 39–43.

Lu Xin and Shi Jingxuan (1991) "Wo guo nüzi xuexiao jiaoyude xianzhuang he zhanwang." *Jiaoyu Yanjiu* 3: 72–76.

Mao Zedong (1977) *A Critique of Soviet Economics* (trans. Moss Roberts; annotated Richard Levy; introd. James Peck). New York, Monthly Review Press.

Marx, Karl, and Engels, Frederick (1975) *Collected Works* (CW). London, Lawrence & Wishart.

Pepper, Suzanne (1984) *Chinese Universities: Post-Mao Enrollment Policies and their Impact on the Structure of Secondary Education—A Research Report.* Michigan, The University Center for Chinese Studies

Perkins, Dwight H. (1969) *Agricultural Development in China 1368–1968.* Edinburgh University Press.

Perkins, Dwight H. (1975) *China's Modern Economy in Historical Perspective.* Stanford, CA, Stanford University Press.

Price, R.F. (1970, 1979) *Education in Communist China.* London, Routledge & Kegan Paul, 3rd. ed. (1979) renamed *Education in Modern China.*

Price, R.F. (1977a) *Marx and Education in Russia and China.* London, Croom Helm.

Price, R.F. (1977b) "Towards Educating Workers with Socialist Consciousness and Culture: The Case of the People's Republic of China." *Asian Profile* 5.6 (December): 519–31.

Price, R.F. (1986) *Marx and Education in Late Capitalism.* London, Croom Helm.

Price, R.F., and Cross, R.T. (1992) "Teaching Science: Between Economic Development and Environmental Damage: The Case of China's Schools." *Studies in Science Education* 20: 65–85.

Prybyla, Jan S. (1970) *The Political Economy of Communist China.* Scranton, PA, International Textbook Company.

Schwab, Joseph J. (1963) *Biology Teachers' Handbook* (Biological Sciences Curriculum Study). New York, John Wiley & Sons.

Stover, Leon E. (1974) *The Cultural Ecology of Chinese Civilization: Peasants and Elites in the Last of the Agrarian States.* New York, Pica Press.

Teng, Ssu-yu, and Fairbank, John K. (1967) *China's Response to the West: A Documentary Survey 1839–1923.* New York, Athenaeum, originally Harvard University Press, 1954.

van der Loo, Hans, and van Reijen, Willem (1992) *Modernisierung: Projekt und Paradox.* München, Deutscher Taschenbuch Verlag.

Walder, Andrew G., and Xiaoxia, Gong (1993) "Workers in the Tiananmen Protests: The Politics of the Beijing Workers' Autonomous Federation." *The Australian Journal of Chinese Affairs,* 29 (January): 1–29.

Wang, Y.C., (1966) *Chinese Intellectuals and the West, 1872–1949.* Chapel Hill, University of North Carolina Press.

Wang Xiaoqiang and Bai Nanfeng (trans. Angela Knox) (1991) *The Poverty of Plenty*. London, Macmillan.

Watson, Andrew (ed.) (1992) *Economic Reform and Social Change in China*. London, Routledge.

Weggel, Oskar (1992) "Wo Steht China heute: Die Rückkehr der Tradition und die Zukunft des Reformwerks, Teil IV: Politicshe Kultur." *China aktuell* (August): 532–55.

CHAPTER 5

Reflections upon Issues of Class and Inequality in Chinese Education*

IRVING EPSTEIN

On April 26, 1992, the Chinese press announced that scientists had developed their own form of the miracle drug interferon that would be mass produced shortly. The announcement came two days after the International Telecommunication Satellite Organization announced that it would use China's "Long March" rocket for satellite launches in 1995–1996 (FBIS April 28, 1992a; FBIS April 28, 1992b), and two-and-a-half weeks after the State Commission of Science and Technology announced a commitment to send its own astronauts into space before the year 2000 (FBIS April 8, 1992). These achievements are remarkable for any developing country, but are especially noteworthy for a country that also admitted to having an illiterate population of 180 million people (illiteracy being defined as the inability to read a minimum of 2,000 characters if one lives in an urban area, 1,500 characters if one lives in rural China) and 2 million children who are not enrolled in school at all (FBIS February 10, 1992). It is the basic assumption of this paper that insofar as the above noted information highlights the existence of increased technological prowess amidst widespread social inequality in China, an analysis of social class issues and their relationship to education not only holds the key to understanding the strengths and weaknesses of the world's largest educational system, but can also contribute to a broader discussion of education and equity in comparative terms.

---

*This chapter expands upon an earlier version that appears in *Compare* 23, 2 (1993): 125–41.

Carnoy and Samoff have argued that Third World states with conditioned socialist economies often develop educational systems that perform contradictory functions (1990). Policies that offer the promise of expanding educational opportunity represent regimes' efforts to reinforce perceptions of political inclusivity. Indeed, providing basic education to a citizenry speaks directly to those issues of distributive justice the state is expected to promote (Connell 1992). However, conflicting demands that encourage the development of skill and expertise in technical terms tend to reinforce inherited traditional hierarchies that are bureaucratic, exclusive, and decidedly undemocratic. The inability of conditioned socialist states to resolve these educational contradictions is reflective of the precarious nature of their political viability and can be explained in part by their inheritance of traditional, state-operated bureaucracies, external threats to their security, and their participation in a world economy dominated by core capitalist countries.

I believe that the Chinese case differs from the Carnoy–Samoff model to the extent that the pretense of using education for the purpose of fostering political inclusivity has been abandoned during the post-Mao era. This may not be surprising, given a climate that has encouraged economic privatisation, commodity fetishism, political decentralisation, growing regional economic inequality, and increased participation in a global economy dominated by core powers under the rubric of commodity socialism. But, an understanding of educational practice in light of these conditions can accomplish a number of aims. It can shed light upon the successful manipulation of formal educational structures so as to reproduce the power and privilege of one's class; it can address the particular, and overtly political, terms through which issues of educational quality and the appropriate standards for measuring quality are defined; and it can inform us about the social constraints that have impeded the creation of a civil society in China, an impediment that has circumscribed efforts to promote successful political reform.

THE NATURE OF SOCIAL CLASS

As it may be useful to view issues of social class in expansive terms, particularly when engaged in comparative analysis, Anthony Giddens' theory of the structuration of class relationships holds specific salience for our purposes. Giddens defines class structuration as the modes in which economic relationships become translated into noneconomic structures

(1980, 105). Of key importance is the extent to which individuals view the possibilities for upward economic mobility as being open or closed, so as to "provide for the reproduction of common life experiences over generations" (Giddens 1980, 105). One notes the similarity between "structuration of class relationships" and Bourdieu's notion of *habitus,* where it is argued that one's future aspirations are internalised according to social practices developed in accordance with the type and quality of one's external environment (Bourdieu and Passeron 1977). In both cases, the role of educational institutions in reinforcing or mediating prevailing social practice results in the sorting out of educational (and social) winners and losers and becomes crucial to our understanding of how social classes are formed and operate.

An expansive view of social class is also sensitive to the ways in which we structure time and space, so as to conform to conventional values and attitudes. Historically, for example, the linkage of time to work encouraged the creation of a capitalist ethic that measured the worth of one's productivity in terms of efficiency (Thompson 1967). Marxist geographers such as David Harvey and Manuel Castells further argue that one must examine social practice with reference to space in light of housing settlement and community formations, if one is to adequately understand how classes appropriate the capital they acquire; patterns of residential differentiation reflect an unequal distribution of space that is not random, but is directly based upon class affiliation. Where one lives, or one's ability to choose where one lives, becomes intertwined with the accumulation of capital for the purposes of defining personal aspiration and class identity (Harvey 1985, Castells 1983).

Under these terms, the political implications of ownership of the means of production or control over the conditions of one's work (even if the work has inherent economic consequence), the ways in which social relations of all types are patterned according to the values and authority relations evident in the work place, and the ways in which we spend accumulated capital determine class composition and class relations. Schools form an extremely important part of the equation since they are expected to prepare prospective workers for the workplace while also instilling in future citizens a respect for the authority of the state. Although these factors bear important consideration in light of the dramatic economic changes that have occurred within China over the past decade, there are unique characteristics of the Chinese social structure that also should be kept in mind.

SOCIAL CLASS IN CHINA

In many respects, Maoist China mirrored the archetype Leninist state, with the party controlling a command-oriented economy, centrally regulating rural and urban markets. In general terms, the Leninist conception of party evolved during the twentieth century to mean more than playing the simplistic role of agent of the working class. The party defined class consciousness and ideological orthodoxy for all groups in historic as well as contemporary terms, according to the experiences of its own members; yet through exercising control of the marketplace, the party not only oversaw the expansion of a centralised state bureaucracy, but its members themselves became part of that bureaucracy, fusing self-interest with state policy (Kraus 1983). Mao's own dissatisfaction with creeping bureaucratism and his reliance upon mass mobilisation techniques to bypass official party hierarchies and destroy class enemies is well known, for it culminated in the Cultural Revolution.

But perhaps the greatest accomplishment of Mao's China was the party's ability to politically penetrate and integrate peripheral areas. In a country with an overwhelming peasant population, political control of rural areas reached its zenith with the creation of communes during the Great Leap Forward, formed according to traditional marketing areas. Vivian Shue describes communal and county organisation as having replicated a honeycomb administrative structure, with both units compelled to respond to provincial and centralised directives without having had direct contact with sister units (1988, 134–35). As is true of many systems with centralised command and policy-making features, local resistance to official directives was quite pronounced, as local cadres used both defensive and aggressive strategies to blunt external aims. Defensive strategies included efforts to protect localities through under-reporting grain production. Local officials used aggressive strategies to enhance their own power base by overtly bending or reinterpreting official rules whenever possible. Shue's conclusion is that by the late 1970s, the administrative center had lost control over the periphery (1988, 137–47).

During the post-Mao era, policymakers have expanded market mechanisms in rural areas and have abolished the former insular political structures such as communes in an effort to defeat localism. As the peasant household has become the central unit of social life, and as rural production has become increasingly commercialised with the growth of peasant-operated enterprises and businesses, lateral relations between members of various villages have been strengthened; relationships outside the village are more contractual today than hierarchical. The result has been the creation of weblike political structures that have replaced the honeycomb, with central authorities more aware of village activities, but able to influence local conditions only indirectly (Shue, 1988, 147–52). At the same time, factionalism and violence have increased, as have clientism and personal patronage (Perry 1985, Oi 1989). Cultivation of market forces has also produced increased regional inequality encouraged by the central government, for when the central government awards affluent coastal provinces more favourable currency exchange rates so as to expedite trade with foreign investors, these provinces exploit their less-favoured counterparts by buying products from the poorer provinces below international market value. They then use for their own purposes the ensuing domestic exchange surpluses that are accumulated (Zweig 1991). An unintended result has been the devolution of central authority, not only with respect to the recapture of local wealth, but with respect to increased dependency upon foreign markets, too.

In urban China, the role of the city was production rather than commercial or consumption oriented during the first thirty years of the People's Republic. As was true of rural areas, urban development was hierarchical; lines of bureaucratic authority were vertically drawn between provincial and municipal authorities. During the post-Mao era, however, there has been an effort to increase networking with sister cities and rural areas as urban commercialisation has been enhanced, as hierarchical characteristics continue to define central government/city relationships (Solinger 1991). Still, since the late 1980s, state enterprises have been eclipsed by the growth of private companies and joint ventures as increased commercialisation of the urban sector continues.

How have these broad developmental changes affected social relations in China? During the first thirty years of the People's Republic, it seems that the peasant village household remained largely intact; external political pressures modified certain aspects of traditional behavior but were most successfully assimilated into local cultures when they were viewed as being nonthreatening to traditional beliefs (Parish and Whyte 1978).

In urban China, the situation was somewhat different. The successful political penetration of neighborhoods and workplaces created pressures for adhering to group loyalties formed outside of the family (Whyte 1974, Whyte and Parish 1984). An effective household registration system along with an enforced sense of collective dependency within the workplace restricted upward and/or geographical mobility (Walder 1986). State-operated enterprises and bureaucracies rewarded the cultivation of personal connections, friendships, and the maintenance of strong social relationships within the work unit. Urban industries, subjected to the "iron ricebowl mentality," were plagued by inefficiency and an underutilisation of staff, as they adhered to commitments guaranteeing workers lifetime employment. Wages and bonuses were universally allocated according to set formulas, creating a rigid stratification system throughout the country. Strategies for obtaining the significant benefits allocated by state-run enterprises—subsidised housing, medical care, guaranteed employment in the city, and so on—were defined by mobility aspirations conditioned by one's class background and presumed party loyalty.

Until the outbreak of the Cultural Revolution, class affiliation was an inherited characteristic, defined in terms of parental status as of 1949. A form of reverse discrimination existed whereby one was considered to have "bad class background" if one's parents were economically privileged in 1949, and "good class background" if one's parents were peasants or workers at that time. Active participation in party affairs provided some of those who were viewed as possessing good class background with the opportunity to secure economic and social benefits; educational achievement was seen as providing those with bad class backgrounds with similar opportunities. Attempts to redefine the "red-versus-expert" equation with reference to university admissions policies and commensurate efforts to reinterpret class loyalty according to ideological criteria (possession of class consciousness) rather than the inheritance of social position (class background) formed a pretext for the factionalism that engulfed the Cultural Revolution (Kraus 1981).

The development of China's educational system mirrored many of these trends, reflecting the inequities of a rural-dominated population, controlled by urban elites, particularly during the 1950s and early 1960s. During the 1950s, the system assimilated many of the characteristics of the Soviet educational model: standardised curricula, heavy emphasis upon technical and specialised education, separation between teaching and research functions, promotion within the system driven by examination, and so on (Pepper 1990, Price 1987, Orleans 1987). In rural areas, periodic attempts were made to address local needs following Mao's Yan'an experiments of the 1930s. They included the establishment of worker–peasant accelerated middle schools (abandoned in 1955) and people's (*minban*) schools during the Great Leap Forward (Pepper 1990, 42–43, 51–53). Yet these efforts were viewed as second-rate alternatives to formal institutions and never received the degree of support afforded conventional urban education structures. Still, by the 1970s, educational access in rural China had expanded; rural schools were supported by state and provincial funds in part; deficits were addressed by local units. As rural schools were considered to be part of the commune political structure, they were generally accepted by the local population as being an important part of village life, except in isolated areas with poor transportation facilities, where the establishment of primary schools and the hiring of teachers was more difficult (Pepper 1990, 75–77, Parish and Whyte 1978, 78–85).

By the 1980s, Cultural Revolution efforts to redress systemic inequality and elitism had been totally rejected. The reinstitution of a national university entrance examination system, provincially administered in 1977 and centrally administered since 1978; the allocation of key schooling designations which legitimised the awarding of disproportionate funds, resources, better teachers and students, and so on, to favoured primary, middle, and university institutions; experiments with strict ability grouping at all age levels; and the centralisation of textbook development and dissemination were some of the policies enacted in order to guarantee educational quality and upgrade standards, by overtly depoliticising the terms through which educational standards were defined.

Two points should be emphasised. First, many of these policies were not new, but were popular during the 1950s and 1960s (Pepper 1990, 1–6). Educational quality was thus defined in conservative rather than progressive terms. Second, in rejecting the ideological messages that accompanied educational reform during the Cultural Revolution, educators sought to link policy with economic development as defined through enhancing collective production capability (Bastid 1984). Efforts to centralise the control and distribution of educational resources thus represented a view of top-down governance that was similar to the way in which other administrative units were operated through the early 1980s.

During the mid to late 1980s, however, Chinese educators confronted pressures for reform that were influenced by the external social developments of which we have spoken–the move from a command to a market economy, a commercial rather than productive urban emphasis, and increased consumerism and cultural commodification. Resulting educational reforms included a compulsory education law in 1986 that acknowledged the limited educational opportunities available in rural areas while calling for their remediation through increased school construction and teacher training so as to effect compulsory universal education by 1995; a move to allow select universities and individual enterprises to play a greater role in directly allocating jobs to graduates, bypassing official labor exchange commissions; efforts to give some school administrators and university officials increased autonomy with respect to decision making; increased responsibility placed upon educational institutions for obtaining financial self-sufficiency; and an increased emphasis upon expanding secondary and tertiary technical and vocational opportunities. Whereas many of the policies encouraging greater institutional autonomy were scaled back in the immediate aftermath of the Tiananmen massacre, the tensions characterising center–periphery economic and political relationships within the country as a whole are evident within the Chinese educational system in particular. The remaining portion of this chapter will examine these tensions in light of social class considerations with specific reference to the exercise of autonomy, and changing views of time and space.

RURAL EDUCATION

The contradictions inherent in a system that centralises curricular decision making, textbook allocation, and the determination of teacher training qualification while decentralising key elements of local management and financial responsibility are sharply felt in rural Chinese schools. While responsibilities for making education decisions are shared among units at various administrative levels—the State Education Commission, provincial education commissions or departments, county education bureaus, township education officers, or the principal of a village school—Cheng Kai-ming notes that a policy of "sponsorship at three levels, administration at two levels," has been in place since the 1980s.

> In practical terms, this means that senior secondary schools should be sponsored by counties, junior secondary schools by townships and primary schools by villages. "Sponsorship" here is taken to mean the financing as well as ownership of schools. In terms of administration, the county authority is expected to administer senior secondary schools; the township authority to administer both junior secondary and primary schools, since there is no administrative structure at the village level. (1991, 7)

With respect to the securing of funds, provincial allocations to local schools only partially subsidise recurring expenses, and the generation of funding through collection of local revenues, taxes, voluntary donations, and institution-generated income is essential if rural schools are to maintain their viability. Professor Cheng notes that in Liaoning Province, in 1986 for example, 74.8 percent of all funding sources were derived from local initiatives as opposed to provincial allocations (1991, 32). At the same time, it is the responsibility of appropriate provincial authorities to insure local compliance with national standards and directives as initially defined by the State Education Commission. Their role includes controlling teacher training, monitoring primary school graduation examinations, and facilitating local planning initiatives that meet compulsory education targets (Cheng 1991, 33).

In China's poorest rural areas, basic education includes no more than a few years of schooling at best, but even in these situations, systemic contradictions sharply define the quality and characteristics of the social experiences of the various educational actors. If one teaches in a rural school, one's categorisation as a *minban* as opposed to *gongban* (public) teacher is crucial in determining renumeration, status, and professional identity. "*Minban*" teachers are considered to lack appropriate teaching qualifications (graduation from a secondary school or formal teacher training program) and, unlike their *gongban* counterparts, are paid solely through local township initiatives. As a result, their pay is irregular, their professional status second class. Certainly, division of labor based upon status hierarchy exists throughout the world. But in the Chinese case, rural teachers of all types confront situations where their work is generically devalued, since so many of the crucial decisions affecting educational policies are made at provincial and state levels. Jean Robinson points out that the continued existence of *minban* schools and *minban* teachers is an embarrassment to central authorities, for their presence highlights the impossibility of implementing compulsory education practices according to predetermined standards and quality levels (1991). But how must rural constituents—teachers, students, peasants— feel when they are asked to contribute to the implementation of a policy knowing that the results of their efforts will be considered inherently inferior? Furthermore, when basic educational practice becomes so standardised as to deny the existence of local cultural and geographical specificity, what then motivates townships and villages to invest in any form of education at all?

Cheng Kai-ming has argued that educational investment at the local level is more likely in areas that view enhanced educational investment as providing inhabitants with the technical sophistication necessary for further economic growth. In this instance, decentralisation of local school management and finances enhances community decision making and is empowering. The overriding concern, however, is that once educated, students and teachers will not return to their native locales (Cheng 1991, 84–85). The corresponding level of village and township economic development certainly is a crucial factor in determining local degrees of educational investment. However, it is not the only factor that is important. The degree of physical isolation, the acceptance of traditional views that value or dismiss the importance of formal education, and the village's own cultural development play important roles in influencing investment decisions. In most cases, drop-out loss has become a greater problem than low initial school attendance, as parents continue to view the singular devotion to farm labor and rural enterprise as a quicker and more likely method of obtaining household affluence (Hao et al. 1989).

It is clear that the worth of rural education is defined in comparative terms by central, provincial, and local authorities, terms which fuse sense of place with more conventional issues of access and upward mobility. One, for example, can view the worst problems rural teachers confront: inadequate and irregular pay, lack of safety and personal protection to the point of facing physical assault, teaching in dilapidated structures without windows or suitable ventilation, and other problems as at least in part due to local resistance to the concept of the externally defined modern school, a generic structure that symbolically situates itself outside of one's traditional sense of place.[1] Alternatively, as village networking is growing, rural peasants themselves are increasingly defining their immediate physical environment in comparative terms. The dilemmas that agricultural middle vocational schools confront—their inability to provide graduates with more favorable employment opportunities along with traditional questions of appropriate fit between the nature of one's training and the actual demands of one's work (Thogersen 1990)—can be viewed within a context where rural/urban differences are more explicit than ever before because rural isolation is eroding. It is not surprising that the lowest end of the educational pyramid would offer its participants a modest degree of status and autonomy. But the uneven commitment to mass basic education in rural areas, in spite of the formation of centrally controlled and provincially administered policy decisions that allow for local consultation, raises questions as to educational effectiveness in promoting both political and social inclusivity along with basic literacy.[2] On the contrary, recent efforts promoting both consolidation and differentiation of rural schooling at the county level have had the effect of closing some schools while differentiating, to an even finer degree, the number of schools at various levels designated as key (*zhongxin*) or non-key, apart from national or provincial designations (Paine and Delany 1991).

URBAN EDUCATION

Chinese urban education can be characterised as confronting a different set of problems. The re-initiation of a national entrance examination system created a meritocratic metaphor that has reverberated throughout all urban social settings, for in light of the supposed linking of opportunities for social reproduction to educational achievement rather than ascriptive criteria (party affiliation, personal connection, etc.), a fundamental change in value orientation affecting social relationships of all types may be occurring. Employers now regularly administer tests as a way of rationalising hiring decisions and worker transfers. And, the possession of educational qualifications has become important even to those seeking to upgrade their party member and People's Liberation Army (PLA) standing (Manion 1985, Latham 1991). Indeed, the effectiveness of reform through labor camps and prisons is now demonstrated by pointing to offender rehabilitation through noting the diplomas and certificates received by inmates (FBIS January 29, 1992, FBIS May 1, 1992). However, the association of educational assessment with the acquisition of competence has had its clearest influence upon educational policy throughout various levels of the formal educational system, with the national entrance examination system driving policy.

Institutional reputation at all levels has been determined by selectivity, as largely defined by examination scores. Key universities have sought to maintain and enhance their status according to the overall examination scores of matriculated students; senior middle schools have sought to enhance their reputations by ensuring that as many graduates as possible who are allowed to apply obtain university entrance; primary school reputation is based upon feeder-school relationships with prestigious middle schools, and so on. To be sure, competition occurs among the key schools only, for one's chances of obtaining university admission are severely restricted if one is affiliated with a non-key school. And, the use of testing at all levels both weeds out marginal students before their future aspirations are set and legitimises early selection patterns at primary and middle school levels.

There are a number of important exceptions to the generalisation. Since the mid 1980s, a number of prestigious senior middle schools, noting that their graduates have not performed as well as had been expected on the university entrance examinations, have negotiated informal feeder networks with select universities, guaranteeing places for some of their graduates (Rosen 1985). In an effort to alleviate financial constraints, some universities have lowered minimum entrance examination scores for commuter as opposed to residential students. The use of testing for primary and junior middle school admission has been criticised and somewhat curtailed, as has the mechanical use of ability grouping at early grade levels to enhance the academic performance of those designated "gifted." In an effort to reduce the importance of the university entrance examination as the sole criterion for determining university admissions, there have been experiments with using more varied forms of student assessment at the senior secondary level (*huikao*), although the result has been an actual increase in testing there (Ross 1991, Yang 1990). Incidences of cheating and corruption related to university examination performance continue to be quite common (Kwong and Ko 1991–1992). And, as universities and secondary schools have been asked to finance a greater part of their budgets themselves, money-making schemes that allow affluent students to buy a place in the desired institution continue to occur.

Still, at least until the mid-1980s, the use of the examination process as a means of selecting future elites held value, particularly for those who no longer viewed party loyalty and the cultivation of personal connections as a legitimate or inclusive means of enhancing intergenerational mobility. An examination-driven curriculum that is standardised masks social differences and resource inequalities that invariably affect individual performance. There are key secondary middle schools that successfully pursue international exchanges and networks with elite sister institutions all over the world, and there are senior middle schools that require security guards to maintain day-to-day order. The universality of the examination process hides these differences, conveying the message that standardisation of assessment guarantees the equality of opportunity to succeed, with failure occurring as a result of personal deficiency. To be sure, attempts to diversify curriculum on a regional basis continue in experimental form, but it appears that they are being implemented in supplemental fashion, rather than as alternatives to their standardised counterparts (Ross 1991, 74). The State Education Commission has decided to institutionalise a differentiated national curriculum reflecting five different socio-economic and educational conditions throughout the country. However, as Paine and DeLany argue, the act of admitting existing regional disparity while still maintaining centralised control of curricular decision making and materials production may do little more than codify existing inequalities rather than begin to resolve them (1991).

Is it the case that schools in urban China can perform the role of social leveler, reducing social inequality? This is perhaps a key question for which there is little good evidence. However, Stig Thogersen, in an important regional study of the Yantai district in Shandong Province, concludes that students from economically disadvantaged backgrounds who are able to attend county or urban key schools have been able to maximise their opportunities for upward mobility through successfully climbing the educational ladder (1990, 132–53). Of course one must be circumspect in generalising the findings. And, the rapid expansion of secondary technical and vocational education over the past decade must be viewed, not simply as a response to external pressures for enhanced economic development, but as an alternative method of facilitating upward mobility apart from schools' contributing to the social reproduction of intellectual elites in traditional ways. If, however, rapid secondary technical and vocational development is an example of institutional accommodation to external pressures for change, one must note that the perceived value of these programs to students is often influenced by external factors influencing their growth—job availability, the conditions of one's work after securing employment, attractiveness of one's earning power in a non-state-supported enterprise, the reputation of the enterprise affiliated with the vocational program and so on—rather than the perceived intrinsic value of the curriculum and training per se. Under these terms, successful vocational programs perform cooling-out functions, preserving the integrity of traditional academic curricula.

Indeed, it can be argued that the curricular and instructional practices of urban schools for the most part remain removed from normal social concerns, as educators themselves express a deep ambivalence concerning their success in enumerating appropriate moral values and concerns within school walls (Ross 1991, 86–92, Davin 1991). Both students and teachers operate within sheltered administrative units that are inflexible and rigid, a rigidity highlighted by the contrasting economic conditions that have been previously described. As those conditions contribute to increases in youth unemployment, the drop-out rate, and ensuing juvenile crime, school authorities receive their share of the blame for these problems (one report, for example, argued that in some detention facilities 80 percent of all adolescent criminals were illiterate or had received substandard education) (FBIS January 14, 1992).

While there has been some movement towards increased decision making by local principals, teachers, and administrators (Paine and DeLany 1991, DeLany and Paine 1991), teacher status, even in urban areas, is not particularly high. Teacher pay remains inadequate; teacher training is afforded an officially prescribed status lower than other tertiary fields of study. It is ironic that the low social status of primary and middle school teachers is conditioned by the hierarchy and elitism of the educational system they serve and promote. Typical responses to these conditions include increased moonlighting or leaving the profession altogether for more lucrative alternatives. It would not be too great an exaggeration to conclude that urban Chinese education alienates both students and teachers in significant numbers.

The irony of such alienation is that for both rural and urban constituents, the post-Mao educational system has at least symbolically represented an alternative to achieving upward mobility through political and ideological ascription as promoted during the Cultural Revolution. The "skidding" that occured in the aftermath of that time period, whereby members of the "Maoist middle class" found themselves in the unenviable if unique position of securing jobs less prestigious than those of their parents (Davis 1992), must be viewed as a contributing factor that has led to the characterisation of personal aspiration in educational terms. However, the degree to which China's current educational system has given the majority of its participants in every sector the opportunity to fulfill their aspirations remains extremely questionable.

UNIVERSITY EDUCATION

In the past, a university education in China provided graduates with an urban job in a state-affiliated enterprise that included some measure of financial security with subsidised housing and other important social benefits. Due to policies of deliberate inbreeding at China's best universities, outstanding graduates were allowed to teach at their home universities and, at least in the ideal sense, the life of the post–Cultural Revolution university professor promised a reasonable degree of comfort and security. More importantly, that life afforded the intellectual elite a measure of autonomy unknown in lower levels of the educational system and included greater opportunities for curricular innovation and study and travel abroad. To be sure, China's universities have lacked the autonomy of sister institutions in the West and were always subjected to strong party and state control. But in the immediate years preceding

Tiananmen, educational reforms gave university officials greater freedom to run their own affairs, provide for financial self-sufficiency and, in some instances, work directly with employers in placing graduates (Hayhoe 1989, 44). Student political organisations after 1986 also became more independent as official surveillance of their activities loosened (Rosen 1990).

Such changes reinforced an independent intellectual tradition that viewed the intellectual as moral–political actor, endowed with the authority to demand political reform by virtue of intellect. It is not surprising that China's intellectuals had embraced the ethic of professionalism by the eve of Tiananmen, an ethic that was appealing in its blending of Confucian autonomy and increasing privatisation induced by a freer market. The curiosity of social scientists organising private companies to conduct public opinion research (Rosen 1991) or journalists conducting independent investigations of official corruption bears witness to the point, although it should be noted that important differences characterised Western and Chinese views of professionalism. In the West, professions grew independently as members imposed upon themselves regulations for accreditation or acceptable standards of ethical behavior that later received state approval. In the Chinese case, professional autonomy devolved from state institutions and was always more limited than in the West. Given the inherently private nature of professional association, the creation of the service ethic was extremely important, for it rationalised the exercise of personal autonomy in the name of helping the greater population. In the Chinese case, however, I would argue that similar service obligations were less overtly expressed because service to the state was considered to be an implicit part of one's intellectual mission.

Certainly, one's professional status and autonomy varied according to the higher education unit with which one was associated, the researcher affiliated with the Academy of Sciences or Academy of Social Sciences possessing greater autonomy than the faculty member associated with the regional teacher training university. But during the years immediately preceding Tiananmen, one finds those intellectual elites at the top levels of the educational pyramid informally networking, creating salon-type study groups that emboldened their critiques of government policy, forming research groups connected to official administrative units but not subject to overt party domination, and using their positions in official research institutes and organisations under the control of the party to offer critical advice (Bonnin and Chevrier 1991). Professionalism in this context meant loosening the patronage ties with official party and government sponsors;

it meant creating a nascent, private media through independently publishing, selling, and distributing research results in newly formed journals and newspapers. Indeed, official government agencies themselves commissioned private research studies, understanding the value of discovering what people actually believed (Rosen 1991, 64–73). Yet in spite of these trends, the ties that bonded intellectuals to the state were never cleanly broken.

Enhanced professionalism within university walls could be seen through attempts to reward professors according to merit in salary and rank allocations, although those efforts conflicted with strongly entrenched seniority systems (Johnson 1991). With respect to curricular change, the natural sciences became the most popular areas for study and research, due to their presumed immunity from political influence, an important consideration in light of Cultural Revolution efforts to overtly politicise the humanities and social sciences. Of course, the pursuit of scientific knowledge according to Western tradition has demanded that one follow a predetermined set of conventions with specific value orientations: the importance of first discovery, the use of prediction to control natural phenomena, and so on. One must also note that for Chinese intellectuals, pursuing serious scientific research held the promise of entering an elite international community of scholars and, in so doing, transcending national as well as parochial borders. More importantly, the scientific paradigm presented an alternative world view that replaced discredited Maoist epistemology with an ideology that saw truth in terms of an ordered rationality that could be mastered, but only by the deserving few. Certainly study of the social sciences and study in the professions derived from the traditional social sciences began to regain popularity when their advocates adopted the positivist assumptions of scientific inquiry to their particular fields.

It has been argued that Chinese education, and Chinese higher education specifically, has historically demonstrated a unique degree of flexibility in borrowing eclectically from foreign models while maintaining traditional normative value claims. Classroom rituals and curricular and pedagogical orientations have gravitated from the expressive to the instrumental, from weak framing and classification mechanisms to strong ones, based upon weak as opposed to strong collection codes (Hayhoe 1989, 11–28). During the early 1980s, the acceptance of scientific and positivist paradigms increased pressures for disciplinary specialisation, the erection of firm disciplinary boundaries, and the implementation of strong framing and classification schemes. But by the late 1980s, there was a greater acceptance of the professions as newly emerging areas of study; interdisciplinary study increased, as did professional, technical, and vocational education. These innovations coincided, rather than conflicted, with the more traditional academic fields. To be sure, economic trends did affect curricula, as the expansion of management, finance, trade, and international and comparative studies attests. But the limits to which such experimentation can affect basic access questions are quite clear, in light of the enforced enrolment restrictions limiting admissions to many social science and humanities areas put in place after 1989 (Hayhoe 1991).

We have previously noted that issues of professional advancement through rank, and the awarding of salary and other benefits, began to be redefined in the early 1980s. It is equally important to recognise that the resurrection of Chinese higher education in the aftermath of the Cultural Revolution also included the awarding of advanced degrees and the creation of credit-generating short-term elective courses. Most recently, nationwide graduate school entrance examinations have been instituted for prospective Master's degree students (FBIS February 18, 1992). All of these developments influence sense of time and place. The introduction of credit-hour systems and shorter-term elective courses in particular symbolically associates the value of acquired knowledge with the divisible time spent pursuing that knowledge; coupled with the awarding of degrees and certificates, the worth of one's academic experience is commodified. Certainly, the internationalisation of university curricula presents interesting and creative possibilities for curricular reform and innovation. But these efforts have also called into question the importance of pursuing traditional areas of study and modes of inquiry: Chinese as opposed to Western methods of treating illness, or studying the practice of law from Western as opposed to traditional perspectives (Burris 1991, Hom 1991).

TIANANMEN AND AFTER

This chapter, in offering an overview of the Chinese educational system, has sought to associate the various components of the system with the relative degree of autonomy they offer their participants and practitioners, defining autonomy in terms of space and time as well as financial remuneration, status, decision-making responsibilities, and so on. It has been argued that curriculum and instructional practices symbolically reflect the conditions of one's work within educational settings and that the same pressures affecting social relations in rural and urban areas—expressed as the country moves from a command, production-oriented economy to a commercial, consumption-oriented one—have affected the educational system too. An underlying assumption is that issues of educational quality were continually defined in terms of audience (quality for whom?), selectivity, and personal autonomy and that in spite of attempts to initiate significant educational reform, the system continued to cater to the aspirations of changing elites on the eve of the Tiananmen uprising. The educational system, during the post-Mao era, influenced by similar considerations that have characterised other Leninist states, never fully articulated a sense of political inclusivity that would have addressed the needs of constituents from every background. Instead, the party leadership understood the need to reproduce intellectuals' expertise as a necessary prerequisite to advancing technologically, while fearing the traditional independence from state control intellectuals sought to preserve for themselves. Whereas the merging of roles—of technocrat and apparatchik—was somewhat successfully accomplished by Soviet intellectual elites in the Stalin period (Fitzpatrick 1978, Konrad and Szelenyi 1991), a similar transformation was never really possible in China, given the traditional independent role afforded China's intellectuals as moral–political scholars, subject to state patronage but also expected to play the role of state critic (Goldman 1981, Lo 1991, Goldman, Cheek, and Hamron 1987). The movement for increased individual autonomy, influenced by freer market conditions from 1986–1989, was a logical consequence of this tradition, as was the resulting crackdown on the part of the state. But unlike the more successful revolutions against party authoritarianism in Eastern Europe in 1989, student and intellectual demands for political reform were unsuccessful, in large part, because of the failure of key institutions, including schools, to create a true civil society. Without the benefit of independent institutions operating within the public sphere, Chinese students and intellectuals forged linkages with other groups that offered the limited prospect of *only symbolic resistance* to government authority. The significant but circumscribed role of the educational process in contributing to demands for political reform can best be seen in terms of government policies that have attempted to regain party control of academic life in the aftermath of the Tiananmen massacre.

Those efforts included jailing active intellectual dissidents, particularly those associated with the Academy of Social Sciences, shutting down the quasi-independent media, forcing college freshmen at elite universities to complete a year of military training, reasserting tighter control our job allocation procedures, initially restricting (but later loosening) study abroad and exchange activities, and increasing party surveillance over university governance. With the exception of economics and management fields, fewer applicants are being admitted into social science areas; strict political litmus tests have been implemented to screen out questionable candidates seeking to study humanities and social science subjects at the graduate level (FBIS January 3, 1992). In fact, dissertations written in the last five years are being scrutinised for political problems as a blacklist of academic work has begun to be compiled (FBIS January 15, 1992).

The success of these efforts is uneven; elite universities in Beijing have suffered the greatest degree of state interference; other institutions have been more fortunate in deflecting efforts to control their operations. It is clear, however, that educational institutions continue to be subjected to the pressures of external manipulation for political ends. One must also note the ease with which some intellectuals have embraced Singaporean and Taiwanese models of neo-authoritarianism, a stance that not only is accommodationist to current political realities, but leads one to question their degree of commitment to democratic reform (Sautman 1992).

In attempting to link issues of educational quality with the perpetuation of social inequalities, two basic questions need to be addressed. First, why is the acquisition of technical expertise inimical to the enhancement of mass, basic education which, with accompanying socialisation messages, would appear to promote greater political inclusivity for all of China's inhabitants? Second, how do the normal curricular and instructional messages common to classroom situations at every level of the education system reify the inequalities of which we have spoken?

It is arguable whether mastery of technical expertise need inherently promote political and social inclusivity. Indeed, Chinese students who were active in the Tiananmen demonstrations showed how technological sophistication could be used to successfully communicate political messages to a mass audience through the use of computer networking and a sophisticated understanding of the electronic media. It has been further argued that during the late nineteenth century, the inclusion of science courses in basic education curricula on an international basis was viewed as a method of enhancing citizenship, as the skills they emphasised— rational calculation and deliberation—were viewed as contributing to an informed citizenry (Kamens and Benavot 1991). Nonetheless, because the sciences and applied sciences are constructed so as to demand mastery of increasingly specialised knowledge areas that are hierarchically positioned, the human and material resources needed to facilitate such mastery are almost always limited, necessitating a selective allocation of those resources in developing world contexts. The political economy of technology transfer has compelled China to pay for increased access to advanced technology through aggressively marketing its exports globally, allowing regional economic inequality to increase while seeking increased foreign investment in favored areas. Disparate educational investment in rural China follows these trends. Furthermore, the promise of obtaining immediate access to and acceptance into the international academic community has heightened pressures that exclusively allocate educational services and materials domestically to those in the best position to take advantage of those resources. In fact, the differential allocation of educational and social services is often rationalised according to criteria labelled as "scientific." The pervasive degree of gender inequality, evident at secondary and university levels, is rationalised as reflecting women's natural and scientific inferiority (Honig and Hershatter 1988, 14–40); in an even more extreme sense, periodic calls for eugenics campaigns offer a so-called scientific rationale for eliminating social burdens altogether (Yang 1990). Stanley Aronowitz has perceptively commented upon the tendency of Western scientific practice to overtly pursue control over the natural world while covertly perpetuating forms of human domination (1988). The quest for power in one domain logically leads to its pursuit in another. Many of the social practices that characterise post-Maoist commodity socialism in the name of science offer evidence for his point, not the least of which include educational policies and priorities.

However, in defining educational quality in terms of selectivity and exclusivity, China's education policymakers also articulate a view of modernity that is quite traditional, in line with historic predispositions that differentiated the importance of manual versus mental labor, argued in favor of a strict demarcation between formal and alternative (*shuyuan*) learning, and reproduced a powerful intellectual elite through the implementation of the Confucian examination system. That system committed itself to the training of a few scholar-officials who could demonstrate an ability to regurgitate classical text. While the terms have been changed, the results are similar. Current efforts to reward those who master scientific and technical expertise demonstrate an acceptance of the vocabulary of positivism as a means of reaffirming traditional elitist tendencies (Price 1990).

Curricular and instructional practices obviously play a crucial role in communicating educational mission and purpose. When children are denied the chance to attend any school at all, they and their communities are placed in a dependent situation, relative to the conditions of more fortunate counterparts. When a standardised curriculum is implemented with insensitivity so as to mask the diverse conditions characterising learning environments throughout the country, teachers' and students' immediate sense of place is implicitly attacked. And, even if specialised curricula are developed for local schools, the failure to link local initiatives with broader priorities isolates and marginalises these efforts. In rural China in particular, the destruction of communal organisation and the inability of the township to command the degree of political authority afforded commune structures has contributed to an inconsistent commitment to schooling. But as horizontal trade linkages continue to develop between rural villages, breaking down rural isolation, awareness of place is also redefined in comparative terms. Sitting in a classroom may mean that one is writing characters instead of working on the family farm or enterprise, but it also means that one is now more aware of other schools in other villages operating in similar or different fashions, an awareness that also influences personal aspiration and educational commitment.[3]

Finally, it is clear that curricular and instructional reform in China has influenced and in turn been influenced by changing views of professionalism that have become popular as the market economy has developed. The use of testing to support meritocratic metaphors, expansion in technical and vocational education at secondary and university levels, and the introduction of positivism to the study of the social sciences and humanities attest to the ability of certain educational structures, particularly at the higher end of the education pyramid, to accommodate themselves to prevailing economic trends. The use of credit systems and short-term courses gives further evidence for their willingness to engage in the commodification of knowledge. Enhanced sensitivity to markets can result in curricular innovation, but if too closely associated with short-term profit, it can also run the risk of damaging long-term institutional credibility. Chinese schools and universities increasingly face this risk as they are forced into expanding their entreprenuerial activities in order to maintain financial viability.

We know that there is a degree of cultural arbitrariness involved whenever certain subject areas are included or excluded from formal study; as Bourdieu notes, the systematic exclusion of any area of inquiry is in itself a form of symbolic violence (Bourdieu and Passeron 1977, 31–32, 67). It is also clear that schools, in selecting specific knowledge areas as being worthy of systematic study, communicate important messages concerning the values and priorities of the state. However, schools do more than simply reflect prevailing social, economic, and political trends, reinterpreting them in their own terms. The receipt of an education offers the possibility for personal and collective empowerment, particularly when the inconsistencies of what is accepted as conventional wisdom become glaring so as to demand change.

The basic incongruity affecting political, economic, and social relations in China today is the existence of state policy that encourages freer markets while restricting human rights and preserving political authoritarianism. The educational system also reflects this incongruity, serving the interests of traditional intellectual and newly emerging professional elites, while still perpetuating an inordinate degree of exclusivity and social inequality in both urban and rural environments. Definitions of educational quality and determinations of appropriate standards for educational progress continue to be defined according to these factors. Educational policies are by no means solely responsible for the failure to create a true civil society in China. Indeed, it has been argued that the significance of the Tiananmen uprising lies in the willingness and ability of its participants to enunciate, through their political demands, a belief in the Habermasian notion of communicative rationality as a prerequisite to the creation of a true civil society, even if the type of institutional autonomy in the public sphere with which the West is familiar was absent (Madsen 1993). Still, the failure of educational and other institutions to promote a greater degree of political inclusivity has ramifications for past and future attempts at initiating significant political reform. One would expect that even after the current gatekeepers of party orthodoxy have been replaced with more pragmatic successors, social schisms between intellectual elites and workers and peasants will remain unbridgeable in the short term. Efforts to encourage the active participation of all of the relevant educational actors in the system would be a step in lessening that gap.

NOTES

(An earlier version of this chapter appeared in *Compare* 23,2.)

1. It should be remembered that "place" in Chinese terms continues to have association with ancestor residence.

2. A case in point is the Prairie Fire Campaign, designed to promote compliance with compulsory education directives throughout the countryside by

improving coordination with all relevant administrative units. The role of the township is recognised as being extremely important in this regard but the degree to which local units are themselves given significant decision-making responsibilities is open to question.

3. A sensitive plea to consider the ramifications of defining sense of place within the American classroom is offered by Theobald (1992).

REFERENCES

Aronowitz, Stanley (1988) "The Production of Scientific Knowledge: Science, Ideology and Marxism." In Cary Nelson and Lawrence Grossberg (eds.), *Marxism and the Interpretation of Culture.* Urbana and Chicago, University of Illinois Press, 519–37.

Bastid, Marianne. (1984) "Chinese Educational Policies in the 1980s and Economic Development." *China Quarterly* 98: 189–219.

Bonnin, Michel, and Chevrier, Yves (1991) "The Intellectual and the State: Social Dynamics of Intellectual Autonomy During the Post-Mao Era." *China Quarterly* 127: 569–93.

Bourdieu, Pierre, and Passeron, Jean-Claude (1977) *Reproduction in Education, Society and Culture.* Beverly Hills, Sage.

Burris, Mary Ann (1991) "Chinese Medical Schooling, Global Science, Local Schools." In Irving Epstein (ed.), *Chinese Education: Problems, Policies and Prospects.* New York, Garland, 255–86.

Carnoy, Martin, and Samoff, Joel (1990) *Education and Social Transition in the Third World.* Princeton, Princeton University Press.

Castells, Manuel (1983) "The New Historical Relationship between Space and Society," In Manuel Castells (ed.), *The City and the Grassroots.* Berkeley, University of California Press, 311–17.

Cheng Kai-ming (1991) *Planning of Basic Education in China: A Case Study of Two Counties in the Province of Liaoning.* Paris, International Institute for Educational Planning/UNESCO.

Connell, R.W. (1992) "Citizenship, Social Justice and Curriculum." Unpublished paper. International Conference on Sociology of Education, Westhill, United Kingdom.

Davin, Delia (1991) "The Early Childhood Education of the Only Child Generation in Urban China." In Irving Epstein (ed.), *Chinese Education: Problems, Policies and Prospects.* New York, Garland, 42–65.

Davis, Deborah (1992) " 'Skidding': Downward Mobility among Children of the Maoist Middle Class." *Modern China* 18 (4): 410–37.

Delany, Brian, and Paine, Lynn (1991) "Shifting Patterns of Authority in Chinese Schools." *Comparative Education Review* 35 (1): 23–43.

FBIS (Foreign Broadcast Information Service)—CHI-92-0009. January 14, 1992. "Juvenile Delinquency, Crime on Increase," 27–28.

FBIS—CHI-002. January 3, 1992. "Education Commission Sets Admission Guidelines," 35.

FBIS—CHI-010. January 15, 1992. "Academic Works 'Blacklist' Reportedly Compiled," 25–26.

FBIS—CHI-019. January 29, 1992) "Prisons Transformed Into 'Special Schools,'" 39.

FBIS—CHI-027. February 10, 1992. "Anti-Illiteracy Campaign to Target 20 Million," 18.

FBIS—CHI-032. February 18, 1992. "Graduate Schools Entrance Exams Begin," 35–36.

FBIS—CHI-92-068. April 8, 1992. "Space Program Unveiled," 33.

FBIS—CHI-92-082. April 28, 1992a. "Large-Scale Production of Interferon to Begin," 32.

FBIS—CHI-92-082. April 28, 1992b. "Contract Signed to Launch Intelsat Satellite," 32.

FBIS—CHI-92-085. May 1, 1992. "Report on Jangsu Reform-Through-Labor Teams," 22.

Fitzpatrick, Sheila (1978) "Cultural Revolution as Class War." In Sheila Fitzpatrick (ed.), *Cultural Revolution in Russia: 1928–1931.* Bloomington, Indiana University Press, 8–40.

Giddens, Anthony (1980) *The Class Structure of Advanced Societies.* London, Hutchinson Publishing, Inc.

Goldman, Merle (1981) *China's Intellectuals: Advise and Dissent.* Cambridge, Harvard University Press.

Goldman, Merle, Cheek, Timothy, and Hamrin, Carol Lee (eds.) (1987) *China's Intellectuals and the State: In Search of a New Relationship.* Cambridge, Harvard University Council on East Asian Studies.

Hao Keming, et al. (1989) "Wo guo nongcun yiwu jiaoyu fazhan de haunjing xianzhuang he qianjing [Current prospects and conditions for developing universal education in rural China]." *Jiaoyu Yanjiu* 10: 39–44.

Harvey, David (1985) "Class Structure and the Theory of Residential Differentiation." In David Harvey (ed.), *The Urbanization of Capital.* Baltimore, Johns Hopkins Unviersity Press, 109–24.

Hayhoe, Ruth (1989) *China's Universities and the Open Door.* Armonk, NY, M.E. Sharpe.

Hayhoe, Ruth (1991) "International Exchanges: Forces of Political, Cultural and Educational Change in China." Unpublished paper. Conference on Chinese Education for the 21st Century, Honolulu, November 19–22.

Hom, Sharon (1991) " 'Beyond Stuffing the Goose': The Challenge of Modernization and Reform for Law and Legal Education in the People's Republic of China." In Irving Epstein (ed.), *Chinese Education: Problems, Policies and Prospects.* New York, Garland, 287–315.

Honig, Emily, and Hershatter, Gail (1988) *Personal Voices.* Stanford, Stanford University Press.

Johnson, Todd M. (1991) "Wages, Benefits, and the Promotion Process for Chinese University Faculty." *China Quarterly* 125: 137–55.

Kamens, David, and Benavot, Aaron (1991) "Elite Knowledge for the Masses: The Origins and Spread of Mathematics and Science Education in National Curricula." *American Journal of Education* 99: 137–80.

Konrad, George and Szelenyi, Ivan (1991) "Intellectuals and Domination in Post-Communist Societies." In Pierre Bourdieu and James Coleman (eds.), *Social Theory for a Changing Society.* Boulder, Westview Press.

Kraus, Richard Kurt (1981) *Class Conflict in Chinese Socialism.* New York, Columbia University Press.

Kraus, Richard Kurt (1983) "The Chinese State and its Bureaucrats." In David Mozingo and Victor Nee (eds.), *State and Society in Contemporary China.* Ithaca, Cornell University, 132–47.

Kwong, Julia, and Kwai Fun Ko (guest editors) (1991–1992) "Bu Zheng Zhi Feng: Corruption in Education." *Chinese Education* 24 (2).

Latham, Richard (1991) "Military Education and Technical Training in China," In Irving Epstein *(ed.), Chinese Education: Problems, Policies and Prospects.* New York, Garland, 316–51.

Lo, Lai. (1991) "State Patronage of Intellectuals in Chinese Higher Education.*" Comparative Education Review,* 35, 4, 690–720.

Madsen, Richard (1993) "The Public Sphere, Civil Society, and Moral Community: A Research Agenda for Contemporary China Studies." *Modern China* 19 (2):183–98.

Manion, Melanie (1985) "The Cadre Management System, Post-Mao: The Appointment, Promotion, Transfer and Removal of Party and State Leaders." *China Quarterly* 102: 203–33.

Oi, Jean C. (1989) *State and Peasant in Contemporary China.* Berkeley, University of California Press.

Orleans, Leo. (1987) "Soviet Influence on China's Higher Education System." In Ruth Hayhoe and Marianne Bastid (ed.), *China's Education and the Industrialized World.* Armonk, NY, M.E. Sharpe, 184–98.

Paine, Lynne, and Delany, Brian (1991) "Authority, Stratification and Schools in China." Unpublished paper. Conference on Chinese Education for the Twenty-First Century, Honolulu, November 12–15.

Parish, William L., and Whyte, Martin King (1978) *Village and Family Life in Contemporary China*. Chicago, University of Chicago Press.

Pepper, Suzanne (1990) *China's Education Reform in the 1980s*. Berkeley, University of California Press.

Perry, Elizabeth (1985) "Rural Violence in Socialist China." *China Quarterly* 103: 414–40.

Price, Ronald F. (1987) "Convergence or Copying: China and the Soviet Union." In Ruth Hayhoe and Marianne Bastid (eds.), *China's Education and the Industrialized World*. Armonk, NY, M.E. Sharpe, 158–83.

Price, Ronald F. (1990) "School Science and 'Modernization.'" In Bih-jaw Lin and Li-min Fan (eds.), *Education in Mainland China*. Taipei, Institute of International Relations, 152–71.

Robinson, Jean (1991) "Minban Schools in Deng's Era." In Irving Epstein, *Chinese Education: Problems, Policies and Prospects*. New York, Garland, 163–71.

Rosen, Stanley (1985) "Recentralization, Decentralization and Rationalization: Deng Xiaping's Bifurcated Education Policy." *Modern China* 11 (3): 301–46.

Rosen, Stanley (1990) "Political Education and Student Response: Some Background Factors Behind the 1989 Beijing Demonstrations." In Bih-jaw Lin and Li-min Fan (eds.), *Education in Mainland China*. Taipei, Institute of International Relations.

Rosen, Stanley (1991) "The Rise (and Fall) of Public Opinion in Post-Mao China." In Richard Baum (ed.), *Reform and Reaction in Post-Mao China*. New York, Routledge, 60–83.

Ross, Heidi (1991) "The Crisis in Chinese Secondary Schooling." In Irving Epstein (ed.), *Chinese Education: Problems, Policies and Prospects*. New York, Garland, 66–108.

Sautman, Barry (1992) "Sirens of the Strongman: Neo-Authoritarianism in Recent Chinese Political Theory." *China Quarterly* 129: 72–102.

Shue, Vivian (1988) *The Reach of the State*. Stanford, Stanford University Press.

Solinger, Dorothy J. (1991) "The Place of the Central City in China's Economic Reform: From Hierarchy to Network." *City and Society* 5 (1): 23–39.

Theobald, Paul (1992) "The Concept of Place in the New Sociology of Education." *Educational Foundations* 6 (1): 5–20.

Thogersen, Stig (1990) *Secondary Education in China After Mao: Reform and Social Conflict*. Aarhus, Denmark, Aarhus University Press.

Thompson, E.P. (1967) "Time, Work-Discipline, and Industrial Capitalism." *Past and Present* 38: 56–97.

Walder, Andrew (1986) *Communist Neo-Traditionalism*. Berkeley, University of California Press.

Whyte, Martin King (1974) *Small Groups and Political Rituals in China*. Berkeley, University of California Press.

Whyte, Martin King and William Parish (1984) *Urban Life in Contemporary China*. Chicago, University of Chicago Press.

Yang Xuewei (1990) "Kaoshi zhidu de zhongda gaige [A Major Reform of the Examination System]." *Jiaoyu Yanjiu* 8: 49–51.

Yuan, Huarong (1990) "Lun Yousi de shehui jingji yiyi he daude de jiuzhi [The Socio-economic Implications and Moral Values of Euthanasia]." *Renkou Yanjiu* 4: 45–48.

Zweig, David (1991) "Internationalizing China's Countryside: The Political Economy of Exports from Rural Industry." *China Quarterly* 128: 716–41.

CHAPTER 6

Education and Mutuality—
An Action Perspective

JANE ORTON

INTRODUCTION

A central concern of comparative educationists has been the dynamics of cultural transactions and interactions and the transfer of knowledge across cultures (Welch 1993). Concerns over the role played by First World countries in the development of Third World countries are an important facet of this book. From a variety of standpoints and interests, the current disillusionment with transfer of the technical means of economic development, which has failed to result in the establishment of a broadly based, indigenous system of quality education, are illustrated. Instead, much of the interaction is perceived largely to have supported existing power structures by maintaining or even strengthening traditional elites. And even these elites have not been liberated in this process from continuing dependence on the First World.

Addressing these problems, Johan Galtung, of the UN-sponsored World Order Models Project, has set the transfer of knowledge between societies within a theoretical framework of values and principles rather than technical structures (Galtung 1975, 1980). These values have been developed into principles for action by Hayhoe with respect to the transfer of knowledge in the field of education between non-Chinese and Chinese (Hayhoe 1986a, 1989b). This chapter examines the dynamics of this area of transfer from an action perspective, with specific examples drawn from the field of educational transfer between non-Chinese and Chinese. The value of using an action perspective lies not only in attempting to forge links between theory and practice. As is shown below, subjecting

Galtung and Hayhoe's proposals to critical scrutiny from an action perspective is an undertaking supported by values fully congruent with the
proposals themselves, and thus may contribute to their development.
An "action perspective" seeks to subject theoretical propositions to
the test of action and to inform principle and theory from practice. The
notion derives principally from the Action Research work of Lewin
(1946), although the influence of Dewey can be perceived in the practical
focus and democratic values. Lewin's work has been developed contem-
porarily by scholars such as Argyris and Schön (1974) in the United
States, Elliott and Ebbutt (1985) in Britain, and Kemmis and McTaggart
(1982, 1988) in Australia. Action Research is concerned with the generation of usable knowledge which will both illuminate what exists and
inform fundamental change (Argyris and Schön 1974). The principal
value underlying this work is "emancipation": an informed change for
the better, brought about by and for the agents of change and achieved
through critical self-reflection. In seeking to serve emancipatory interests, Action Research thus falls within the "critical social science" category of Bernstein (1976), Habermas (1981), and Gouldner (1981).
Although as different from Marxism and Freudian psychotherapy as they
are from each other, like them Action Research may be seen as a form of
critical theory which seeks to transform the self-awareness of the subjects so that they may more freely choose whether and how to transform
their world (Argyris et al., 1985, 70).

In order to bring about this transformation, the actors—those who
act in the situation—must learn to "know better," a state which exists
outside their present awareness. In a fundamental departure from traditional science, critical theory thus must go beyond informing actors how
they would behave if they had certain interests, to inform them what
interests it is rational for them to have (Geuss, 1981, 58). Argyris argues
that critical theory justifies advocacy of a normative position by adhering
to the principle of internal criticism. That is, the critical theorist claims
that the normative views in question are implicit in the beliefs and practices of the agents to whom the critical theory is addressed. Critical theory
proceeds by making explicit the epistemic principles the agents already
use but of which they are unaware, and by showing that the agents' world
view is false by the criteria of these epistemic principles. (Argyris et al.,
1985, 70–72) Validity of the critical theory rests on confirmation of the
actors who find on reflection that they wish to give up a part of their previous world view (Geuss 1981, 76). It is important to realise that validity
in no ways entails that the actors are "right" but that they arrived at their

position freely. The test of truth is thus convergence between investigators who begin with a difference of view.

MUTUALITY IN THEORY

The Power Differential and the Process of Mutuality

In *The True Worlds: A Transnational Perspective,* Galtung (1980) sets the goal of development as a society where power takes the form of power over oneself, at individual and societal levels. This is *autonomy.* The opposite is submissiveness to whatever is introduced, which is *penetration.* Attainment of the goal of autonomy, Galtung proposes, must be tackled at both the system level of structure and the individual level of action. In structures it may be achieved through realisation of the guiding values of *equity, autonomy, solidarity,* and *participation,* and in action, through the guiding values of *personal growth* and *equality. Equity* means achieving an equal net benefit on either side of an interaction relation in *having* (that is, in material benefits) and *being* (that is, in nonmaterial benefits). *Autonomy* is also a relational construct. It is the power to be able to withstand the power of others over others (that is, over oneself), in all its forms including ideas. *Solidarity* is the opposite of fragmentation and is the extent of direct relationship among those involved at the bottom of a vertical division of labour. *Participation* is the extent of integration into multilateral relations. It opens the way for two-way input and influence. At the individual level, as stated, the values are personal growth and equality. *Personal growth* can manifest itself in a number of ways. It is brought about through diversity, freedom, and access to mobility, information, and communications. A negation of personal growth is alienation. *Equality* does not mean equal gains to all, but gains to all which fall between a lower and upper limitation. Work which does not lead to personal growth and equality for the individual actors is *exploitation.* Work which does not lead to equity, autonomy, solidarity, and participation for the society is *penetration.*

Galtung points out that the starting reality for a project (between any range of two "sides") in which participants are aiming to realise autonomy is the power differential between them. This may exist at the individual level, with one actor high in *being* power (personal realisation) and/or *having* power (material wealth) and very often both; and at the system level, with one system high in resource power and/or structural power, and, again, very often high in both; and, finally, the differential may exist and very often does, in favour of one side at both individual and system levels. To work towards the realisation of the espoused values is thus to work to reduce the power differential at all levels.

The Process of Mutuality in a Chinese Setting

In *Penetration or Mutuality? China's Educational Cooperation with Europe, Japan, and North America,* Hayhoe (1986a) seeks forms of educational engagement between non-Chinese and Chinese which "promise development without domination," or *mutuality.* Mutuality is the opposite of penetration and Hayhoe proposes Galtung's values of equity, autonomy, solidarity, and participation as the guiding values for an undertaking which achieves mutuality. Hayhoe applies the values to an East–West educational undertaking and develops their meaning in such a context.

Equity, she proposes, would be realised by the aims and patterns of organisation for the undertaking being set by full mutual agreement from both sides; *autonomy* would mean a respect for the theoretical perspectives rooted in Chinese culture, realised by foreign participants' gaining a deep and genuine understanding of Chinese scholarly culture and participating in intelligent dialogue over differences between it and their own; *solidarity* would mean the development of a network of interaction among Chinese participants in the project and between them and their fellows in other institutions, leading to a critical reinterpretation of the theory and technique being introduced; and *participation* would mean allowing Chinese discourse and contributions to enter the field and be integrated into and influence the dominant paradigms, which in turn would mean being open from the very beginning to the possibility of a creative Chinese contribution to the field.

In another article, Hayhoe sees this process of mutuality as the means to resolve the internal dilemma embedded in China's aspiration for economic development: the need to transform "the rigid Confucian regimentation of knowledge, on the one hand, coming up against notions of political order that were conceived entirely in terms of the regulation and control of knowledge, on the other" (Hayhoe 1989b, 162). She, too, sees a place for "critical theoretical interaction which will stimulate and strengthen a problem-solving environment in both the developed and developing world" (Hayhoe 1989b, 171). Hayhoe sees the kind of communicative action envisaged by Habermas with its view of reason "characterised by passion and morality" as offering a new dimension to a study of international educational relations, an interaction among systems which, while "characterised by fixated scientific-technical rationality, is linked back to its cultural life-world and gradually modified through a redefinition of rationality." In international interaction this process "could provide a vision of the redemption of Western modernity that comes not only through the internal critiques of its own scholars but also through the contribution of other sociocultural values and aesthetic sensitivities" (Hayhoe 1989b 171–73).

The practitioner who espouses mutuality thus adopts the goal of a reduction in the power differential to be realised in a transfer of knowledge guided by the values of equity, autonomy, solidarity, participation, personal growth, and equality. The means proposed are full agreement in planning and aims; informed discussion of cultural differences; collegiality among members of the recipient society; and openness of the knowledge to influence from the recipient culture which occurs, through "a balanced and non-dominating knowledge interaction process that . . . provide[s] conditions for mutual transformation" (Hayhoe 1989b, 174).

In the remainder of this chapter, the process of mutuality is examined from an action perspective. Certain modifications are seen to be needed to take into account critical features of practice which have not been raised in the above theoretical considerations. Further principles and concrete actions for realising the process are identified. A practical definition of mutuality is then proposed.

MUTUALITY IN ACTION—CONTACT

Putting Empowerment on the Agenda

In accordance with the views set out above, the practitioner who espouses mutuality begins a project intending to reach full agreement on aims and to raise for discussion matters of significant cross-cultural difference. Both these goals are seen to be necessary in order to reduce the power differential between participants. Both goals, therefore, need to be pursued in ways which themselves are congruent with this intention. Right from the start of any project, however, there are some factors which impinge on these goals.

One key feature of an action setting is that it is particularised: there is no longer "a non-Chinese participant" and "a Chinese participant"; there is only "you and her"; "he and I." These are real people, who have not appeared from nowhere: someone has arranged for them to come together, perhaps they themselves, but more often it is other people, who may not share the goal of mutuality, who have made the initial contact and negotiated a contract for the project. In any event, when actual participants in an international project meet for the first time, the aims and even some of the organisation and procedures for the project will have already been set, some perhaps immutably. Furthermore, there will be external pressure on both participants to carry out the work in a way approved by those who negotiated it—usually their employers—and a pressure to do so in a manner congruent with professional competence as it is understood in their different societies. Thus they begin the project not only with the attributes which constitute the power differential between them, but also with pressures on the scope of acceptable action open to them.

At the first meeting, and throughout the project, the practitioner who espouses mutuality is wanting to reduce the power differential, which may exist at personal and system levels, in having and being, and often occurs in all four categories in the one relationship. It will be manifest in differences between, for example, participants' material wealth, their formal position in employment, and their book knowledge; in the esteem granted to the groups of which they are members; and in their greater and lesser ability to access and present their interests and negotiate on their own behalf with others. Despite an intention to set the aims and patterns of organisation of the project *by full mutual agreement,* even with respect to matters which participants do have control over, an imbalance in the ability to access and argue one's interests will interfere with the intention to initiate the equitable exchange of opinion needed to reach full mutual agreement. Furthermore, given that the project is about transferring knowledge, an imbalance in knowledge and decision-making power over substantive issues is likely, and this will also interfere with setting the aims and processes of the project by full mutual agreement. Even in respect of cultural matters, the diligent visiting practitioner who wishes to *discuss intelligently* relevant differences in cultural perspectives may find that he or she will be more articulate and more developed in comparative understanding of local culture than those who live in it.

The existence of the power differential in having and being thus appears in its various guises from the outset of a project and creates an immediate challenge to the values of mutuality and a consequent dilemma for the practitioner who espouses it: to achieve full agreement about planning on the surface, while ignoring an imbalance in negotiating facility, substantive knowledge, or cross-cultural understanding will be to use the power differential to achieve domination and thus only to prolong and increase it; yet attempting to take the imbalances in knowledge into account by acknowledging them brings difficulties of its own, as it also risks reinforcing them. What causes the problem in this move is another power issue: differences in the internal power differential of the cultures to which the participants belong, which Hofstede (1991) calls "the power distance."

Although power distance is universally present in relationships, it is managed differently from one social group or culture to another. Thus, for example, in China, all relationships are hierarchical and what is expected and preferred, to a relationship where participants behave as equals in a discussion, is that the guest, or teacher, is placed by both parties in a superordinate role, deferred to and agreed with by the other, and expected to lead by command rather than consensus. In the planning of an international project in China, the Chinese party can therefore be expected to be more comfortable with a power distance greater than that required by the Western counterpart for useful conversation on joint planning and the consideration of cultural differences. This will be the case most particularly when to do otherwise would expose local ignorance of substantive matters or entail the "expert" 's appearing not capable of the decision making appropriate to a leader. In such a case, seeking to reach full agreement on aims and processes may be experienced as an attempt at unacceptable intimacy; or an arrogant assertion of superiority in scientific knowledge or about local beliefs and customs; or a humiliating exposure of local inadequacies rooted in either malicious superiority or a mindboggling insensitivity to *face*. It is thus a move which risks damaging the relationship from the start.

A similar contradiction with local values may arise over the value of *solidarity*, which advocates the development of a network of interaction among local participants in the project and between them and their fellows in other institutions. In some societies, the culturally acceptable power distance factor may preclude, or at least put limits on, what can be achieved in solidarity among the locals involved in a joint undertaking, or in their collective participation with the foreign practitioner. In China, for example, competition for privilege may limit what participants are willing to share among themselves, and fears for political safety may limit how prepared participants are to be seen by compatriots to be engaged with ideas introduced from abroad.

In addition to the above matters concerning the values of the process, there is another factor present from the beginning of any project which, although not raised by the proponents of mutuality, plays an important role in maintaining the power differential and thus must also be taken into account from the start if there is any intention to work to reduce it. This is the matter of the values embedded in practical knowledge and the consequent limitations on its successful transfer beyond cultural boundaries. Most international exchanges are based on a technical rationalist view of practice (Shils 1978, Schön 1987) in which "rigorous professional practitioners solve well-formed instrumental problems by applying theory and technique derived from systematic, preferably scientific knowledge" (Schön 1987, 4), that is, knowledge which is universal. (And it is this technical rationalist view of practice which is transferred when the knowledge being transferred is professional competence itself.) Such a view assumes that the knowledge and skills of the competent practitioner in one society can be transported and introduced into another by arranging for the practitioner to spend some time in the new society telling and showing professionals there what to do. As professionals, these latter will understand and appreciate the knowledge once they are introduced to it and, provided they are given the resources, the outcome of the project should be satisfactory to all. In such a view of the task, the notion of submissiveness, or penetration, does not arise.

In some cases this may be how exchanges work, but in reality, not many projects are so simple. Whether the practitioners are encouraged to consider the issue or not, the greater part of even the technical knowledge they have to offer is far from being universal and value free. It is the result of decisions to undertake research in some fields, not others; to fund research into certain questions rather than others; to study problems which arose in particular societies; and to find solutions which are compatible with the beliefs and values of those societies and their culture. This can become particularly apparent when these solutions leave their native shores and are implemented abroad. In health care, education, and agriculture, for example, solutions to problems in postindustrialised countries often provide a doubtful fit for the problems of countries where the fundamental issue in hygiene and food production is simply staying alive and basic schooling barely exists. In China, the new knowledge from the West which arrived 150 years ago did not lead to the development of the broad, popular education system it advocated, nor did it enable even those trained abroad to be progressive-minded American reformers to make a contribution to solving local problems on their return. Instead they found themselves "ignorant about the things that affect our daily lives, and we neither know their causes nor the conditions surrounding the causes" (Tsiang, in Fairbank 1982, 86).

There is one aspect of this situation—otherwise well documented and discussed by others—which needs to be recognised by those seeking mutuality. It is that acknowledging the cultural shaping of the knowledge one has and the values embedded in it means admitting that it may have relative rather than absolute value. When brought to bear on problems which arise in another society and culture, it cannot be considered to be the answer, but must once again be put to the test. It is obviously critical to a process intended to reduce the power differential between participants that right from the start they share an understanding that the usefulness of the knowledge being offered is yet to be proven. Unfortunately, due to the prevailing belief in a scientific vision of knowledge, such a view may also add strain to interpersonal dealings, as those in the host country may become anxious to think that perhaps their visitor is not the expert they had hoped for, or that despite the cost, the knowledge being brought may not be the certain solution to their problems. In China, the view that knowledge generated in the West needs critical scrutiny before adoption in China was accepted in theory long ago, with recognition of the class base of knowledge. However, there has been little or no recognition of other values being embedded there which may conflict with local ones; nor even agreement as to where the class nature of knowledge will be expressed. (See, for example, the discussion in Shanghai Shifan Daxue 1979, 2, on whether class values are necessarily embedded in superstructure or not.) The non-Chinese practitioner seeking mutuality will be anxious to foster critical reflection on the new knowledge in order to ensure that what the Chinese adopt is consonant with Chinese culture as they wish it to be. In this way, the new knowledge can lead to modernisation without necessarily requiring Westernisation: a position espoused by many and deemed feasible by writers such as Hu (1986), Xu (1987), and Li (1987).

WHAT IS TO BE DONE?

From the outset, then, the practitioner seeking to establish a process of mutuality may be confronted by a number of places where he or she is uncertain what to do to realise it. The solution suggested here is that the fundamental process for reducing the power differential in a manner congruent with the espoused values is one in which participants must share decision making about the conduct of their joint work *and* of the relationship between them. Thus at the first meeting, face-to-face with a counterpart, the practitioner beset with uncertainties such as those set out above does not make unilateral and private decisions about how to proceed, but opens the process to being constructed and controlled bilaterally, that is, by both parties to the discussion.

The first step towards sharing the creation of their relationship is raising for discussion the participants' expectations. How this is done is also critical to its actualisation: the power differential will not be lessened by a visiting practitioner who is a proponent of mutuality's inviting the local to disclose his or her expectations, but by the visiting practitioner's opening for scrutiny and comment the expectations on which he or she has come to the job. The practitioner must include in this initial disclosure the goal of mutuality which forms the value base of his or her participation. And that will entail a second important step towards lessening the power differential: the practitioner must disclose also his or her uncertainty as to how it might be realised and thus uncertainty as to how the pair (or group) might proceed from now on.

It is important to note that it is not the public espousal of the process of mutuality with its intention to put empowerment on the articulated agenda which begins a reduction in the power differential, but rather the acknowledgement by the practitioner of uncertainty about how to proceed. It is this which opens the process of decision making to bilateral control and offers the possibility of constructing a collaborative relationship: an open-ended dialogue where neither party is in control (Bernstein 1983, 144), the only way out of the dilemma.

Such a move is an invitation. It provides evidence that the averred goal of power sharing is true and it provides a model of how power sharing may be realised. But, like all action, it is a move undertaken with no guarantee of success. Counterparts must be free to decline to transcend the bonds of their traditional values by admitting their own ignorance; and to maintain the culturally preferred power distance by not joining in bilateral discussions of value conflicts or accepting some authority in the relationship and for the joint undertaking. The underlying assumption in proposing the move, however, is that participants will tend to accept the invitation, if it is offered as outlined above. Accepting the invitation may be no more than not rejecting it. Even a positive acknowledgement of imbalances in knowledge and mutual ignorance of cultural values, however, does no more for the present than joining in the opening of a bilateral relationship. These are not states which can be dispelled simply at will or by request. In the end, whether the invitation is accepted or turned down, the question of what to do must be posed anew.

In suggesting a mode of relating beyond what is normal in the local society, the practitioner is enacting that part of critical theory which attempts to inform counterparts what interests it is rational for them to have. At the same time, the practitioner who raises these topics for discussion is testing his or her own theory of how things are and ought to be against reality. If the counterparts decline the invitation to collaborate, then at least in part the theory is proven to be inadequate. Without yet abandoning the goal, the practitioner would need to investigate the situation further so as to understand it better and subsequently to remake the offer with a greater chance of success. Whether successful earlier or later, the goal of the action is a change in the counterpart's behaviour towards convergence with the practitioner's proposed course of action. In Habermas' view people will do this because they are actually being made aware of implicit beliefs they already hold. Congruently but more practically, Argyris claims that it is because people can see that the offer to be different provides an opportunity to learn that they are willing to change: to lower defensiveness, to reflect publicly, and to discuss touchy issues (Argyris 1985, 63).

In the first conversation, the value base of the knowledge being brought for transfer must also be disclosed as an issue. In this way, too, the power differential begins to be reduced as the foreign expert becomes recognised by both parties as not possessing some knowledge essential to creating a satisfactory outcome, knowledge in which the local, as local, is rich. As well, the expert knowledge the foreigner brings becomes recognised as only potentially valuable, having to be put to the test in a new situation, which may also lead to its modification. The goal of such a project cannot be the production of an outcome which only satisfies the prior expertise and values of the foreign practitioner, but must be one which also is feasible for the local practitioners and which, likewise, satisfies their values. This does not preclude their being educated to perceive the value of something new, but it also opens the visitor to being educated further and his or her values to being modified as well.

In such a project, the basic contract is not a one-way transfer of knowledge, but rather a bilateral endeavour to see if the two parties can make the knowledge of the one party, firstly, accessible; secondly, usable; and, thirdly, perhaps even valuable, within the practical setting of the other. Such a way of working opens the knowledge itself to the possibility of being transformed by the common engagement and by the encounter with new perspectives and new contexts. At the same time, in a process like that advocated by Freire (1974), participants are also transformed as their critical awareness is aroused through engagement with substantive issues and one another.

MUTUALITY IN ACTION—DEVELOPMENT

The Need for Action in the Exchange of Meaning

Founding a project on an espousal of mutuality which recognises limitations to the outsider's knowledge and agrees to create bilateral control does not remove the imbalance in being and having between participants. Agreeing to make joint decisions, for example, does not deal with an imbalance in the knowledge required to make the decisions, or in clarity of vision for the project. This has three consequences. Firstly, it means that participants will have to discover how they can achieve a collaborative relationship which lessens the power differential while actually operating their relationship; secondly, this will have to be learned while in a situation where one party is dependent on the other; and, thirdly, it means that they will have to turn to action before being able to reach full agreement on some significant matters. There are other factors, too, such as the cultural framing of talk itself and the nature of practical knowledge, which pose limitations on what can be achieved in creating mutuality through discussion. These matters are examined more fully below.

IGNORANCE

A fundamental obstacle to joint discussion with shared power is substantive ignorance. For example, where the substantive content of the project concerns one party's introducing knowledge or ways of working which have been developed in a very different and unfamiliar society, and where so much to be considered is radically new to the other party, there is a limit to how much and how well the latter will be able to comprehend the choices available, or to access the considerations on which decisions could genuinely be based. Likewise, there is a limit to how much the former will know of what it might be relevant to consider when familiar work is placed in a new setting. As a consequence, there will be a limit to the consensus which can be reached in discussion. It is only as they work together in concrete situations that new ideas and foreign meanings can be perceived. Participants in a process of mutuality will therefore proceed to action largely in the roles of teacher and learner, with the task of bringing the learner to that level of equality with the teacher which Buber (1958) calls "I and Thou."

THE INNER CONTRADICTION IN THE PROCESS

Establishing an explicit teacher–learner relationship may satisfactorily deal with the imbalance of power based on knowledge present at the beginning of the project and offer a way to reverse this state in the future. However, it also brings difficulties of its own as it will mean having to acknowledge the value clash inherent in any teaching situation. That is, that in order to bring learners to autonomy with respect to the knowledge presented, a teacher must require them to open themselves to the new largely in blind faith, dependent on the teacher. Developing the ability to withstand imposition thus begins with submission to it. Practitioners who avow mutuality cannot avoid this and can only seek to minimise the extent of the imposition by constant mutual monitoring which fosters in the learners the critical skills which underpin the exercise of autonomy. The contradiction in values is accepted, of course, in the hope that submission on a small scale now will mean autonomy on a grand scale later. But both parties must recognise that, even with the best will and skill in the world, there can be no guarantee that mistakes will not be made, or that damage will not be done. It is a realisation which should lend a spirit of humility to the teaching.

CROSS-CULTURAL INTERFERENCE

At the planning stage and throughout the joint undertaking, discussion of issues will be surrounded by culturally determined frames of meaning which impose constant limitations on what can be achieved through talk. Discussion of cultural differences is particularly difficult by being, itself, open to the bias and interference of the very same differences. Thus issues may be raised and apparently agreed upon in discussion, but turn out in practice to reveal very different meanings for the terms agreed upon. For example, in a non-Chinese–Chinese educational exchange, there may be consensus that what is to be sought is promoting students to be *active* and to *participate.* In practice what one side means by that may look more like *busy* and *obedient* to the other; while in reverse, the latter group will term what the former had in mind as *unruly* and *unacceptably opinionated.*

Differences in these matters once revealed in practice are, however, then accessible for discussion. An even greater difficulty in communication across the cultural divide will stem from differences which cannot be discussed because neither side is even aware of their very existence. These are matters so taken for granted that they simply are not raised and so go undetected in conversation. Earnest and intelligent participants then reach agreement without having raised what will prove to be some of the most important issues between them. Because they are so unanticipated, participants are often bewildered when these differences appear in the practice of the other party; and because they concern matters so deeply embedded in the participants' sense of how the world is and what the right course of action is that they have not even been raised, they cause considerable shock, disappointment, even disgust, on both sides when suddenly perceived. This can easily lead to the erosion of trust.

Unless participants are aware of the depth of interference from cultural framing and ethnocentricity and recognise the limitations on the effectiveness of talk to resolve them, their goodwill and best efforts may go badly awry and lead to a breakdown in the process of mutuality. Just knowing that there may be unraised matters which should be discussed is insufficient to prevent the problem of undiscussed difference: however much the participants have broadened their minds about their partners' culture and society, they must reach a point where they cannot think outside the frameworks of their own culture base and social experience. Furthermore, the cultural shaping of some parts of one's own or another's basic beliefs and values is simply not perceivable until exposed to a new environment. One thus quite literally does not know what should be said. It is only, for example, as actual texts are selected, actual classes taught, and real students spoken to that some of the tacit assumptions on which these actions are based become apparent.

At several levels of conversation in a cross-cultural setting, therefore, there are obstacles to the successful transfer of knowledge which can only be remedied by recourse to action. And at the deepest level, it is only through action that some essential pieces of the knowledge can even be discovered.

THE NATURE OF PRACTICAL KNOWLEDGE

In discussions of the transfer of knowledge, little attention has been paid to another factor which entails recourse to action if the transfer is to be successful, that is, the nature of practical knowledge. There are several constraints on the use of talk to transfer practical knowledge effectively. Some, as noted above, are most acute in a cross-cultural situation, where the exotic nature of certain factors in a new approach to work will require demonstration and examination over time before they can be perceived, understood, assessed, and mastered. Other constraints on transfer through talk are permanently present and are the result of limitations of the human brain faced with the complexity of practice situations. In these matters, the sheer quantity, complexity, and simultaneity of what makes up a piece of practice preclude its being fully articulated even by those who can practise it competently. As Argyris and Schön (1974) have pointed out, humans can do more than they can say. As they can also perceive more than they can say, demonstration is often a successful way of conveying practical knowledge.

Schön (1987) has also pointed out in detail a further limitation on talk to transfer practical knowledge, a limitation which stems from the nature of practical competence. This is the component of *artistry,* the knowledge whereby a professional is able to design new strategies to bring to bear on the unique, uncertain, and unknown features of a novel practice situation. Schön proposes that this ability to respond to the new is the key competence of professional practice and thus it is an essential component of any professional learning. The difficulty in the transfer of this knowledge is that, being a creative response to a situation, it is knowledge which does not exist outside of an actual practical action. Schön proposes a process of coaching while doing for the transfer of the knowledge underpinning artistry, knowledge which he calls "knowing-in-action" (1987, 22).

The imbalances in having and being which are present from the beginning of a project put a number of limitations on the use of talk to raise, discuss, and plan the substantive issues in a project: one side may not have the knowledge or skills to represent its own interests sufficiently; neither side can ask or say all that needs to be known in a new situation; neither side knows all the matters it is essential to raise for discussion outside the participants' own culture; and, by its very nature, the knowledge to be transferred is only partly accessible through words and is, anyway, only partly sayable. While the parties may begin with discussion and some agreement, for the teachers to provide it and for the learners to gain access to it, the complex, culturally framed, practical knowledge from outside their own experience requires *doing.*

From a practical perspective, then, the power differential manifest as an imbalance in knowledge and the consequent aspects of dependence within the relationship between participants, combined with the constant limitations to talk as a vehicle for the exchange of meanings, show mutuality, firstly, to be a process which can be espoused at the start of a project, but which cannot be realised outside of a recourse to action. Action is needed for identifying and displaying knowledge and meanings, illuminating the context of decisions and fostering critical awareness through reflection on actual practice. Secondly, like other practical processes, the process of mutuality is uncertain. Realising it will require of the practitioners artistry to meet the unknown, the unique, and the uncertain. Finally, essential to the success is participants' understanding that mutuality does not exist outside themselves: it is the process of their own relationship, a relationship in which they engage together in attempts to negotiate meanings for the values as they engage in the transfer and adaptation of substantive knowledge. What the values mean in reality can only be discovered as they proceed and will have to be constantly discovered anew as they continue.

MUTUALITY IN ACTION—PRACTICE

The Means for Creating a Collaborative Relationship

The implication for an actual project of the above way of framing it is that, to be successful, practitioners who avow mutuality will need to be able to create a collaborative relationship in and through their joint undertaking. To do this requires expertise in more than the technical knowledge and professional artistry of their substantive field. In skill terms, they will need also to have developed interpersonal skills to lead and to take part in the conversations suggested; and in psychological terms, they will need to have developed a self-esteem which is not dependent on the privileged status and personal self-confidence of the technically competent professional. Indeed, framing the task in terms of mutuality, as set out above, redefines in some significant aspects the notion of a competent professional practitioner.

At the start of a project, the first matter to be discussed by participants is expectations, including the aspiration to create a collaborative relationship and to realise the process of mutuality. As noted above, there will be limitations on what can be exchanged through talk alone, and all conversation will need to be supported and extended by jointly observed action. At the same time, whether they are discussing their relationship or the substantive matters of a project, participants will need a framework for managing a conversation equitably and for facilitating using talk to negotiate meaning. One such framework, which the author has found useful, is Argyris and Schön's Theory of Interpersonal Interaction, which they call Model II (Argyris and Schön 1974, 18). The model sets out the values and strategies they believe will tend to lead to successful interaction, that is, interaction which generates valid information, reduces defensiveness, and leads to reliable bilateral decision making. It will be noted that these values and goals are congruent with those espoused for the process of mutuality.

The first column of Table 6.1 lists the governing variables—the goals the actor strives to fulfil in interactions. The second column identifies the action strategies that participants adopt to achieve these goals. The third column describes the interpretation of the actor's behaviour by others involved, the kind of response they are likely to make to it, and the consequent features of the relationship likely to be established between those involved. Argyris and Schön claim, and it has been the author's experience that this is justified, that Model II goals and strategies tend to allow others to see the actor as minimally defensive and open to learning. Participants will tend to test publicly their assumptions and tend to be open to possibilities for change that may result from that testing. Thus Model II tends to lead to a behavioural world in which learning and growth are the consequences.

As noted among the limitations to talk, producing and exchanging new and complex knowledge is difficult. Model II provides a technique for exchanging meaning by speaking in observable categories, anchored in observable behaviour.

Thus in identifying how one feels in talk, one also reveals what action or behaviour underlies the feeling, rather than simply providing a judgement. For example, instead of saying, "Yes, well, I think you need to pay a little more attention to drawing out the students' own opinions" [*A judgement with no clues as to its source*], a participant would say, "Do you remember the point where that tall student had suggested one likely result of the problem and you began to talk about several others?" [This is what I saw you do: *identifies the behaviour from which the inference is to be made and allows the data to be confirmed or contested.*] ("Yes.") "Well, I see that as you taking over and telling them what they should think. [This is what I thought of that: *identifies the inference made.*] We have said we want them to be more active in providing opinions. [This is the value we espoused: *identifies a goal jointly agreed upon in talk.*] Well, I would like to see you probe more at this point, rather than providing answers yourself." [Allows own meaning of term to be seen: *identifies a concrete, observable meaning for "being more active" and provides a concrete observable behaviour as a strategy for realising it.*]

The other participant may then agree with the validity of the description of what actually happened, contest any of the points made—that the student was interrupted, that he or she did talk as much—or introduce other factors, such as pressure of time, which conflicted with the espoused

Table 6.1. Model II

Governing Variables	Action Strategies	Consequences for the Behavioural World	Consequences for Learning	Consequences for Quality of Life	Effectiveness
1. Valid information.	1. Design situations or environments where participants can be original and can experience highly personal causation (psychological success, confirmation, essentiality).	1. Actor experienced as minimally defensive (facilitator, collaborator, choice creator).	1. Disconfirmable processes.	1. Quality of life will be more positive than negative (high authenticity and high freedom of choice).	
2. Free and informed choice.	2. Tasks are controlled jointly.	2. Minimally defensive interpersonal relations and group dynamics.	2. Double-loop learning.	2. Effectiveness of problem solving and decision making will be great, especially for difficult problems.	Increased long-run effectiveness

Governing Variables	Action Strategies	Consequences for the Behavioural World	Consequences for Learning	Consequences for Quality of Life	Effectiveness
3. Internal commitment to the choice and constant monitoring of its implementation.	3. Protection of self is a joint enterprise and oriented toward growth (speak in directly observable categories, seek to reduce blindness about own inconsistency and incongruity).	3. Learning oriented norms (trust, individuality, open confrontation on difficult issues).	3. Public testing of theories.		
	4. Bilateral protection of others.				

Source: From Chris Argyris and Donald A. Schön, *Theory in Practice: Increasing Professional Effectiveness.* San Francisco, Jossey Bass, 1974, 87.

goal. Once they have established a common view of what happened, the two can have a meaningful conversation about the incident, or, for example, open a discussion on strategies viable for the practitioner, or differences in their meanings of the notion of students' being *active in providing opinions.*

In this way of working, the common practical experience provides the essential reference for the discovery of many of the meanings of participants' own behaviour, which they would never have been called on to articulate before; and being common, it provides the reference for meanings of notions not shared and not otherwise accessible, as well as for alerting either side to differences in the meaning of terms which in speech were apparently shared. Using a Model II framework will not prevent participants from getting confused or making mistakes, but it will allow these to be detected and corrected. As the model shows, the key to the detection and correction of error is drawing on the common experience of a practical situation, speaking in observable categories, being vigilant in examining inferences, and constantly testing assumptions in practice.

In keeping with the espoused Model II value of "speaking in directly observable categories," and mindful of the limitation of words to convey meaning across even narrow cultural gaps, extracts from actual practice are included below which provide examples of how the process of mutuality can be created. The extracts are all taken from the case study of a 3-month consultancy the author undertook in China, working with university teachers of English seeking to improve their teaching of English (Orton 1990). The consultancy was initiated by the author as a means of investigating some communication problems encountered while teaching in China a couple of years earlier. The extracts have been chosen because they each illustrate points raised in this chapter. They are offered not as recipes, but simply as concrete examples of how the process of mutuality may be enacted, with the intention of assisting others in making clearer links between theory, principle, and individual behaviour.

1. Joint Control from Day One The following excerpt is from an account of the introductory meeting with department teachers in which the author was seeking participants for a consultancy to be undertaken on a return visit. The personal dissatisfaction with earlier work in China and curiosity over the causes of difficulties which prompted the consultancy were explained fully but have been largely omitted here. The excerpt illustrates the visiting practitioner's taking the lead in disclosing expectations and aspirations and, from the very beginning, frankly raising issues and opening the project to joint control.

After greetings and amid assurances on both sides that we could just be informal, I put a small tape recorder on the table and began:

> "I am looking for a conversation. I am looking to start a conversation. My purpose is to investigate how to be a foreigner in China and help improve the teaching and learning of English in, for example, Beijing Middle Schools. . . ."

I went on to say that I wanted to work with them in their real-life situations and to take real-life contingencies into account. I finished by saying:

> "What I'd really like to find is a group of people—say 4 or 5 or 6— who would be interested in continuing this conversation in the area of ignorance, difference and value clashes. And, I don't know, this may be unrealistic—and I'd like to be told so—ideally that group could meet 4 or 5 times before I go back, perhaps for one hour, or an hour and a half, with an agenda. . . . I would take the responsibility for beginning that conversation, but I would expect you people would be able to help direct it by what you are interested in. But we'd start on what seem to me to be some basic differences [in our practice]."

As agreed on before, once I had made my proposal, I left them in the library to discuss among themselves who and what might be arranged.

2. Putting Empowerment on the Agenda The three-month consultancy consisted of classroom observation and a one-to-one weekly discussion session with each client teacher. At the first session each was given the Values piece presented below. It was discussed at the second meeting. The piece sets out a value framework for the work, attempts to make a link between it and Chinese Marxist values, and provides some concrete, observable procedures for doing what is proposed. The consultant acknowledges that there may be failings in her own realisation of the values and invites the client teachers to take joint responsibility for enacting the values by holding the consultant to account for her own behaviour. The suggested way of relating was very new to the Chinese but, as will be shown in later excerpts, they did take up this invitation to challenge the consultant's behaviour. In doing so, they tested for themselves the reality and value of the espousals in the piece and the trustworthiness of the consultant.

VALUES

When working with you I have, of course, my values which guide me in choice of event to pay attention to, how I look at the event, and what kinds of things I try to draw your attention to.

My primary value is "emancipation": that is, literally, to help make you free. This means that when we are discussing your teaching I am not trying to get you to adopt a particular course of action but, rather, trying to help you discover as large a set as possible of alternative courses of action to choose from and to understand what you see these realistically to be, as far as that can be done. Thus it needs to be a dialogue in which we try to reach a common understanding of the events and their environment, the issues at stake for the actor (you), and then to see what possible courses of action we can design and what the implications of these are when we consider them. But the choice of action is yours.

In Marxist terms I understand working in this way as consciousness raising: seeking to transform our self-awareness through critical self-reflection, so that we may more freely choose whether and how to transform our world.

The problem, of course, is how to make these ideas reality and not just pretty-sounding but empty! I use the following rules:

1. Participants (=us) are jointly in control of what happens.
2. Choices are made jointly and not suddenly, without consultation.
3. Talk about what happened is in ways that both can share: i.e.,
    i.   Begin with an actual event and see if agreement can be reached that it happened.
    ii. If we can agree that such-and-such happened, then try to reach understanding of how that event is seen from our separate cultural viewpoints.
    iii. If there has been mutual understanding so far, discuss evaluation of the event.

Examples of this way of working will occur all the time and I will make these steps clearer as we proceed (I believe a little *zhiguanxing* [concrete example] and *ganxing renshi* [sensory perception] are a great help to giving meaning to abstract ideas like these!) See also attached example.

The underlying assumption is that we can have this kind of dialogue. This rests on the assumption that two people can communicate if they have a genuine interest in doing so. It demands that both sides be willing to be responsible for what they do (and say) and willing to examine their actions and speech publicly (i.e., with the other person). To continue, it requires, in fact it assumes, that free and open discussion will produce agreement or at least an agreed understanding as to what is not agreed on.

Discussing our teaching is a complex business. Actions do not always have clear and easily reached motives. When we make great efforts to do a good job, it is often painful to face our shortcomings! And when we reflect on our work with another person, this becomes complicated by our feelings for that person. These feelings might include embarrassment that they should know our shortcomings or irritation and anger because they themselves are not apparently suffering from the same shortcomings. These feelings are normal. There is no easy way around them, but they are less damaging to oneself and to the relationship if they are acknowledged—firstly to oneself and then to the other person.

If you find that such feelings occur it may help to remember that the only reason I am asking the kind of questions I am asking is because I know the problems—not from books, but from my own teaching. Keep in mind that it was because I was dissatisfied with my teaching in China that I have come back to try again. And the reason I am sitting here trying to help you work through your problems in this way is because someone did that for me, too, and I found it most useful. So useful I felt able to come back and try again by trying to share this way of working with you.

Another thing this way of working means is that I will not be hiding things from you. I will not say "I did not see any issues" this week and then two weeks later or in the report, suddenly say "Well, actually there were some things but I didn't want to tell you."

Much of the success of this way of working relies on how you think of what you are doing when you admit that some aspect is not as effective as you would like. An "error," meaning something happening that you do not want to happen, or did not expect would happen as a consequence of what you did, can be looked at as a puzzle, as something to engage with intellectually, emotionally, and physically. In this way you accept yourself as a learner—for life—and feel excitement, interest, curiosity, and confidence about tacking the problems. This is the attitude of a reflective practitioner. Alternatively, you can think of these ineffective aspects as crimes, as actions to be covered up and hidden, and you will feel frustrated, embarrassed, anxious, and ashamed of them. This way is closed to change because the event is not available for examination. You cannot change something if you do not know what it is.

"I see my role as a person who is trying to help you minimise the bad feelings so that you can look at the places where you feel your work is ineffective with the greatest openness and confidence possible. I will be working hard to keep to the rules I have set above. However, it is both our responsibility to see that I do so. Anything I say or do is open for you to challenge and disagree with. I welcome your pointing out to me my failings with respect to my rules and values and assumptions. I hope you will put this to the test whenever you feel it is necessary.

"I have drawn my ideas from several sources, but in particular from the work of Chris Argyris and Donald Schön."

* * *

3. Detecting and Correcting Error It has been emphasised throughout this chapter that mutuality has to be created through a process of trial and improvement by participants working within the reality of their situation. What is important in this process is not that errors will be made—this is inevitable—but that errors be detected and corrected. In the following excerpt from the consultancy journal, the handling of a major error in consultant behaviour is described.

XIA, WEEK 4

. . . Our meeting which followed this class immediately was a complete contrast to the one before. I was angry over Xia's handling of an interchange with one of his students during the class and I took him to task about it directly. In fact I went at him about it in what an hour afterwards I recognised as an almost comical replay of the same event: I berated, lectured, and hectored until he was as silent, red, and jammed as she had been. The comical part was that it had been done in a spirit of "Don't you treat people like that."

Before we met again I had apologised in a note to Xia for behaving as I had. At our next discussion we spent some time on my behaviour and Xia protested that I had been quite within my rights, that he had deserved to be berated, and that he had not felt angry with me, but rather with himself. I suggested if it happened again, he should point it out to me and ask me to stop. This was the first time we discussed our relationship directly.

The incident above occurred at the end of the first month of the consultancy. The Chinese teacher, Xia, responds to the consultant's self-criticism in a manner congruent with traditional Chinese norms of courtesy and face towards a superordinate: he takes the blame on himself. However, as shown below, two months later there have been significant changes in his way of dealing with consultant behaviour he dislikes and in relating to the consultant. Points of particular note are: (1) When asked by J. for comment on her work, Xia begins with typical Chinese behaviour when asked for a value judgement: he simply describes what has happened. But he then moves on to an issue of his own and this he handles differently. (2) It is Xia who raises the above "error" incident for discussion, and he feeds back that it made a good impression on him, something not clearly apparent at the time. (3) Despite the error, J.'s behaviour over it and in subsequent contact has led him to feel confident in the sincerity of the invitation in the Values piece, and reiterated above by J., that there is room for him to take some responsibility for shaping the conduct of their work and relationship. Thus in Week 7 he made a radical intervention. Based on belief in the sincerity of the invitation, his intervention also put that sincerity to the test. (4) J. points out to him that it was a success: when he intervened she did as he asked. She thus confirms her approval of his action. At the same time, J. is pushing him to reflect on a concrete meaning for the abstract notions set out in the Values piece. (5) Although still shy about his new role, in making the intervention and in having this meta-dialogue about the conduct of their relationship, Xia is placing himself in an "I and Thou" relationship with J. and thus enabling them for the moment to realise mutuality.

XIA, WEEK 13

J: So, we've worked together for three months—have you got anything to say? Can you give me some feedback?

XIA: Yeah. [*Pause*] . . . How time flies, huh? . . . I think the time we have been spending together is meaningful . . . because we have been discussing some methods, right? Or some new approaches—at least, some new approaches for me, in my teaching . . .

J: Mmmm.

XIA: And I am very impressed by your ways of . . . ah . . . giving advice . . . suggestions . . .

J: By the *way*?

XIA: I mean, by the frankness.

Xia was referring to our "incident." I said I was pleased and interested that he had found frankness a useful feature of working with me.

J: And I think you're right: that particular time when I was upset was a very important point in our relationship . . .
Xıa: Mmm.
J: . . . and the best thing you did between us, you did last week. When [*that time*] I was upset . . .
Xıa: Mmm.
J: . . . afterwards I said to you, "If I'm ever like that again, you say to me, 'Ok, Jane, that's enough,'" right?
Xıa: [*laughs*] Yeah.
J: And last week you said that to me.
Xıa: [*giggles*] Yeah.
J: After I'd been explaining to you how you should teach vocabulary, yeah?
Xıa: Yeah.
J: You said to me, "*Ok, I get it!*"
Xıa: Yeah.
J: And I was so pleased . . .
Xıa: You were pleased [*giggles*], yeah?
J: Absolutely! I was so pleased. I heard you and I thought, "Oh, yeah, what am I doing? I'm just going on and on—
Xıa: [*laughs*]
J: . . . shut up Jane!"
Xıa: [*laughs*] That's what I really meant, last week.
J: I got the message: I shut up, if you noticed.
Xıa: But I learned it from you: you told me to do that.

4. Using Model II in Conversation The excerpt below shows the transfer of a small piece of substantive knowledge achieved within the emancipatory framework set out in the Values piece of trying to help Fu "discover as large a set as possible of alternative courses of action to choose from." To transfer the knowledge, the participants must both engage in using action to make exchangeable meaning for ideas and practices unknown to the other. They must also resolve several difficulties and in doing so provide one another with new information on the inner workings of their different world pictures and professional frameworks. The outcome is convergence. There is no suggestion that this will be all that is needed to have Fu adopt the technique proposed, only that Fu has come to understand what it is, and that she thinks it is an option worth trying out.

FU, WEEK 8

J: Quite a lot of them didn't give you that
sentence, you had to ask for it each time.
Now . . . when you'd had about eight or
nine examples and almost all of them you
had then to ask for that last piece, were
you aware of that? Sort of having to push
them to do that extra piece?

*citing an event by
describing it; checking
that it happened +
giving own judgement*

[*Pause ? Fu nods*]

J: Because at one point I felt kind of impatient
myself and I felt sure, if it were me, I
would have said to them, I'd have stopped
the ordinary proceedings and, as it were,
stepped aside and said, *Hey, come on
you people! I said when you give your
evidence you must also give the concluding
sentence. Now I don't expect to have to ask
for that every time.* Do you know what I
mean?

testing assumptions

FU: Yeah.

J: [*drawing a circle*] If you're here with a class
and you've got an activity going on which
is giving the answer plus evidence plus
conclusion, right? That's the activity. Now
if they're not doing this unless you push
them, what I would do is kind of step out
of that role and talk to them about this
activity. I feel somehow that's not a
Chinese thing, but I may be quite wrong.

*suggesting a new
technique*

*advocating combined
with enquiry:; sharing
control: this is my way,
it's ok if it doesn't fit
here*

FU: I do realise that I had had to do it. I notice
one student used the sentence I gave . . .
sometimes I had to say, *So..?* and lead
them to do that.

J: Uhuh. But while you're doing that, you're
still within this activity like that [*circle*],
but it's also possible to kind of step out of
that activity and kind of look at it, and say,
*Look, when we're doing that, what I'm
expecting you to do is* . . . and then you can

go back and be the teacher again. But it's
kind of looking . . . you're asking them
to look that way [*indicates*] back at the
activity and say, *Do you see what we're
doing? Do you see that there's a problem
here?* Now, it's sort of a *Let's look at what
we've been doing* kind of an activity, do
you follow that?

*in the light of Fu's
apparent non-
recognition of the
technique, J. fumbles
to access a piece of
own artistry*

FU: Yeah, yeah.

J: Now you can say that in an ordinary kind of
voice, or you can be scolding them, I don't
know, it depends on . . . I probably would
have said in English at least—and that's
with the social relations in English—I
probably would have said something like
[*in mock exasperation*] *Just a minute. Huh!
I thought I said up here I'd like evidence
and conclusion, right? So if you're going
to give the answer, I expect answer,
evidence, and conclusion.* So you sort of
stop that activity, step outside, have a
conversation about the activity . . .

*feedback: she gets the
point of the problem,
not clear she gets the
suggestion*

FU: And then go back.

Later in the same session

J: Quite often you say, *Can anybody argue
against him?* And there's silence. And
what I want to know is what do you see are
possible choices for you at this point? What
can you do or say?

*investigating Fu's
world*

FU: Put the question in another way, in different
words.

J: Uhuh. [*writes Put Q another way*] What else?

FU: Ask one student to . . . call on one student
to answer.

J: [*writing Name S*] Ok, anything else?

FU: I think those are the possibilities I use all
the time. [*laughs*]

J: Ok, then there are two questions I have for
  you. One is, um, you are saying that those
  are what you do do . . .

FU: Mmm.

J: . . . Ok, is there anything else you *could* do
  that you can think of? A reasonable thing
  to do?

FU: It's not good to wait. [*laughs slightly
  tightly*]

J: That's a comment. I'm asking you what you
  would do.   *a meta-comment, itself
                                                               an example of stepping
                                                               aside*

FU: [*laughs*] Uhuh.

[*Pause*]

J: Do you feel you can't wait?   *picks up where Fu is at*

FU: I cannot.

J: [*writing*] Ok, just stand there?

FU: [*burst of laughter*]

[*Pause*]

J: So that option is out, right? So, anything else
  you could do that you can think of?

[*LONG PAUSE*]

FU: I cannot see it.

J: Ok, well let's . . . so let me ask you, what for
  you . . . putting the question in another
  way, what would be the purpose of that?
  [*That = her #1 answer: Putting the Q in
  another way.*]

FU: To give them some hint of the question,
  lead them on the track.

J: Uhuh. When I hear you say that, I think   *reveals own
  there's another reason, therefore: that you   judgements and checks
  think . . . what? That they can't do it? That   it out; thinking aloud
  they are not doing it because they can't do   = passing on
  it. Is there some link there with that or not?   knowledge of process
                                                               by modelling it*

FU: Perhaps they don't come to the point . . .
  the purpose of this question.

J: I'm sorry, I'm not sure what . . .

FU: Oh, if I ask them to argue against such a
  point, they don't see the . . . the . . . the
  link of this wrong one with this correct
  one, how . . . it's difficult for them.

J: So, this is . . . you're giving them a hint
   because you think . . .
FU: . . . it is difficult.
J: . . . they're not answering because it's
   difficult.
[*Pause*]
J: So, I understand the silence as meaning *It's*   *feeds back and checks*
   difficult, so I'll give them a hint and the   *publicly the picture of*
   way I'll do that is to put the question in   *underlying motivation*
   another way. Ok, that's one possibility.
   I'm curious about this one, of course.
FU: Why cannot I wait? It's a waste of time
   [*laughs*].
J: Yeah?
[*PAUSE*]
J: So when that happens you feel impatient, you
   want to get moving?
FU: Yeah.
J: What about feeling uncomfortable?   *confronts*
FU: Why I feel . . . ?
J: No, I said, Do you also feel uncomfortable   *checking her world*
   when that happens?
FU: Yes.
J: So it's . . .
FU: Very awkward.
J: Why? What word would you use in Chinese   *opens up a touchy*
   for that?   *topic*
FU: *Leng chang.*
J: *Leng* . . . ?
FU: *Chang*: the complete silence on that
   occasion, *leng chang*, embarrassed. *Leng* is
   cold . . .
J: I know.
FU: *Chang* is occasion: a cold occasion, no
   response.It can mean many things,
   disagreement, um . . . [*laughs slightly*].
J: So then that's very uncomfortable?
FU: Uhuh.
J: Yeah, most people feel like that. Again, I have   *lessens defensiveness,*
   a feeling . . . sure, I know the feeling   *acknowledges the*

myself, but I have a sense that in China that's somehow worse than it is in the West, that people tolerate less well, they get much more anxious about it.

difficulties, raises possibility of cultural difference

FU: If they talk very much I feel very . . . um . . . easy to get into them, but if nobody speaks, especially on these occasions, I feel *I* am lost, I don't know how to deal with it.

Fu is prepared to open up on a touchy issue

J: Mmm. Yes, it's very powerful, isn't it? Because you can feel you're really locked out, right?

FU: Yes.

J: Nobody's looking at you, nobody wants to talk to you.

FU: But if I feel it's really not that difficult, I'm sure someone can answer, I make one of them.

J: So the way out of this is to . . . so that goes back to [*2 options stated above: rephrase Q or name another S*], depending on whether you think it's difficult or not, you'll do one or the other, uhuh. Um . . . one other possibility there is to—and it may not be for you, it is for me—would be to do the same kind of thing: [*indicates circle.*]

FU: Ah! Now I see. Talk about it, the activity [*laughs*]. I have never thought of this third possibility . . .

meaning of the new has finally been exchanged through recourse to a practical example

FU: . . . I feel if I said this, some of the students will shut up for the later questions.

J: Why is that?

FU: They will feel—I can say this: "I don't mean that you are bad, I want to know the reason or the . . . ," but they will take it as a criticism.

Fu reveals new meaning for J.'s strategy in the local context

J: Mmm.

FU: As a scold.

J: Well, ok, I'm not suggesting you rush out and do it . . .

J. open to influence from local context

Fu: Uhuh, no . . .

J: . . . and I don't mean you should say *that,* say   *modifies strategy*
something that's comfortable for you.

Fu: Step out and look at it. I think I should do   *convergence*
this.

CONCLUSION

The theory of mutuality is premised on the possibility of partnerships being genuine although unequal. It has been shown in this chapter that a genuine partnership can be realised only if the relationship allows the power differential between participants to begin to be addressed by opening it to bilateral control. This kind of relationship cannot be achieved instantaneously, but must be developed over time. It will require mutual commitment to learning by doing, using the practice situation to reveal inner working and thus inform and assist communication. A genuine partnership will also require more than avowed good intentions to be egalitarian: it will require participants to acquire frameworks for conducting their work and conversations in a manner consistent with the values espoused.

The aim of this chapter has been to inform the theory and principles of mutuality by subjecting them to the test of a practical setting and an action perspective. In the course of this test, mutuality as a process of reducing the power differential between participants by realising the values of equity, autonomy, solidarity, and participation has been found to be more complex than set out in theory by Galtung or Hayhoe. In particular a practice setting reveals limits on (1) the scope of open-ended dialogue, due to the pressure of a real-life work contract; (2) the agreements and exchanges of view that can be achieved before commencing a project; and, (3) the successful exchange of essential information in the medium of words alone. This last stems from the fact that educational practice is not an applied science, so not all of competent practice is conducted on a rational basis, or even accessible to the practitioner; and this is true even of a piece of practice which can be justified rationally. In practice, mutuality is shown to be only feasible as a dynamic process of discovery, a journey without end, of collaborative, responsible, interactive engagement with the substantive problem and the interpersonal relationship created to work on it. As such, mutuality does offer practitioners a process worth exploring in working towards the goal of international educational exchange and development without domination. In doing so, it also fulfils the essential requirements of critical theory for a process of mutual self-transformation through critical reflection and freely adopted change.

In this chapter, pieces of actual practice have been made available for critical scrutiny with the intention of demonstrating some of the dynamics of mutuality raised above, illustrating problems likely to be encountered and offering some possible solutions to them, including a conversation framework which may be used for negotiating meaning effectively and equitably. At the same time it is recognised that this is only a beginning. More work needs to be done on actual practice, and, in particular, the voices of Chinese and other recipients in projects aimed at the transfer of knowledge across cultures need to be heard on the subject as well.

REFERENCES

Adelman, C. (1985) "Who Are You? Some Problems of Ethnographer Culture Shock." In R.G. Burgess (ed.), *Field Methods in the Study of Education.* Barcombe, Lewes E. Sussex, Falmer Press.

Allender, Jerome S. (1986) "Educational Research: A Personal and Social Process." *Review of Educational Research* (Summer) 56 (2): 173–93.

Argyris, Chris (1985) "Making Knowledge More Relevant to Practice: Maps for Action." In Edward E. Lawler III, Allan Mohrman, Jr., Susan A. Mohrman, Gerald E. Ledford, Jr., Thomas G. Cummings and Associates, *Doing Research That Is Useful for Theory and Practice.* San Francisco, Jossey-Bass.

Argyris, Chris, Putnam, Robert, and Mclain Smith, Diana (1985) *Action Science.* San Francisco, Jossey-Bass.

Argyris, Chris, and Schön, Donald A. (1974) *Theory In Practice: Increasing Professional Effectiveness.* San Francisco, Jossey-Bass.

Bao, Zunjia (1984) "Bijiao. Jiaoliu. Fazhan" [Compare. Exchange, Develop]. *Dushu*, 7: 78–83.

Barlow, Tani E., and Lowe, Donald M. (1985) *Chinese Reflections.* New York, Praeger.

Benveniste, Guy, and Ilchman, Warren F. (eds.) (1969) *Agents of Change: Professionals in Developing Countries.* New York, Praeger.

Bernstein, R.J. (1976) *The Restructuring of Social and Political Theory.* Philadelphia, University of Pennsylvania Press.

Bernstein, R.J. (1983) *Beyond Objectivism and Relativism.* Oxford, Basil Blackwell.

Berg, David N., and Smith, Kenwyn K. (eds.) (1985) *Exploring Clinical Methods for Social Research*. Beverley Hills, Sage.

Biggerstaff, Knights (1975) *Some Early Chinese Steps Towards Modernization*. San Francisco, Chinese Materials Center Occasional Series, No. 23.

Bloom, Alfred (1981) *The Linguistic Shaping of Thought: A Study in the Impact of Language on Thinking in China and the West*. Hillsdale, N.J., Lawrence Erlbaum.

Blumenthal, Peggy (1981) *American Study Programs in China: An Interim Report Card*. National Academy of Sciences Committee on Scholarly Communication with the PRC.

Bochner, Stephen (1982) *Cultures in Conflict: Studies in Cross-Cultural Interaction*. Oxford, Pergamon.

Bond, Michael Harris (ed.) (1986) *The Psychology of the Chinese People*. New York, Oxford University Press.

The British Council (1982) *English Teaching Newsletter*. Beijing, The British Council.

The British Council (1983) *English Teaching Profile: China*. London, The British Council.

Buber, Martin (1958) *I and Thou*. New York, Charles Scribner's and Sons.

Buck, Pearl (1955) *My Several Worlds*. London, Methuen.

Burnaby, Barbara, and Sun, Yilin (1989) "Chinese Teachers' Views of Western Language Teaching: Context Informs Paradigms." *TESOL Quarterly* 23 (2) (June): 219–38.

Carr, Wilfred, and Kemmis, Stephen (1986) *Becoming Critical: Knowing Through Action Research*. Geelong, Deakin University Press.

Chan, Wing-tsit (1967a) "Chinese Theory and Practice, with Special Reference to Humanism." In Charles Moore (ed.), *The Chinese Mind*. Honolulu, East-West Center, University of Hawaii Press, 11–30.

Chiao, Chien (ed.-in-chief) (1983) *Proceedings of the Conference on Modernization and Chinese Culture,* March 7–11. Hong Kong, Faculty of Social Science and Institute of Social Studies, The Chinese University of Hong Kong.

Chin, Yueh-lin (1980) *Chinese Philosophy. Social Sciences In China* 1. Beijing, Social Science Publishing House of China.

Cowan, J. Ronayne, Light, Richard L., Matthews, B. Ellen, and Tucker, G. Richard (1979) "English Teaching in China: A Recent Survey." *TESOL Quarterly* 13 (4) (December): 465–482.

Crossley, Michael, and Burns, Robyn (1983) "Case Study in Comparative and International Education: An Approach Bridging the Theory-Practice Gap." *Comparative and International Studies and the Theory and Practice of Education,* Proceedings of the 11th Annual Conference of the Australian Comparative and International Education Society, Hamilton, New Zealand.

Cua, Anthony S. (1982) *The Unity of Knowledge and Action: A Study in Wang Yang-Ming's Moral Psychology.* Honolulu, University Press of Hawaii.

Curle, Adam (1969) "The Devil's Advocate View." In G. Benveniste, and W.F. Ilchman, (eds.), *Agents of Change: Professionals in Developing Countries.* New York, Praeger.

De Bary, William Theodore (1982) *The Liberal Tradition in China.* New York, Columbia University Press.

De Bary, William Theodore, and Bloom, Irene (eds.) (1979) *Principle and Practicality: Essays in Neo-Confucianism and Practical Learning.* New York, Columbia University Press.

Deng Xiaoping (1985) *Build Socialism with Chinese Characteristics.* Beijing, Foreign Languages Press.

Elliott, J., and Ebbutt, D. (1985) *Facilitating Action Research in Schools.* New York, Longman.

Fairbank, John K. (1982) *Chinabound.* New York, Harper Colophon Books.

Fairbank, John K., and Teng, Ssu-yu (1967) *China's Response to the West: A Documentary Survey, 1839–1923.* New York, Atheneum.

Fan, Maoyuan (1986) "Chuantong Jiaoyu yu Jiaoyu Gaige" [Traditional Education and Educational Reform]. *Hongqi* 13: 35–41.

Fan, Maoyuan, and Ye, Zhihong (1988) "Xiandai Jiaoyu yu Jiaoyu Xiandaihua" [Modern Education and the Modernisation of Education]. *Hongqi* 5: 22–28.

Fitzgerald, C.P. (1969) *The Chinese View of Their Place in the World.* Oxford, Oxford University Press.

Franke, Wolfgang (1967) *China and the West.* New York, Harper and Row.

Frankel, Boris (1979) "Jürgen Habermas: The Relationship of Communication to Learning." In J.V. D'Cruz and Wilma Hannah (eds.), *Perceptions of Excellence.* Melbourne, Polding Press.

Freire, Paulo (1974) *Pedagogy of the Oppressed.* London, Falmer.

Furnham, Adrian, and Bochner, Stephen (1986) *Culture Shock: Psychological Reactions to Unfamiliar Environments.* London, Methuen.

Galtung, Johan (1975) "Is Peaceful Research Possible? On the Methodology of Peace Research." In J. Galtung (ed.), *Peace: Research, Education, Action.* Copenhagen, Christian Ejlers.

Galtung, Johan (1980) *The True Worlds: A Transnational Perspective.* New York, Free Press.

Gasster, Michael (1983) *China's Struggle to Modernize.* (2nd ed.) New York, Alfred A. Knopf.

Gernet, Jacques (1985) *China and the Christian Impact.* Cambridge, Cambridge University Press.

Geuss, R. (1981) *The Idea of a Critical Theory.* Cambridge, Cambridge University Press.

Gouldner, A. (1981) *The Two Marxisms.* Oxford, Oxford University Press.

Grabe, W., and Mahon, D. (1981) "Comments on a Methodology-oriented Teacher Training Program in China." *TESOL Quarterly* 15 (2): 207–09.

Grabe, W., and Mahon, D. (1982) "Teacher Training in China: Problems and Perspectives." *ON TESOL '82.* Washington, D.C., TESOL, 447–59.

Grove, Cornelius Lee (1984) "U.S. Schooling Through Chinese Eyes." *Phi-Delta-Kappa* 65 (7) (March): 481–82.

Grove, Neal (1986) *Teaching Language and Literature in the People's Republic of China.* Occasional Papers in Intercultural Learning, No. 11, AFS International/Intercultural Programs, Inc.

Habermas, Jürgen (1972) *Knowledge and Human Interests.* London, Heinemann.

Habermas, Jürgen (1981) *The Theory of Communicative Action.* Vol. 1. Boston, Beacon Press.

Hadfield, Charles, and Hadfield, Jill (1986) *Watching the Dragon.* London, Impact Books.

Harvey, P. (1985) "A Lesson to Be Learned: Chinese Approaches to Language Learning." *English Language Teaching Journal* 39 (3) (July): 183–86.

Hawkins, J.N. (1983) *Education and Social Change in the People's Republic of China.* New York, Praeger.

Hayhoe, Ruth (1984a) "Chinese-Western Scholarly Exchange: Implications for the Future of Chinese Education." In Ruth Hayhoe (ed.), *Contemporary Chinese Education.* London, Croom Helm, 205–29.

Hayhoe, Ruth (ed.) (1984b) *Contemporary Chinese Education.* London, Croom Helm.

Hayhoe, Ruth (1984c) "The Evolution of Modern Chinese Educational Institutions." In Ruth Hayhoe (ed.), *Contemporary Chinese Education.* London, Croom Helm, 26–46.

Hayhoe, Ruth (1986a). "Penetration or Mutuality? China's Educational Co-operation with Europe, Japan and North America." *Comparative Education Review* 30 (4) (November): 532–59.

Hayhoe, Ruth (1986b) *Thoughts about Research into Chinese Education in the Late 20th Century.* Paper. Conference on Chinese Education, La Trobe University, Melbourne, November 1986.

Hayhoe, Ruth (ed.) (1987a) "Chinese Educators on Chinese Education." *Canadian and International Education* 16 (1): 7–11.

Hayhoe, Ruth (1987b) "Review of Tani E. Barlow and Donald M. Lowe, *Chinese Reflections.*" *Comparative Education Review* 31 (2) (May): 308–10.

Hayhoe, Ruth (1989a) *China's Universities and the Open Door.* Armonk, N.Y., M.E. Sharpe.

Hayhoe, Ruth (1989b) "A Chinese Puzzle." *Comparative Education Review* 33 (2) (May): 155–75.

Hayhoe, Ruth, and Bastid, M. (eds.) (1987) *China's Education and the Industrialized World: Studies in Cultural Transfer.* Toronto/Armonk, N.Y., OISE Press/M.E. Sharpe.

Heyman, Richard (1979) "Comparative Education from an Ethno-methodological Perspective." *Comparative Education* 15 (October): 241–49.

Hofstede, Geert (1991) *Cultures and Organizations.* London, McGraw-Hill.

Howards, Melvin (1985) *Teaching in China: From Ideograph to Alphabet and Back.* Paper. Northeast Regional Conference of the Comparative and International Education Society, Boston, Mass., November 22.

Hsu, Francis (1953) *Americans and Chinese: Two Ways of Life.* New York, Henry Schuman.

Hsu, Francis (1985) "The Self in Cross-cultural Perspective." In A. Marsella, G. Devos, and F. Hsu (eds.), *Culture and Self, Asian and Western Perspectives.* New York and London, Tavistock.

Hu, H. (1948) "The Chinese Concept of Face." *American Anthropologist* 46: 45–64.

Hu, Wenzhong (1986) "Why Bother about Culture in English Language Teaching?" In Neil Grove (ed.), *Teaching Language and Literature in the People's Republic of China.* Occasional Papers in Intercultural Learning No. 11, AFS International/Intercultural Programs, Inc., 212–23.

Hynes, Maureen (1981) *Letters From China.* Ontario, The Women's Press.

Jacobson, Harold W. (1980) *The Education System and Academic and Technical Exchanges of the PRC.* Research Report. International Communication Agency, Washington, D.C.

Jiaoxue Shiyan Yanjiu Xiaozu (1982) *Jiaoxue Gaige Shiyan Baogao* [Report on Experiments in Teaching and Learning]. Beijing, Jiaoyu Kexue Chubanshe.

Jie, Tao (1980) "Comments on the Article 'English Teaching in China: A Recent Survey'" *TESOL Quarterly* 14 (2) (June): 257–60.

Journal of Asian Pacific Communication 1. (1990) H. Giles and H. Pierson (eds.). Clevedon, Pa., Multilingual Matters Ltd.

Kallgren, Joyce K., and Simon, Denis Fred (eds.) (1987a) *Educational Exchanges: Essays on the Sino-American Experience.* Berkeley, Institute of East Asian Studies, University of California.

Kallgren, Joyce K., and Simon, Denis Fred (1987b) "Examining Exchanges: An Overview." In J. Kallgren and D. Simon (eds.), *Educational Exchanges: Essays on the Sino-American Experience*. Berkeley, Institute of East Asian Studies, University of California.

Kahn-Ackermann, Michael (1982) *Within the Outer Gate*. London, Marco Polo Press.

Keenan, B. (1977) *The Dewey Experiment in China: Educational Reform and Political Power in the Early Republic*. Cambridge, Mass., Harvard University Press.

Kemmis, Stephen, and McTaggart, Robin (eds.) (1982, 1988) *The Action Research Reader*. Deakin Victoria, 3217, Australia, Deakin University Press.

Kong, Lizhen (1986) "Cong Xiandai Kexuede Guandian Kan 'Dui Wai Kai Fang' " [Looking at "Opening to the Outside" from a Modern Scientific Viewpoint]. *Guangming Ribao* (September 19): 3.

Kristeva, Julia (1986) *About Chinese Women*. London, Marion Boyars.

Lancashire, Douglas (1967) "Confucianism in the Twentieth Century." In Nicholas Tanling (ed.), *China and Its Place in the World*. Auckland, Blackwood & Janet Paul Ltd., 26–41.

Lawler III, E. E., Mohrman Jr., Allan M., Mohrman, Susan, A., Ledford Jr., Gerald E., Cummings, Thomas G., and Associates (1985) *Doing Research that Is Useful for Theory and Practice*. San Francisco: Jossey-Bass.

Lehmann, Winifred (ed.) (1975) *Language and Linguistics in the People's Republic of China*. Austin,University of Texas Press.

Leonard, Deborah L. (1986) "A Walking Footnote: Teaching American Literature To Chinese Students." In Neal Grove (ed.), *Teaching Language and Literature in the People's Republic of China*. Occasional Papers in Intercultural Learning, No.11, AFS International/Intercultural Programs, Inc., 3–11.

Levenson, J.R. (1958, 1964) *Confucian China and Its Modern Fate*. Vols.1 & 2. London, Routledge and Kegan Paul.

Lewin, Kurt (1946) "Action Research and Minority Problems." *Journal of Social Issues* 2 (4): 34–36. Reprinted in Stephen Kemmis and Robin McTaggart (eds), *The Action Research Reader*. Deakin University, Vic. 3217, Australia, Deakin University Press.

Li, Jiangang (1987) *Xiandai Jiaoyu He Chuantong Jiaoyu San Ti* [Modern Education and Traditional Education: Three Issues]. *Waiguo Jiaoyu* 3: 1–5.

Li, Yiyuan, and Yang, Guoshu (eds.), (1971) *Zhongguorende Xinge, Kejizong Hexingde Taolun* [Symposium on the Character of the Chinese: An Interdisciplinary Approach]. Taiwan, Institute of Ethnology, Academica Sinica, Monograph Series B, No. 4.

Liang, Shuming (1986) *Fazhan Zhonghuaminde Chuantong Jingshen* [Develop the Ethnic Spirit of the Chinese People]. *Guangming Ribao* (July 21): 2.

Liao, Kuang-Sheng (1984) *Antiforeignism and Modernisation in China 1860–1980.* Hong Kong, The Chinese University Press.

Liu, Fan (1982) "Developmental Psychology in China." *International Journal of Behavioural Development.* 5 (4) (December): 391–411.

Liu, James, and Tu, Wei-Ming (1970) *Traditional China.* Englewood Cliffs, N.J., Prentice Hall.

Liu, Zongren (1984) *Two Years in the Melting Pot.* San Francisco, Books & Periodicals, Inc.

Lu, Weiyuan (1986) *Jiangshoufa Guoshile Ma?* [Is the Lecture Method Out of Date?]. *Zhongguo Jiaoyubao* (August 3): 3.

Mackerras, Colin (1987) "Western Images of China." *Australia-Asia Papers No. 41.* Nathan, Queensland, Centre for the Study of Australian-Asian Relations, Griffith University.

Maley, A. (1982) "XANADU—A Miracle of Rare Device: The Teaching of English in China." *Language Learning and Communication* 2 (1): 97–104.

Maley, A. (1984) "On Chalk and Cheese, Babies and Bathwater and Squared Circles: Can Traditional and Communicative Approaches Be Reconciled?" In P. Larson, E.L. Judd, and D. S. Messerschmitt (eds.), *On TESOL '84.* Washington, D.C., TESOL, 159–69.

Mao Zedong (1937) "On Practice." In *Mao Tse-tung: An Anthology of His Writings.* New York, Mentor, 1962.

Marsella, Anthony J., De Vos, George, and Hsu, Francis L.K. (eds.), (1985) *Culture and Self: Asian and Western Perspectives.* London, Tavistock Publications.

Masemann, Vandra Lea (1982) "Critical Ethnography in the Study of Comparative Education." *Comparative Education Review* (February): 1–15.

Matthews, M. (1987) "Current Educational Practice in the People's Republic of China." *Asian Affairs* 17 (October): 277–87.

Merson, John (1981) *Culture and Science in China.* Sydney, Australian Broadcasting Commission.

Metzger, Thomas A. (1977) *Escape from Predicament: Neo-Confucianism and China's Evolving Political Culture.* New York, Columbia University Press.

Mohan, B., and Lo, W.A. (1985) "Academic Writing and Chinese Students: Transfer and Developmental Factors." *TESOL Quarterly* 19 (3) (September): 515–534.

Moore, Charles (ed.) (1967) *The Chinese Mind: Essentials of Chinese Philosophy and Culture.* Honolulu, East-West Center, University of Hawaii Press.

Munro, Donald J. (1969) *The Concept of Man in Early China.* Stanford, Stanford University Press.

Munro, Donald J. (1977) *The Concept of Man in Contemporary China.* Ann Arbor, University of Michigan Press.

Murphy, Gardener, and Murphy, Lois B. (eds.) (1968) *Asian Psychology.* New York, Basic Books Inc.

Orton, Jane (1984) "From Principles to Practice." In R.F. Price (ed.), *English For China.* Melbourne, Committee for Australia-China Relations, 29–66.

Orton, Jane (1990) *Educating the Reflective Practitioner in China.* Unpublished Ph.D. dissertation. La Trobe University, Bundoora, 3083, Australia.

Osbourne, Andrea G. (1987) *Chinese Students and Methodology Courses.* ERIC Document Reproduction Service No. ED 2877 296.

Patrie, J., and Daum, D.N. (1980) "Comments on the Role Oof Foreign Expertise in Developing Nations: A Summation of the Findings of an Exchange of ESL Specialists with the People's Republic of China." *TESOL Quarterly* 14 (3): 391–94.

Pederson, Paul B. (1976) *Counselling Across Cultures.* Honolulu, University Press of Hawaii.

Price, R.F. (1979) *Education in Modern China.* London: Routledge & Kegan Paul.

Price, R.F. (ed.) (1984b) *English For China.* Melbourne, Committee for Australia-China Relations.

Sampson, Gloria Paulik (1985) "Exporting Language Teaching Methods from Canada to China." *Waiyu Jiaoxue yu Yanjiu* [Foreign Language Learning and Research] 1: 44–51.

Schön, Donald A. (1987) *Educating the Reflective Practitioner.* San Francisco: Jossey-Bass.

Schram, Stuart R. (ed.) (1973) *Authority, Participation and Cultural Change in China.* Cambridge, Cambridge University Press.

Scovel, T. (1983) "The Impact of Foreign Experts, Methodology and Materials on English Language Study in China." *Language Learning and Communication* 2(1): 83–91.

Shanghai Shifan Daxue Jiaoyuxue Bianxiezu (1979) *Jiaoyuxue* [Pedagogy]. Beijing, Renmin Chubanshe.

Shera, Wes (1985) *Resource Bibliography on Cross-cultural Consultation.* Unpublished manuscript. Honolulu, East-West Center, Hawaii.

Shils, E. (1978) "The Order of Learning in the United States from 1865 to 1920: The Ascendancy of the Universities." *Minerva* 16 (2): 159–95.

Smith, K.K., and Corse, S.J. (1985, forthcoming) "The Process of Consultation: Critical Issues." In Mannino, Fortune, Trickett, Kidder and Levin (eds.), *The*

Handbook of Mental Health Consultation. Washington, D.C., National Institute of Mental Health, U.S. Government Printing Office.

Spence, Jonathan (1969) *To Change China: Western Advisers in China 1620–1960.* Boston, Little, Brown.

Stover, Leon E. (1974) *The Cultural Ecology of Chinese Civilization.* New York, Pica Press.

Suttmeier, Richard P. (1980) *Science, Technology and China's Drive for Modernization.* Stanford, Hoover Institution Press.

Tang, Lixing (Undated. c. 1984). *TEFL in China: Methods and Techniques* (in English). Shanghai Foreign Language Education Press.

Tanling, Nicholas (ed.) (1967) *China and Its Place in the World.* Auckland, Blackwood & Janet Paul.

Tao, Xingzhi (1981) *Zhongguo Jiaoyu Gaizuo* [The Transformation of Chinese Education]. Hefei, Anhui Renmin Chubanshe.

Teng, Ssu-Yu, and Fairbank, John K. (1963) *China's Response to the West.* New York, Atheneum.

Ting, Y.R. (1987) "Foreign Language Teaching in China: Problems and Perspectives." *Canadian and International Education* 16 (1): 48–61.

Tseng, Wen-shing, and Wu, David Y. H. (1985) *Chinese Culture and Mental Health.* Orlando, Fl., Academic Press, Inc.

UNESCO (1981) "Educational Research and Training in Asia and the Pacific." *Report of a Regional Seminar, October 22–November 5, 1981.* Bangkok, UNESCO, National Institute for Educational Research, Tokyo.

Valdes, Joyce M. (ed.) (1986) *Culture Bound*: *Bridging the Cultural Gap in Language Teaching.* Cambridge, Cambridge University Press.

Waley, Arthur (1958) *The Opium War Through Chinese Eyes.* London, George, Allen & Unwin.

Wang, Gungwu (1977) *China and The World Since 1949.* London, Macmillan.

Wang, Y.C. (1966) *Chinese Intellectuals and the West, 1872–1949.* Chapel Hill, University of North Carolina Press.

Weber, Max (1964) *The Religion of China.* New York, The Free Press.

Weiler, Hans (1984) "The Political Dilemma of Foreign Study." *Comparative Education Review* 28 (May): 168–79.

Welch, A.R. (1993) "Class, Culture and the State in Comparative Education: Problems, Perspectives and Prospects." *Comparative Education* 29 (1): 7–29.

Williams, Angela, Giles, Howard, and Pierson, Herbert (1990) "Asian Pacific Languages and Communication: Foundations, Issues and Directions." H. Giles and H. Pierson (eds.), *Journal of Asian Pacific Communication* 1: 1–25. Clevedon, Pa., Multilingual Matters Ltd.

Wilson, Richard (1970) *Learning to be Chinese: The Political Socialization of Children in Taiwan.* Cambridge, Mass., M.I.T. Press.

Wilson, R., Greenblatt, S.L., and Wilson, A.A. (eds.), (1981). *Moral Behaviour in Chinese Society.* New York, Praeger.

Wu, K.C. (1982) *The Chinese Heritage.* New York, Crown.

Wu, Zhaoyi (1986) "Wenhua Yanjiude Shiye" [The Field of Cultural Research]. *Guangming Ribao* (August 20): 3.

Xu, George O. (1989) *Instruction of EFL Composition in China.* ERIC Document Reproduction Service No. ED 304 019.

Xu, Guozhang (1987) "Tantan Xuexi Yingyude Mudi he Cezhongdia" [A Talk on the Purpose and Major Concerns of the Study of English]. Talk. National Conference for Excellent Young Teachers of Foreign Languages, May, 1987. Edited and published in *Zhongxiaoxue Waiyu Jiaoxue* 11 (5): 6–7.

Yao, Shuping (1985) "Butong Wenhua Jiazhi Guannian Dui Kexue Fazhande Yingxiang" (The Influence on Scientific Development of Different Cultural Values). *Guangming Ribao* (July 17): 3. Reprinted from *Ziran Bianzhengfa Tongxun* (Natural Dialectics Newsletter) 1.

Ye, Xiaoqing (1985) "Dongxi Wenhua Bijiao Yanjiu Sixiang" [Some Thoughts on the Comparison of East and Western Cultures]. *Dushu:* 88–89.

Zhang, Zhen-bang (1983) "TEFL at the Shanghai Foreign Language Institute." *Language Learning and Communication* 1 (3) (Fall-Winter): 289–93.

Zhang, Zhifang (1986) "*Ting Waijie Jiaoshi Jiangke de Yidian Qishi*" [Some Revelations Watching Foreign Teachers Taking a Class]. *Zhongguo Jiaoyubao* (China Education News) (August 30): 3.

Zhao, Hongzhou, and Zhuang, Guohua (1985) "Dangxin na! La Pulasi Juedinghua" [Beware! La Place's Determinism]. *Guangming Ribao* (July 8): 3.

Zhuang, Jiaying (1984) *English Teaching in China's Colleges.* Paper. Annual Meeting of the California Association of Teachers of English to Speakers of Other Languages, San Jose, Calif. April 13–15.

CHAPTER 7

"Post Marxist" Discourse and the Rethinking of Third World Education Reform

ANNE HICKLING-HUDSON

In the contemporary rethinking of educational philosophies, educators who have moved into "postmodern" and "poststructuralist" paradigms are increasingly challenging paradigms informed by Marxist-inspired "critical theory." This coincides with the collapse of the Soviet Union in the 1990s, which has accelerated the rethinking of socialist views of the world. This chapter examines the practical implications of this rethinking for issues of quality and equality in education. It considers some of the strengths and weaknesses of socially critical theory and practice in education, explores some of the emerging systems of postmodern/postcolonial thought, and reflects how new or syncretic theoretical perspectives might affect education practices. For this chapter, I have chosen two examples of educational problems within a Caribbean context as practical referents for discussing various perspectives from which to analyse educational reform.

The first example is that of the present secondary school reform process taking place in Jamaica. The project aims to reform secondary education in such a way as to be a step towards equalizing the severely stratified school system. The second example considers the work undertaken to lay the basis for educational transformation during the Grenada Revolution, and the postrevolutionary approaches taken to education. My knowledge of these processes is based in the first case on selected documents as well as involvement in one of the planning exercises midway through the project. In the second case it is based on two years' involvement (1981 to 1983) in teacher education change and other educational reforms during the revolution, and on several visits after the collapse of the revolution to maintain a knowledge of developments in the educational system. Reflecting on my experience has left me with questions stemming from the world view of socially critical theory, on the process and role of educational reform.

The socially critical discourse about education is associated in policy analysis with the work of educators such as Martin Carnoy and Henry Levin, and in pedagogy with the work of educators such as Paulo Freire and his disciples Ira Shor and Henry Giroux. As Svi Shapiro (1991) suggests, it is perhaps the only discourse which makes a serious and sustained attempt to relate education to problematic issues in contemporary society and philosophy. This theoretical outlook suggests to me that projects to "equalize schools" are largely rhetoric, in the absence of any commitment or planning to equalize society. These projects may improve the quality of education in some schools compared to the previous situation, but they do not equalize educational quality for the children of privileged and of disadvantaged families. If school reform occurs in the absence of a broader movement struggling for egalitarian social change, then these attempts will be rendered at best partial and perpetually limited, at worst marginal and meaningless by powerful constraining factors evident in both the Jamaican and Grenadian attempts at educational reform.

JAMAICA: THE "REFORM OF SECONDARY EDUCATION" PROJECT

In Jamaica, the reform of secondary education (ROSE) has been, since 1988, a major focus of education reform organised by the Ministry of Education in collaboration with international overseas loan agencies such as the World Bank. The project is well under way in implementing its aims of restructuring the secondary education system. The major achievement of ROSE is to begin to upgrade the standards of education for the most disdavantaged group of students in society. These are the thirteen to sixteen year olds who, not having "passed" the Common Entrance (11+) examination into secondary high schools, end up in the senior forms of All-Age elementary schools, those shockingly neglected schools of the poor which Hyacinth Evans (1988) describes with sympathy and sensitivity. ROSE has put into many of these schools a new curriculum that upgrades the education of thirteen to sixteen year olds to a junior secondary level (grades seven, eight, and nine), comparable to the curriculum in forms one, two and three of the traditional elite high schools.

The improved curriculum is being specially prepared by teams of curriculum experts from the Ministry of Education, Teachers' Colleges, and the University of the West Indies, in collaboration with selected schoolteachers. Very different from the old remedial/vocational curriculum in the All-Age schools, it provides students with five periods weekly of language arts, mathematics, science, social studies, and the performing arts, six periods of a new subject called resource and technology, which can include components such as product design, resource management, home and family management, and agriculture and the environment, and two periods each of a foreign language, religious education, and physical education. Curriculum redesign was placed at the centre of the reform effort because, as Johnson (1993) points out, clear curriculum goals define the kind of graduates that the school system needs to produce and the kind of educational experiences children must share if they are to develop valued qualities, as well as giving parents and other interest groups a basis for relating actively to the schools, assessors a basis for test design, textbook developers guidelines for producing acceptable materials, and administrators a basis for effective administration. The redesigned curriculum is of such high quality that much of it has been voluntarily adopted for grades seven to nine in other secondary schools, including the comprehensive high schools (as the former 'New Secondary' schools have now been renamed) and many of the elite traditional high schools. It is hoped that it will become the basis of a national curriculum, which all secondary schools will follow. Teachers in the All-Age schools were offered short upgrading workshops to help them to implement the new curriculum.

The proposed new curriculum is indeed of a high quality, but some knotty contextual questions have not been addressed at a policy level in the process of reform. These questions, recognised by many concerned educators, relate to an endemic inequality in the resourcing of the education system. When the new curriculum is in place in all schools (the target date is about 2014), the All-Age senior forms will have been reorganised as junior high grades. But students in them will still be poorer students in poorer schools. They will still face the material hardships of coming from extremely poor families unsubsidised by welfare payments, and therefore will be less able to access a full range of opportunities in schools. These inequalities show in the differential qualifications of teachers (those in the poorer schools are almost invariably not university or college graduates), and in the differential chances of proceeding to grades ten to thirteen (a minority of students from the junior high grades, who do well in the grade nine examinations, will be allowed to transfer to other secondary schools to prepare for the Carribean Examination Council exams at grade eleven). It is more than likely, therefore, that in spite of the efforts of ROSE, the majority of Jamaica's school students do not have a hope of accessing equal educational opportunity, or of achieving a similar spread of academic performance levels, as their peers in elite schools.

Like most Caribbean countries, Jamaica suffers from an insufficiency of funds on the scale needed to equalize per capita funding and resourcing throughout the school system. In the Strengthening of Secondary Schools project, the funds available as loans from international agencies only suffice for the pilot stages of the project. Given limited resources, elected governments in Jamaica, as elsewhere in the Caribbean, have always perceived themselves politically unable to carry out a comprehensive and serious redistribution of educational benefits, for fear of backlash from the influential vested interests of the educated classes. Education bureaucrats operating in this framework are understandably reluctant or unable to recommend any meaningful challenge to the entrenched and powerful instruments which select out an elite minority for the top levels of high quality secondary education. Among the most important of these instruments are elite and expensive private primary schools, an insufficiency of places in 'top' elite high schools, and selective exams limiting entry into these schools to about one quarter of the cohort. Not surprisingly, it is mainly the children with the best primary education who comprise the quarter that perform best in these selective exams. The recent abolition of the Common Entrance Exam will not change this. Two outcomes have occurred. Firstly, broader and better exams (in the National Assessment Program, or NAP) have replaced the narrow 'intelligence tests' of the old Common Entrance Exam. Secondly, all children in grade six are now required to sit the NAP exams. But the elite high schools will still be able to select those with the highest marks—who are likely to continue to come from the private primary schools. Thus, the pattern of old could continue: 25 percent of the cohort may go to the 'top' high schools, another 25 percent to the vocationally-oriented comprehensive high schools, and 50 percent restricted to the junior high grades of the former elementary schools.

Reforming the curriculum while allowing the continuation of a framework of stratified schooling, as is being done in the Jamaican project, would not be acceptable in a politically revolutionary context. Equalizing access to education in such a way as to bring about an equal spread of outcomes for those from elite and those from poorer families is a revolutionary concept which would undoubtedly need radically innovative strategies if it were to be realized. What would be necessary is a rethinking of the entire school curriculum, examination system and resource allocation to schooling, bringing about a reorganisation of the education structure in a way that better meets the society's needs for more effective productive and cultural strategies than those marred by the colonial heritage of stratified maldevelopment. For example, education change might have to include abolishing any kind of selective exam that determines access to school type, and some of the immensely complex problems associated with this are discussed in a government document (Ministry of Education, Jamaica 1990, 37–39). The government might then have to consider making all schools comprehensive, putting in place a national curriculum that insists on a combination of meaningful practical work and study, providing equal qualifications and salaries to all teachers, guaranteeing fair opportunities to all students to take exams of high market value, requiring means-tested contributions from families to education, establishing affirmative action for the most disadvantaged students, zoning schools, and/or bussing groups of children so that all schools have a mixture of wealthy, middle class, and poorer students.

Any of this would so challenge established conservative norms and privileges in a resource-poor environment that little of it is likely to be done. It would need to be supported by a broad movement working for egalitarian change. For reasons to be discussed later in this paper, this movement would have to address questions of the injustices in the international economy which constrain the development of Jamaica and other Third World countries and may also have to take an interventionist approach to the question of developing the national economy— an approach different from the laissez faire privatisation and free-market doctrine that is now prevalent. When the new, improved secondary curriculum is established in an education system that continues to be stratified (even if disadvantaged schools are somewhat upgraded) and within an economy that continues to be crippled by neocolonial dependency, past experience suggests that it is highly likely that the relative failure of students from poorer schools will be blamed on them, with the familiar "blame the victim" charge that even when their schools were improved, they did not try hard enough.

GRENADIAN EDUCATION:
THE REVOLUTION AND AFTER

The second example of a Third World educational process that needs careful thought is that of educational change during the Grenada Revolution and its legacies in the society today. Grenada ended the decade of the 1970s with a ramshackle education system fashioned by over three hundred years of French and British colonialism and some five years of a kind of political "independence" which had not moved beyond neocolonialism. As in Jamaica, the Grenadian education system was characterised by rigid stratification of school type—elite academic high school, vocational government secondary, and All Age—but in the aspects of curriculum reform, teacher education, supervision, and tertiary education, Grenada's system was even less developed than Jamaica's. The Grenada Revolution, from 1979 to 1983, set out to tackle the enormous problems left by colonialism and to construct a society which would take a path of "socialist orientation" (see, for example, Jules 1992, Meeks 1993).

A brief overview of the educational change that took place during this short period in Grenada would have to take account of three angles: direction, structures, and content. In direction the revolution pursued goals of modernising the system, including curriculum, pedagogy, and administration, instituting changes and policies which would eventually lead to equalizing access and equalizing the spread of outcomes for different classes and strata in the society, and, finally, laying foundations for moving towards what was seen as revolutionary or "anti-imperialist" consciousness.

The People's Revolutionary Government established new structures and developed existing ones at each level of the system. In the formal sector of education, an in-service teacher education programme was established to train the island's untrained primary teachers (amounting to 67 percent of the total), and policies were in place to start the in-service education of the 72 percent of unqualified secondary teachers. Access to secondary education was widened in that high school fees were abolished, and 2,000 of the 9,000 new secondary school places needed were provided, while the rest were planned for in systematic phases. Subsidies for food, books, and uniforms were provided for the neediest schoolchildren, which particularly benefited children at the infant and primary levels. As far as content was concerned, the government encouraged Grenadian high schools to introduce the programme required by the Caribbean Examinations Council (CXC), so that Caribbean school-leaving examinations would replace British ones. New texts exploring issues of radical social change were produced in early childhood and adult education (see Jules 1991, 1992). The production of more such texts and courses was planned, and there was a definite commitment to phase out the All Age schools and unify/comprehensivise the secondary school system (Hickling-Hudson 1989).

The strongest emphasis of the revolutionary government was on providing for the training and education of adults who were in or who would enter the labour force. Professional education was put in place on a scale never seen before. Besides the approximately three hundred teachers studying in the local in-service teacher education programme, more than three hundred young Grenadians were given scholarships to go overseas to study medicine, engineering, agriculture, languages, social work, economics, and other disciplines essential to the country's development, most of these new university places being negotiated with the help of Cuba and other socialist countries. At the same time, the island's existing link with the regional University of the West Indies was strengthened by the phased payment of the debt arrears that had been accumulated by the previous government, and a plan was envisaged to seek the assistance of Canadian universities to merge all of the island's tertiary education institutions into a national university. Workers in nonprofessional occupations in agriculture, fisheries, and tourism had their skills upgraded through short in-service courses in expanded vocational institutions. In the nonformal sector of education, an adult literacy programme was established with aims to provide opportunities for society's least advantaged people to move through various stages from literacy to school to postschool or tertiary education, and there was also informal education through the mass organisations of women and youths (Hickling-Hudson 1989, Jules 1992).

Nearly all these changes, except for the aims to move towards revolutionary consciousness and content, were of the kind of which even conservative Caribbean societies might have approved in the sense that they tackled key areas of backwardness in education, replanning and modernising the system. There are two concerns. One: the Revolution collapsed internally, having imploded into fratricidal conflict and killings, which provided the excuse for the United States government to invade Grenada in October 1983, with the cooperation of some neighbouring Caribbean governments which had from the start been uneasy at the revolution and which now expressed their horror at the violent events.

Grenada reverted to its former system of government, this time with the assistance and tutelage of the U.S. government. The new Grenadian governments tried to reverse or erase memories of the programmes of the revolution, even while continuing with some of them. But all this has not erased the burning question still in Caribbean minds: what was there about the process of revolution which could lead at one and the same time to such morally and socially necessary changes in systems as those which occurred in education, health, housing, and production, yet also to the kind of horrific conflict that forgot or ignored the revolution's idealistic goals?

The second concern is how to interpret the postrevolutionary educational process in contemporary Grenadian society (see Ferguson 1990, McAfee 1991, 95–109). Most of the revolution's experimental structures in nonformal education which benefited the least advantaged adults have been abandoned. Disbandment immediately occurred of the complex structure of the Centre for Popular Education, which organised adult literacy, postliteracy, and catch-up programmes. Substitute adult education programmes are now coordinated by the Grenada Teachers' College, but basic vocational in-service education for workers as well as adult literacy education have been greatly reduced. There has also been a dramatic reduction in opportunities for adults to undertake professional diplomas and degrees, mainly because of the cutting of ties with Cuba, which had provided hundreds of scholarships. Without Cuban educational assistance, only about twenty Grenadians a year could access university scholarships, out of some 160 who apply with adequate matriculation. The University of the West Indies has expanded its provision of local part-time courses through which people can start a degree, but many of these part-time students will be unable to afford to finish their degree as this entails paying fees and living expenses in one of the three "campus" territories of UWI: Barbados, Jamaica, or Trinidad.

Since 1986, there has been a realization of the vision of the revolution to amalgamate selected tertiary institutions into one national college, but this has not necessarily guaranteed sufficient professional education even at certificate or diploma levels for the needs of the island's economy. For example, the provision of teacher training within the new national college has once more been scaled down to serve about forty trainees a year, as it did before the revolution. A high teacher turnover and insufficient provision of initial teacher education means that the problem of a high proportion of unqualified teachers in the schools is as bad as before. This may be one of the reasons why school performance in general continues to be weak, both in elite and in disadvantaged schools. Grenada and Jamaica both demonstrate this weakness. For example, in the relative ranking of national performance of the elite minority of 16 to 18 year olds taking the regional school-leaving exams of the Caribbean Examinations Council, 1984 to 1990, Grenada ranks thirteenth and Jamaica fourteenth out of fifteen Caribbean countries (OECS Report 1991, 23). In the senior forms of All-Age schools to which the Grenadian poor are consigned, between 85 percent and 88 percent of school-leaving candidates regularly fail the annual school-leaving examinations (Brizan 1991, 63).

On balance, the present education system in Grenada has gone back to being very similar to the education systems of most other Caribbean territories in structure and goals. Within an educational framework constrained by poverty and characterised by massive failure of the majority of its students, the rhetoric of all well-meaning educators articulates the desire for reform, modernisation, and more egalitarianism. But there is no sign of the radical educational planning and dialogue, and of the changes in the socioeconomic base, that would be necessary to achieve this. That was an option when socialist countries were willing to give the kind of support in scholarships, infrastructure, and trade development that wealthy capitalist ones offer the Caribbean only in a very restricted way. Today, it may be the case that only a U.S.-approved path, with all its proven deficiencies (not to imply that there were not also deficiencies in the other path), is available.

So we are left with the question: is the kind of socioeconomic change that benefits disadvantaged majorities only on the agenda of radical governments such as the Grenadian revolutionary government? Today, when the possibility of that kind of revolution has been abruptly halted, is it possible to fashion approaches to change which make a real socio-educational difference, or is educational egalitarianism only consistent with a certain radical context? The aim for the socially critical scholar is to understand how educational reform happens and what its potential and actual effects are at particular moments of history, so that our knowledge of practical strategies of change within social contexts becomes sharply honed and more effective for action.

Socially critical theory provides some guiding ideas as to what can be done to achieve genuinely egalitarian reforms. Many of these ideas were put into practice in the educational reforms and planning process of the Grenada Revolution. What I want to consider is whether the ideas that stem from this theoretical base would be added to in any way *that is meaningful for action* by postmodern and postcolonial theories, which see themselves as being "post-Marxist" in the sense of claiming or inferring that they go beyond the insights that neo-Marxist educational theory was able to achieve.

POSTMODERN/POSTSTRUCTURAL THEORY

A useful way of understanding postmodern theory is to consider how its perspectives differ from "modernist" ones and how postmodern perspectives would critique the kind of neo-Marxist theory that underpins the analyses of the two educational problems described above.

Postmodernism has emerged as a theory to explain the complexities of society in the new and fast-developing context of postindustrialism and its global effects on all social and economic systems. Aronowitz and Giroux (1990) summarise these new contexts as including the changes in production methods caused by technological developments, the spread of global communication, the displacement of blue-collar labour together with the rising demand for technologically skilled workers in post-Fordist enterprise, the decentering of economic and political power as the formerly firmly Western multinational corporations disperse production through other countries in search of cheaper labour, the increase in assertive cultural pluralism in the First World, and the challenges to old hierarchies of power such as patriarchy and electoral politics. "Modernist" theories, that is, those which stemmed from the eighteenth-century Enlightenment with its faith in the individual or collective pursuit and achievement of reason and freedom, are seen to be no longer effective in explaining society or shaping goals in today's world. Western educators of both liberal and radical politics as widely separated as John Dewey and Martin Carnoy have, say Aronowitz and Giroux, assumed the basic world view and assumptions of modernism in its ideal of remaking the world. To challenge it, and them, as postmodern theory does, is to call into question "the very basis of our history, our cultural criticism and our manifestations of public life."

Postmodern theory critiques modernism on grounds of its univocal perspective (the voice of Western, male intellectualism) and its totalizing metanarratives ("universal" stories such as those told by liberalism and Marxism, both rooted in a Eurocentrism which pretentiously claims to speak for all of "mankind"). Modernist philosophy is limited by a putative scientific rationality grounded in a Western concept of progress, a positivist empirical approach to research which inferiorizes other ways of knowing, and a teleological view of the world. Postmodernism offers, instead, ways of seeing which are polyvocal, local, and contextualized, encouraging the voice of individuals and diverse groups and foregrounding experience rather than theory. It uses techniques of poststructuralism to deconstruct all texts, rejecting any canonising of Eurocentric scholarship and any educational requirement that "great canons" of such scholarship necessarily be studied.

Postmodern educational theorists such as Giroux, Aronowitz, and McLaren see great strength in these insights that encourage diversity of voice and techniques of deconstructionism, yet warn against the limitations of "right-wing postmodernism," which renounces engagement with political activity. Their choice of critical, postmodern pedagogy is embedded in a "postmodernism of resistance" which would aim at shifting power from the privileged and powerful "to those groups struggling to gain a measure of control over their lives" (Aronowitz and Giroux 1990, 115). This "emancipatory postmodernism" sounds like Marxism, but difference is claimed by the argument that postmodern resistance is not constrained by modernist images of progress and history. It recognises the disintegration of modernist culture in a postindustrial world in which electronic communication is radically altering traditional notions of time, community, and history, and which is "at once more global and more differentiated" (Aronowitz and Giroux 1990, 115).

Since the nihilistic, pessimistic postmodernism of the right (see Shapiro 1991 for a clear summary of this philosophy) is useless and irrelevant for people living in the Third World of oppressed and exploited communities, how would an emancipatory (or left-wing) postmodernism of resistance analyse a socially critical or neo-Marxist interpretation, such as the one above, of the problems of Third World educational reform? It would first have to apply deconstructionist techniques which would necessitate identifying the "privileged themes" as well as the spaces in that account. The "privileged themes," those explored in detail in a socially critical analysis, would include the role of capitalism in the underdevelopment of the Third World, the oppression of the majority of populations by means of many institutions including the school and the educational system, the way social class conflict is played out, the resistance and the creative solutions of the oppressed, and the assumption of binary distinctions including between "developed" and "underdeveloped." The spaces, that is, themes which are silenced or not adequately explored include those of gender, race, and culture, personal relationships and impulses, and ethics based on the rights of the individual (see Mills 1991).

According to poststructuralist theory, the privileged themes of this account would constitute different aspects of a neo-Marxist "metanarrative." The focus of the narrative is on the class struggle. The teleological assumption is that the outcome is predictable: the oppressed classes will eventually be victorious and will construct a better society. Applying a poststructuralist viewpoint to the deconstruction and rethinking of this metanarrative could well be an enriching exercise. Using some of the techniques set out by Cherryholmes (1988, 151–53), the rethinking process would include the goal of identifying the spaces and silences in the narrative and filling them with a variety of voices and experiences, and this might either rejuvenate commitment to existing goals, or lead to something different. The vision of the future, the strategies on the road ahead, will emerge from this dynamic interplay.

An emancipatory postmodern reading of the situations described above in Jamaica and Grenada could, then, be quite useful in arriving at an analysis which might be both more richly textured and inclusive and more open-ended than one based on critical theory. However, I feel that in real situations of strategic policymaking and planning it would be in danger of losing sight of the commitment to work towards changing the situation of the oppressed, which is the major strength of critical theory. The tradition from which this commitment is drawn is neo-Marxist, and in the Third World, this means anti-imperialist. While postmodernism might usefully remind those in the socially critical tradition of the necessity of being open-ended and inclusive so as to avoid the dangers of replacing the existing hegemony with a new orthodoxy, we have to turn to insights drawn from neo-Marxism, postcolonialism, and feminism to consider substantive goals which might guide policy and realistic strategies for implementation.

POSTCOLONIALISM

Postmodernism's rejection of the modernist claim to exclusivity of correct insight, its deconstruction and subversion of accepted texts, and its counterposing of a plurality of voices to replace "totalizing metanarratives" is hardly new. Radical Third World scholars and movements have long been doing this in their challenging of global capitalism, Eurocentrism, and racism, both during and after the colonial period. Much scholarship and creative writing and many practical careers in the Third World have been based on such challenges. In the centres of capital, too, multiculturalism, the more radical antiracism, feminism, and other challenges have faced and resisted the hegemonic and totalizing impositions of conservative and liberal capitalism. Some of these challenges may have fallen within other metanarratives or totalizing visions (such as Marxism) rooted in Eurocentric modernism, but some challenges, particularly in Third World scholarship, operated to contest and subvert modernist tradition in a way that might very well today be called *poststructuralist*.

Although there are several usages of the term *postcolonialism*, this chapter will discuss the usage adopted by Ashcroft, Griffiths, and Tiffin (1989). The referent in this usage is thematic, the term *postcolonial* being used "to cover all the culture affected by the imperial process from the moment of colonization to the present day. This is because there is a continuity of preoccupations throughout the historical process initiated by European imperial aggression." The authors argue that this usage is particularly appropriate in referring to the literature of the colonial empires, because they emerged "out of the experience of colonization and asserted themselves by foregrounding the tension with the imperial power, and by emphasizing their differences from the assumptions of the imperial centre" (Ashcroft, Griffiths, and Tiffin 1989, 1–2).

At the early stage of development, literatures in so-called peripheral countries, that is, the colonies, were characterized by a mimicry of the "centre" or the metropolitan country, a mimicry proceeding from "a desire not only to be accepted but to be adopted and absorbed. It caused those at the periphery to immerse themselves in the imported culture, denying their origins in an attempt to become 'more English than the English'" (Ashcroft, Griffiths, and Tiffin 1989, 4). This type of postcolonialism, then (though I would myself prefer to describe it as neocolonialism) would be characterized, as far as individual identity is concerned, by the pain of an obsessive denial of self and attempt to identify with forces that constituted themselves as the "centre" of all that is valuable. The later stage of self-assertion comes when the "privileging norm" of canonical English literature and language is challenged and displaced with a questioning and rejection of the assumptions underlying claims to a special status, a refusal to accept marginality, an exploration of the crisis of postcolonial identity focusing on place and displacement, a subversion of the conventions and philosophy of the centre, and a deliberate incorporation into literature of regionally unique language codes referred to as "englishes" to distinguish them from the standard code of "English," the language of the erstwhile colonial centre.

As a result of these challenges, the postcolonial world, although shaped by oppressive power, has become "the site of the most exciting and innovative literatures of the modern period" (Ashcroft, Griffiths, and Tiffin 1989, 8). The alienating process which relegated that world to the "margin" became an unprecedented source of creative energy when the challengers pushed into a position from which they claimed that all experience was "uncentred, pluralistic and multifarious" (12). This postcolonial impetus towards decentering and pluralism came much earlier than the same impetus in the movement of poststructuralism in European thought—in fact, "these notions are implicit in post-colonial texts from the imperial period to the present day" (12), and are skillfully explored in novels, poetry, and scholarly texts produced in the last thirty years by writers such as Wilson Harris, E. Kamau Brathwaite, Jacques Alexis, Salman Rushdie (see Ashcroft, Griffiths, and Tiffin 1989, 33–37, 147–154). Another kind of challenge to Eurocentric arrogance came from Third World communities such as Jamaica's Rastafarians, who, starting from the 1930s, deconstructed the negatively distorted Eurocentric view of black culture and established their unique religion, culture, and mode of production, which draws inspiration from African and Creole ideas and experiences. Yet another challenge comes out of the postcolonial feminist perspective. This includes writers such as Jean Rhys, Margaret Atwood, and Paule Marshall, who draw an analogy between the relationships of men and women and those of the imperial power and the colony (Ashcroft, Griffiths, and Tiffin 1989, 31), and others who argue that no widespread changes in gender roles and statuses will take place unless there are also changes in the system of global capitalism which exploits and oppresses both men and women (see Johnson-Odim 1991, Russo 1991).

Thus, the deconstructive postcolonialist tradition of trends such as these in Third World scholarship, art, and culture infused at least some of the anti-imperialist challenges of the 1960s and 1970s with proudly held cultural difference. Even if some Third World movements of resistance to Euro-American imperialism had not fully developed their positions of deciding what to incorporate, what to reject, and what to re-create, the postcolonial tradition in its self-assertive stage has given rise to educators who have for decades been practising the kind of pedagogy now advocated by U.S scholars such as Peter McLaren (1991). He states that a critical postmodern or postcolonial pedagogy (he uses these as complementary and interchangeable terms) is dedicated to the subversion of the " 'official knowledges' of colonialism—pseudo-scientific, typological, legal-administrative, eugenicist" and explains that a critical postmodernist or postcolonial resister needs to be able both to "create . . . double readings of social texts and effect changes in the material and structural conditions which make such double readings necessary" (McLaren 1991, 138).

Let us take the meaning of "social text" to refer not only to literary and artistic works but also to social practices such as the educational reform processes which I presented at the beginning of this paper. Such "double readings" as McLaren calls for can be effected by a socially critical analysis which scrutinises the rhetoric and exposes the assumptions and functions of those educational reform policies, then moves to discussing a radical alternative which aims at challenging power structures from the perspective of the disadvantaged. That analysis is grounded in an anti-imperialist (and postcolonial, if you like) perspective which is not simply abstract textual analysis, but implies a commitment to action that aims, as McLaren desires, to "effect changes in the material and structural conditions which make such double readings necessary." What would McLaren's "postmodern or postcolonial resister" add to this? Perhaps a sensitivity about the limitations of universalistic answers and a willingness to engage with a wider variety of voices in working out solutions. Applied to education, all this would undoubtedly add to the quality of the teaching and learning process. But in order to contribute to practical changes in the context of the society, it would have to be based on some understanding of global and local economic structure, which so far has been provided by analyses influenced by Marxism in recognising the entrenched nature of global inequalities based on capitalism.

In thinking about postmodernism/postcolonialism, I do not wish to succumb to what Wendy Kholi (1992, 41) points out is an "either/or" position based on "dualistic thinking that makes it difficult to see and hear freshly." However, I fear, as Kholi does, that the present agonising over "post-" this and "post-" that may represent a kind of paralysis that is gripping the "academy" in the First World, and I empathise with the lament of African-American professor Hazel Carby that "theories of difference and diversity in practice leave us fragmented and divided but equal in our inability to conceive of radical social change" (see Kholi 1991, 44). From a Third World perspective, this inability seems to characterise some of the writing of "emancipatory" postmodernists such as Giroux, Aronowitz, and McLaren. Although the excellent collections of papers that they have edited (such as the ones in *Education and Society* 9. 1 and 2) and some of their arguments suggest that they are sympathetic to a radical postcolonial stance, much of the educational discourse in their writings cited in this paper displays a propensity towards verbal convolution which avoids engaging with specific material and social problems such as the ones posed at the beginning of this chapter. Postmodern/ postcolonial philosophy as they express it seems of little *practical* use for thinking about problems of Third World countries enmeshed in an international system which severely constrains their development. Indeed, their mode of expression seems related to that nihilistic postmodernism which stems from "the insularity or political impotence of intellectuals that leads us to consign all notions of reality to what for intellectuals is the more manageable terrain of discourse, signs and texts" (Shapiro 1991, 119). To prevent itself from being rendered meaningless by this nihilism, emancipatory postmodernism as put forward by these educational theorists appropriates neo-Marxist and Third World interpretations and approaches which help to guide action in the educational arena, but their conception of the arena appears limited, focusing on questions of cultural identity far more than on those issues of material change which Third World educators do not have the luxury of avoiding.

"THE DISTANCE FROM THE CLASSROOM TO THE STREETS"

Kholi (1991) says: "As important as it is to 'de-center' and to interrogate our given assumptions about politics and social change, I think it urgently important that we move beyond the paralysis . . . and move towards building alliances to end the exploitation that Sweet Honey (an African-American singing group) so poignantly and accurately conveys." This song *Are my Hands Clean?* by Sweet Honey, quoted by Kholi (44), should remind educators of the daily realities of global capitalism in which we must position the social text of educational reform.

ARE MY HANDS CLEAN?

> I wear garments touched by hands from all over the world, 35 percent
> cotton, 65 percent polyester, the journey begins in Central
> America
> In the cotton fields of El Salvador
> In a province soaked in blood, pesticide-sprayed workers toil in a
> broiling sun
> Pulling cotton for two dollars a day.
> Then we move on up to another rung—Cargill
> A top-forty trading conglomerate, takes the cotton thru the Panama
> Canal

Up the Eastern seaboard, coming to the U.S. of A. for the first
    time.
In South Carolina
At the Burlington mills
Joins a shipment of polyester filament courtesy of the New Jersey
    petro-chemical mills of
Dupont.
Dupont strands of filament begin in the South American country of
    Venezuela
Where oil riggers bring up oil from the earth for six dollars a day.
Then Exxon, largest oil company in the world
Upgrades the product in the country of Trinidad and Tobago
Then back into the Caribbean and Atlantic Seas
To the factories of Dupont
On the way to the Burlington mills
In South Carolina
To meet the cotton from the blood-soaked fields of El Salvador.
In South Carolina Burlington factories hum with the business of
    weaving oil and cotton into miles of fabric for
Sears
Who takes this bounty back into the Caribbean Sea
Headed for Haiti this time
May she one day soon be free
Far from the Port-au-Prince palace
Third-world women toil doing piecework to Sears' specifications
For three dollars a day my sisters make my blouse
It leaves the Third World for the last time
Coming back into the sea to be sealed in plastic for me
This Third-World sister
And I go to the Sears department store where I buy my blouse
On sale for 20 percent discount
Are my hands clean?

(Bernice Reagan, 1985)

Third World peoples, daily in the vortex of these injustices, need to utilise a theoretical base which is substantive rather than abstract in interpreting the material world and its "social texts." I want to turn now to an interpretation which recognises and names the processes and effects of global capitalism in this era with a clarity that illuminates where we are, thus helping to bridge what Henry Louis Gates calls "the distance from the classroom to the streets" (see Shapiro 1991, 119).

A. Sivanandan (1989) sets the stage for his article "New Circuits of Imperialism" by asserting that "imperialism is still the highest stage of capitalism—only, the circuits of imperialism have changed with the changes wrought in the production process" (1989, 1). The information-technology revolution has changed employment patterns, pointed to the end of the nation state, forced the "socialist" centres into modernising their economies, and, most fundamental of all, initiated a process whereby microelectronics is replacing intellectual labour just as the old machines replaced manual labour. Sivanandan argues that these momentous changes have given far more strength and mobility to capital, owned by Euro-American (and Japanese) multinational corporations, to intensify advantages for the few at the expense of the many. He discusses the situations of various countries to illustrate how the path of global capitalism "ravages, consumes and destroys physical and social environments in order to survive" (1989, 1). In the global assembly lines of production scattered all over the world, domestic capital in the poorer countries is (still) constrained by and servile to metropolitan capital; in the sphere of this capital he sees "no autonomous growth, no development that speaks to the needs of the people," and the situation for the "captive labour pools of the Third World" is even more precarious than in the past because "capital can take up its factory and walk any time labour gives it trouble or proves costly" (1989, 1).

The global hierarchies of production maintain the power hierarchy of world capitalism, with DCs (developed countries) controlling the new high tech industries, devolving the older heavy industries as well as many onerous aspects of high tech production to the NICs (newly industrialising countries) and relegating light industries to the UDCs (underdeveloped countries in the sense of Walter Rodney's use of the term, which highlights the responsibility of Europe and the United States for deliberately underdeveloping them). Sivanandan does not see this scenario as providing hope for the lessening of the exploitation and poverty in which oppressed communities have so long been enmeshed. He argues that most of the NICs, in spite of their capitalist growth, have not been able to break out of the impasse of low and medium technology, or in some cases, strangling debt, so as to benefit the masses of their people. And many of the governments of the UDCs, desperate to lessen the unemployment which threatens their regimes, enter into competition with each other in offering the global multinational companies "cheaper and cheaper labour, de-unionised labour, captive labour, female labour and child labour—by removing whatever labour laws, whatever trade union rights have been gained in the past" (Sivanandan 1989, 9–10). Increasing concessions in property and resource ownership accompany labour concessions, until the interests of the governments of the UDCs "are no longer the interests of their people but of metropolitan capital, of which they are the servitors" (11). What spreads and anchors this scenario is "the installation and maintenance of authoritarian Third World regimes by western powers" (12), together with the insidious impact of mind-dwarfing American corporate culture, or, if that is not enough, then direct military force or indirect "low-intensity warfare" which is becoming a fine art of U.S. military operations (12–13).

To summarise, most developing countries are caught in a position in which the previous raw material mainstays of their economies are likely to become less relevant and less in demand. The structure of global production is changing along lines made possible by developments in micro-electronics and information technology, fields in which most of them are barely at the margins. Multinational corporations are becoming stronger rather than weaker in their ability to exploit the cheap labour of these countries.

The education system borrowed from the colonial era, even if expanded and improved, is unlikely to produce a population that is highly educated and skilled enough to respond effectively to the present global changes, and to design creative solutions to the problems they cause. In this situation, poverty and dependence are likely to increase rather than decrease. This has indeed been the case with many of the countries of the "South," including Jamaica, Grenada, and most other Caribbean countries, in the 1980s. This is why I argued earlier that any movement working for egalitarian change on a national scale has to include, as a major part of their work, efforts to challenge and overcome the kind of injustices embedded in the international system since colonial times. Brazier (1989) points out that most of the formerly colonial countries, having attempted during independence to follow a Western-prescribed path of "development" in the 1980s, have had to, in the 1980s and 1990s, pay dearly for this attempt in the shape of crippling interest on loans from the institutions of the rich world. He shows that more than seventy countries have had to "restructure" their economies along the path prescribed by U.S.-dominated international agencies such as the International Monetary Fund (IMF), of devaluations, increases in prices and taxes, and drastic reductions in government expenditure. Some have also had to suffer the fact that prices for their raw material exports by 1988 had stabilized at a rate of 30 percent lower than their value in 1979.

The case of Jamaica illustrates the extent of the erosion that can be suffered by a developing country as a result of, among other things, the severe economic restructuring imposed by the IMF. Polanyi-Levitt (1991) sets out a detailed analysis to demonstrate this, showing, for example, that income per capita fell by some 35 percent in the 1970s, and that in the 1980s income disparities between rich and poor widened, that grinding poverty for the majority worsened, with women and children suffering the greatest deprivation and about 41percent of the rural population living below a poverty line of US$199 annually (45). She points out that per capita spending on the social-welfare sectors of health and education declined by over a third. One result was a shortfall of some 2,000 teachers who made an exodus from the teaching profession because of poor morale and low salaries. Another is that up to 50 percent of children who finish primary school may be considered functionally illiterate insofar as they read simple texts with extreme difficulty, and failure rates in external exams have increased. This is the discouraging context in which the Jamaican Ministry of Education is trying heroically to implement its "Strengthening of Secondary Schools" project described in this paper.

Without the sort of understanding articulated by Sivanandan of global structures and their relationship to historical and contemporary capitalism, it would be difficult for Third World educators and students to see the contextual constraints in which they have to operate and which they must challenge and manipulate. It is this perspective which shows that while the educational reforms in the NICs and UDCs may modernise curricula and increase access for growing numbers of students, there is serious distortion and deception in the underlying assumption of these reforms. That is, making no reference to the local and international economy, they perpetuate the myth that formal schooling, Western style, will enable the poor to emerge from what is seen as their backwardness and ignorance to join the modern world. This myth is debunked by economic analysis of the kind put forward by Sivanandan and others, who insist that it is not just schooling or lack of it that causes poverty—it is the context of international capitalism. Socially critical educational theory borrows from and adds to this with its stress on participatory mechanisms for change, and it is also enriched by those elements of postcolonial philosophy which have challenged Western assumptions of having the correct answers. "For critical pedagogy, cultural struggle finds its ultimate validation in the struggle to transform the lives of ordinary people, especially the most marginal and oppressed among them" (Shapiro 1991, 120).

But even the Freireian type of participatory education and "cultural struggle" in this tradition (Freire 1970, 1978, Hickling-Hudson 1988) is often not enough to overcome the spaces and silences and distortions, particularly about race, gender, and the environment, embedded in the neocolonial society which produced the challengers (Morrow 1990, 53–54, Mayo 1993, 16–20, Weiler 1991). Those who contest the injustices of imperialism often have not renounced the arrogance which leads them to arrogate only to themselves the capacity to find and articulate what they see as true and real. Seeing themselves as the forces of liberation trying to overthrow domination, they can easily fall into the trap of behaving like those forces of repression which have traditionally crushed the "Other" in the name of freedom. This analysis throws light on areas of failure in many revolutions including that in Grenada. The Grenadian revolutionary party's internal conflicts over strategy, leadership structure, and pace of reform were not resolved because each faction, convinced it had the correct view, took this to the point of armed struggle against each other. "I have thought, often, over the past five years," reflects one of the imprisoned survivors of the struggle,

> what would have happened if either the minority or the majority faction had taken the matter in a principled manner to the masses. And what better fora for doing it than the Zonal Parish and Workers, Women, Youth . . . Assemblies (and) meetings? With copies of all relevant minutes printed and distributed to the people; with representatives of both trends in the leadership putting their view forward to the people in the Assemblies . . . and being questioned and grilled by the people in return and hearing their views . . . what better way could there have been for resolving our differences? (Coard 1989, 10–11).

It is in their criticism of the inflexibility of the totalizing view that, as Shapiro points out, "postmodern ideas and insights provide a series of cautions to critical pedagogy which cannot be easily dismissed." He quotes Sharon Welch's account of a feminist theology of liberation as putting forward one of the clearest warnings that the temptation of defining others' hopes for liberation must be avoided.

The oppressed, says Welch, must name their own oppression and liberation. . . . The struggle against oppression gains power by drawing . . . peoples' heritage and experience of liberation into dialogue with other interpretations. Only in this way can the dialogue avoid being one-sided (Shapiro 1991, 121).

CONCLUSION

Educators, planners, and communities working for change in the Third World have long been deeply concerned with what is uppermost in the writings of educators in the postmodern tradition—that is, questions of cultural identity in plural societies. However, it could be argued that the only realistic context in which to understand the role of Third World countries and their education systems in global capitalism is that described by Sivananda from a neo-Marxist perspective. The postmodernist and postcolonial perspectives are not sufficiently informed by the sort of analysis that deals with the realities that Sivananda delineates and that people in Third World communities have to deal with daily. To struggle for a more just and democratic global economy is absolutely vital for countries made poor by the international system: this political and economic struggle has to take place at the same time as we strive to develop our education systems to provide quality education for increasing numbers of students. Otherwise, those on the bottom rungs of world capitalism will experience little or no economic expansion or change which will enable them to provide employment and an egalitarian place in society for the new graduates holding their secondary school certificates. The growth in educated unemployment will limit social development in the way pointed out by Kazim Bacchus (Bacchus 1980).

The Grenada Revolution provided an important example of a way to develop the economy and the education system at the same time, so that the growth of one nourished and was strengthened by the growth of the other (see Hickling-Hudson 1989). But this kind of change is of little use if it is going to be destroyed by the kind of modernist arrogance and totalizing views that underlay the power struggles which brought the Grenadian Revolution to its violent end. It is here that emancipatory postmodernism/postcolonialism has the important message that in working for change, it is vital to throw off the limitations of the metanarrative and the univocal voice, and to empower the voices of the present in a collective struggle out of the past in our attempts to construct a viable future.

REFERENCES

Aronowitz, S., and Giroux, H. (1990) *Postmodern Education: Politcs, Culture and Social Criticism.* Minneapolis, University of Minnesota Press.

Ashcroft, Bill, Griffiths, Gareth, and Tiffin, Helen (1989) *The Empire Writes Back: Theory and Practice in Post-Colonial Literatures.* London, Routledge.

Bacchus, M. K. (1980) *Education for Development or Underdevelopment?* Canada, Wilfred Laurier.

Brazier, C. (1989) "Two Decades in the Life of the World." *New Internationalist* 200 (October): 4–7.

Brizan, G. (1991) "Education and Society in Grenada." In E. Miller (ed.), *Education and Society in the Commonwealth Caribbean.* Kingston, Jamaica, University of the West Indies.

Cherryholmes, Cleo (1988) *Power and Criticism: Thinking about Education Post-structurally.* New York, Teachers' College Press.

Coard, B. (1989) *Grenada: Village and Workers, Women, Farmers and Youth Assemblies During the Grenada Revolution: Their Genesis, Evolution and Significance.* London, Caribbean Labour Solidarity and Karia Press.

Evans, H. (1988) *Strengthening of Secondary Education (General Curriculum): A Study of Five Parishes.* Unpublished report, University of the West Indies.

Ferguson, J. (n.d.,1990?) *Grenada: Revolution in Reverse.* London, Latin American Bureau.

Freire, Paulo (1970) *Pedagogy of the Oppressed.* New York, Seabury Press.

Freire, Paulo (1978) *Pedagogy in Process: The Letters to Guinea-Bissau.* New York, Continuum.

Hickling-Hudson, A. (1988) "Towards Communication Praxis: Reflections on the Pedagogy of Paulo Freire and Educational Change in Grenada." *Journal of Education* 170 (2).

Hickling-Hudson, A. (1989) "Education in the Grenada Revolution." *Compare* 19 (2).

Johnson, J. (1993) "Neither Unreasonable Nor Irrational: Response to a Critic of Jamaica's New Curriculum for Grades 7–9." Paper. 1993 annual conference of the Comparative and International Education Society, Kingston, Jamaica.

Johnson-Odim, C. (1991) "Common Themes, Different Contexts: Third World Women and Feminism." In C. Mohanty, A. Russo, and L. Torres (eds.), *Third World Women and the Politics of Feminism.* Bloomington, Indiana University Press, 315–27.

Jules, D. (1991) "Building Democracy: Content and Ideology in Grenadian Educational Texts, 1979–1983." In Michael Apple (ed.), *The Politics of the Text Book.* New York, Routledge, 259–88.

Jules, D. (1992) *Education and Social Transformation in Grenada, 1979–1983.* Ph.D. dissertation, University of Wisconsin-Madison.

Kholi, W. (1991) "Post-Modernism, Critical Theory and the 'New' Pedagogies: What's at Stake in the Discourse?" *Education and Society* 9 (2): 39–46.

Mayo, P. (1993) "When Does It Work? Freire's Pedagogy in Context." *Studies in the Education of Adults* 25 (1): 11–30.

McAfee, K. (1991) *Storm Signals: Structural Adjustment and Developement Alternatives in the Caribbean.* London, Zed Books.

McLaren, P. (1991) "Post-Colonial Pedagogy: Post-Colonial Desire and Decolonized Community." *Education and Society* 9 (2): 135–58.

Meeks, B. (1993) *Caribbean Revolutions and Revolutionary Theory: An Assessment of Cuba, Nicaragua and Grenada.* London, Macmillan Press.

Mills, C. (1991) "Marxism and Caribbean Development: A Contribution to Rethinking." In Judith Wedderburn (ed.), *Rethinking Development.* University of the West Indies.

Ministry of Education, Jamaica (1990) *Jamaican Primary Education Policy Study: Final Report,* Vol. 2. Jamaica, Trevor Hamilton & Associates, and USAID.

Mohanty, C., Russo, A., and Torres, L. (1991) *Third World Women and the Politics of Feminism.* Indiana, Indiana University Press.

Morrow, R. (1990) "Post-Marxism, Postmodernism and Popular Education in Latin America." *New Education* 12 (2): 47–57.

OECS [Organisation of Eastern Caribbean States] Education Reform Working Group (1991) *Foundation for the Future: OECS Education Reform Strategy.* St. Lucia, OECS Secretariat and CIDA.

Polyani-Levitt, K. (1991) *The Origins and Consequences of Jamaica's Debt Crisis.* Kingston, Jamaica, University of the West Indies.

Russo, A. (1991) " 'We Cannot Live without Our Lives': White Women, Antiracism and Feminism." In C. Mohanty, A. Russo, and L. Torres (eds.), *Third World Women and the Politics of Feminism.* Bloomington, Indiana University Press, 297–313.

Shapiro, S. (1991) "The End of Radical Hope? Postmodernism and the Challenge to Critical Pedagogy." *Education and Society* 9 (2): 112–122.

Sivanandan, A. (1989) "New Circuits of Imperialism." *Race and Class* 30 (4): 1–18.

Weiler, K. (1991) "Freire and a Feminist Pedagogy of Difference." *Harvard Educational Review* 61: 449–474 .

CHAPTER 8

Qualifications, Quality, and Equality
A Political Economy of Sri Lankan Education 1971–1993

ANGELA LITTLE

Much of the debate about equality and quality in education focuses on the tension between access to education and the ensuing quality or standard of that education. Arguments revolve around whether democratised access decreases quality, whether restricted access increases quality, or whether democratised access and enhanced quality can be achieved simultaneously.

A rather different argument about the relationship between equality and quality was presented by Dore (1976). His controversial book titled *The Diploma Disease* anticipated much of the late 1980s international interest in the quality of mass education. The book and a programme of related research (Little 1992) suggested that educational quality is determined in part by the pattern of use of educational certificates for labour market recruitment, a pattern whose development varies with the point in world history at which a country begins its drive towards industrialisation. The argument was based on a series of country case histories of the development of educational traditions, educational provision, educational quality, assessment procedures, and job allocation mechanisms.

The diploma disease thesis asserts

> the later development starts (i.e. the later the point in world history that
> a country starts on a modernisation drive) the more widely education
> certificates are used for occupational selection; the faster the rate of
> qualification inflation and the more examination-oriented schooling
> becomes at the expense of genuine education. (Dore 1976, 72)

In the third world today the importance of qualifications is greater than in the advanced industrial countries. Educational systems are more likely to be geared to qualification-getting, and the consequences for the society and its pattern of development are likely to be even more deplorable. (83)

schooling in developing countries seems . . . *much* less effective at developing those attitudes which make people find *intrinsic* satisfaction in creative mental activity. (95)

The thesis focuses on educational qualification as a criterion of future access to education and occupation. Where future access is determined by examination scores, then teachers and students orient their classroom practice towards tests and examinations. The "tyranny of testing" and "teaching to the test" are familiar complaints in many contemporary educational systems but the history of these complaints is long. They can be traced in England to the 1911 Report of the Consultative Committee on Examinations; in Colonial Ceylon to the 1867 Morgan Committee; and in China to the Tang Dynasty (618–907) when the civil service examinations were criticised for overemphasising literary skills at the expense of skills having practical utility (Cleverley 1985).

The significance of the diploma disease thesis lies in the location of this traditional concern within a comparative analysis of education and the impact of the economy on education. With respect to the quality and equality debate, the following proposition and its converse can be derived:

the more that access to future resources (whether educational or economic assets) is restricted, the more the quality of the educational process will be determined by the criteria which determine that access.

the more that access to future resources (whether educational or economic) is democratised, the less the quality of the educational process will be determined by the criteria which determine that access.

These propositions focus on *future* access to employment and education resources, as perceived by students already selected into the system. The focus is on access *from* the present education cycle rather than access *to* it and the implications for quality. The diploma disease thesis, however, does not examine *why* employment and economic resources are scarce. Rather it examines the impact on educational quality of the criteria used to determine access *when* resources are scarce.

By focusing on those criteria which determine student's future access in conditions of resource scarcity, the proposition extends analyses of the determinants of the quality of education in developing countries. Such analyses have tended to focus on teacher education, curriculum, professional support, and financial resources available for education (Beeby 1966, Hawes and Stephens 1990, Lockheed and Verspoor 1991).

This chapter examines the case of Sri Lanka in the light of educational quality and access, in the light of the propositions presented above. The discussion contrasts with others writing on a similar theme in the context of Sri Lanka. Jayeweera (1991) suggests that there is no necessary incompatibility between notions of "equity" and "excellence":

> As high abilities and talents are not confined to a socio economic elite, it is not possible to provide opportunities for the fullest development of human potential in the total population without ensuring equity (3).

Her discussion therefore presents the issue in terms of a possible tension between democratising education and maintaining standards, that is, between the quality of education and access *to* it, rather than *from* it.

Gunawardene (1993) distinguishes equality from equity and suggests that equity is achieved only when democratised access to a level of education leads to equality of outcome and economic opportunity. She questions whether the democratisation of access to university has in fact led to increased opportunity for high quality education and subsequent employment opportunity for those from lower socioeconomic groups. Her conclusion, that neither has occurred, is interpreted as confirmation of the universities' role in legitimating inequality through relegating students from lower social groups to less prestigious curricular tracks. Employers too reinforce the necessity of acquiring qualifications but then "suppress achievement" by emphasising English proficiency and other skills characteristic of students from higher social classes. Increased equality of access through entry criteria has not led to an increase in equality of provision and hence jeopardises increased equality of outcome.

This chapter provides a complementary rather than contradictory perspective on the tension between equality and quality. It focuses on the role of exit rather than entry criteria in determining the quality of educational experience and examines change in this relationship in the context of economic and political change in Sri Lanka over the past two decades.

EDUCATION IN SRI LANKA: A CHANNEL OF SOCIAL MOBILITY

In contrast to the development of education in some industrialised countries, the history of Sri Lanka's educational development was characterised by discontinuity in the nineteenth century, followed by a rapid development of mass education and participation in qualification systems in the early twentieth century.

In the nineteenth century schools which had been put in place during the Dutch period of colonisation were replaced by those sanctioned by the British colonial government. A dual system emerged in which students in elite schools and bound for mid-level posts in government and commerce studied in the English medium while students in the mass schools bound for lower-level employment studied in Sinhala or Tamil, the languages of the majority and minority populations, respectively. Catholic schools, legacies of the earlier Portuguese period, and Buddhist schools, legacies of the precolonial period, were officially discouraged.

The school system expanded rapidly between the late nineteenth century and the mid-twentieth. The importance of this period for the diploma disease thesis is the creation of a broad social and political consensus about the role of education as a "channel of social mobility, [via] a single peaked pyramid which everybody could climb" (Dore 1976, 64). This egalitarian ideal emerged in reaction to colonial education policies which had created religious, ethnic, regional and social-economic imbalances.

> The dual system of education of elite, English schools and minimal mass education in the local languages, the Christian domination of the power structure in education, uneven socioeconomic development in the country and the advantaged status of the southwest and northern sectors of the country, and the demands of the colonial economy were components of the legacy transferred to local policy makers in the nineteen thirties (Jayeweera 1989, 7).

Universal franchise introduced in 1931 created the momentum for social change and Dr. C.W.W. Kannangara, the first Minister of Education, provided the political force for the egalitarian ideal in the years immediately preceding independence in 1948.

ASYNCHRONOUS DEVELOPMENT
OF EDUCATION AND THE ECONOMY

The growth of education and the economy in the mid-twentieth century was asynchronous. The creation and consolidation of a unified system of education post independence occurred in an economy which grew too slowly to absorb the numbers emerging from the education system with the expectations of modern-sector, largely government, jobs. By 1971, at the time of the youth insurgency, the imbalance between inputs and outputs was critical. Nearly 20 percent of the labour force was openly unemployed (Alailima 1991). Four-fifths of the unemployment was concentrated among those aged under 25 years; and among the 20–24 year olds with at least three "O" level passes 55 percent of males and 74 percent of females were unemployed.

EDUCATIONAL QUALIFICATIONS,
EXAMINATIONS, AND JOBS

Research conducted in 1975 confirmed that educated youth in the early 1970s aspired to modern-sector jobs and that access to these depended on possession of educational qualifications. The estimated imbalance in the labour market was of the order of 3:1. Between 150,00 and 200,000 job seekers with grade 10 education (i.e., General Certificate of Education (GCE) "Ordinary" level sat after a minimum of 11 years of education) were pursuing an estimated 60,000 jobs in medium- to large-scale modern-sector enterprises. If only white collar wage employment was examined the imbalance was 7:1. Not surprisingly, proof of a minimum educational level reached was required even for entry to the very lowest grade of unskilled labour (Deraniyagala, Dore, and Little 1978).

Qualification escalation, or the raising of qualification levels for a particular job, was a trend common across many jobs during the 1960s and early 1970s. The trend was clearer when the qualifications of selectees rather than eligible recruits were examined. Escalation was apparent in both the public and private sectors of employment, though it was particularly apparent in public-sector recruitment. The escalation was of two types, vertical or horizontal. Vertical referred to an increase in the level of education required, while horizontal referred either to an increase in the performance demanded at a given level, or the addition of a supplementary criterion, for example "years of experience." The dominant rationale for qualification escalation expressed by employers was logistical—the need to reduce applicants to a manageable number, itself a symptom of the underlying structural imbalance between qualified applicants and economic opportunity.

The major qualifications used for labour market recruitment in the early 1970s were the public examinations held at the end of eleven and thirteen years of schooling, respectively (including the kindergarten year), reduced in the period 1972–1977 to ten and twelve years, respectively. In 1972 the ministry was sufficiently concerned about the influence of examinations on the curriculum to establish a committee of enquiry. Its findings were clear on the purposes served by these examinations:

> The characteristic function of public examinations is that of selection . . . Public examinations are social devices for screening the candidates in such a way that favouritism, thuggery and low cunning are set at nought in selecting persons for jobs or further education . . . there are many other functions which public examinations serve—such as providing the educational system with a measure of the schools' efficiency, providing the candidate with information regarding his attainments, and providing teachers and pupils with incentives to do certain kinds of work. But these are subsidiary functions besides the main function of selecting persons for jobs. (Ministry of Education 1972)

SELECTION, CURRICULUM, AND PEDAGOGY

The function of public examinations as determinants of access to future resources is undisputed. The implication which is asserted for curriculum and pedagogy is both controversial and difficult to establish empirically. The assertion is that

> examinations *dominate* the curriculum, that all learning is ritualised, that curiosity is devalued, that no one is allowed to stray from the syllabus, that no one inquires about the usefulness, the relevance, or the interestingness of what is learned. (Dore 1976, 61)

The problem resides in the displacement of knowledge and skills which could be of potential use to the *majority* of children, who will leave the system before reaching the apex of the educational pyramid, by knowledge and skills which are assessed through examination (e.g., quadratic equations and memorisation of the length of the world's largest rivers). It also resides in the compromise of the development of the abilities of the *minority* who do reach the top, "the future controllers of Sri Lanka's destiny." How, Dore wonders, are they to become "imaginative managers and administrators noted for their independence and integrity" if they have completed sixteen years of training in the "docile acceptance of the authority of teachers and examiners" and the production of answers "which we expect those in authority to expect?" (Dore 1976, 64).

Dore's views on the influence of the selection function of schools on educational quality resonated in the early 1970s with those of senior educational professionals and politicians. As a Director of the Sri Lankan Curriculum Development Centre was to comment,

> the qualifying function . . . tended to become exalted at the expense of the educational functions. Educational qualifications and not real meaningful education have emerged as the major determinant of success in life . . . such a situation has grave implications . . . firstly, the function of education is reduced to that of an expensive means of distinguishing the academically able from the less able, hoping that such a distinction will enable the nation to develop its manpower most effectively. Secondly, the kinds of knowledge, skills and attitudes imparted by such a process, have little relevance to socio economic development. (Ranaweera 1975, 16)

Speaking shortly after the youth insurrection of April 1971, the Minister of Education commented on the socialisation of youth into feeling "rejected" by an education system focused on access to University:

> From the time the child enters school, the target is set on the university. Each year only one percent of the school population enters the universities. So all the efforts, expenditure and preparations are for the benefit of this one percent . . . the school instead should concentrate on the vast majority. They should be made to feel that the society wants them, and they are doing something useful to the betterment of their country. They should not be made to feel that they are rejects who could not enter the university. (*The Nation,* 30 May 1971).

And in his analysis of educational change at the time of the insurrection and published some years later, a former director of educational planning commented:

It is a hard fact that in our country each segment in the educational
ladder is viewed by the pupils and parents primarily as a route for
entry into the next. These values of the clients naturally influence the
order of priorities among school authorities. Stipulations laid down
for crossing a hurdle are likely to have a backwash effect on what goes
before that hurdle. (Wijemanne 1978)

The most systematic evidence of the backwash of public examinations on
curriculum and pedagogy in secondary schools was collected in 1974–
1975 by Lewin (1984) who explored the influence of the innovative
National Certificate of General Education (NCGE) examination on curriculum. This examination, which is taken at the end of junior secondary
school, was designed to reinforce an innovative curriculum having a
prevocational bias and claiming to have greater relevance for the lives of
the majority of students. In practice the new examination was very similar
to the earlier GCE examination "in spite of intentions to the contrary"
(Lewin 1984, 126). Because of its continued role as a hurdle in the competition for scarce resources there was public pressure to retain compara-
bility with the earlier examination. Teacher involvement in assessment
and practical assessment was ruled out because of the public legitimacy
accorded closed-book and controlled-examination conditions. Despite
statements that the new integrated science curriculum should emphasise
the development of scientific concepts, patterns, and processes rather than
facts, the examination comprised a proportion of items testing knowledge
higher than the average of the earlier single-subject science papers (Lewin
1984, Table 4.3). Moreover, because of low pass marks (estimated raw
scores of around 30 percent) and multiple choice format, it was possible
for students to pass the examination purely on the basis of the recall of
memorised facts.

CHANGE OVER TIME?

If this was the picture of examination backwash in the early 1970s, has it
remained constant in the intervening years? Is test tyranny a universal
educational phenomenon invariant across time and space, impervious to
change in context such as economic development?

   In 1977 the United National Party came to power and introduced policies designed to liberalise the economy. Estimates of per capita growth
in the economy suggest that the slow annual average growth in GNP of
1.3 percent between 1970 and 1977 was replaced by an annual average of

4 percent during the period 1977–1987 (de Silva and de Silva 1990). Between 1971 and 1980–1981 the labour force grew at an annual growth rate of 2.5 percent and between 1980–1981 and 1990 at a rate of 2.2 percent. The female labour force grew more rapidly than the male, at an annual rate of 3 percent between 1971 and 1980–1981 and 5.4 percent between 1980–1981 and 1990 (Alailima 1991).

In 1971 the open unemployment rate was almost 20 percent. Members of the labour force aged between 20 and 24 and with GCE "O" Level qualifications experienced an unemployment rate of 62 percent. By 1981 the open unemployment rate had reduced to 15.3 percent and in 1990 to 14.4 percent (Alailima 1991). In 1985 the unemployment rates for GCE "O" level qualified youth aged between 20 and 24 had reduced to 43 percent. Between 1970 and 1985 the unemployment rate for those aged 20–24 and having grade 8 education had reduced from 39 percent to 31 percent.

One of the major changes in economic opportunity over the past twenty years has been the volume and composition of overseas employment. In the early 1970s the numbers seeking employment abroad were small and comprised mainly professionals seeking work in the new and old Commonwealth. During the 1980s, however, there was growth of employment in skilled and unskilled work for men and women in West Asia. Nadarajah and Wijemanne (1991) estimated that nearly 50,000 women, mostly from rural areas and with grade 5–10 education, would find work as housemaids in West Asia in 1991 alone. By the late 1980s remittances from West Asia constituted the major source of foreign exchange, capturing the preeminent position held by plantation crop revenues for over a century.

EDUCATIONAL PARTICIPATION

If the economy has expanded during the past twenty years then so too has the education system and with it the numbers of teachers employed. Between 1971 and 1986 the proportion of the population aged over 5 years with less than five years of primary education had declined from 24.5 percent to 11.6 percent . For those with "O" level it increased from 3.7 percent to 10.8 percent and with "A" level from 0.9 percent to 2.1 percent. This reflected a major expansion of the upper levels of schooling during this period. University enrolment did not grow at the same rate and the percentage of the population with a university degree grew from only 0.38 percent to 0.53 percent. Although the expansion of government-supported universities was carefully controlled, the private sector of tertiary, especially part-time, education has grown. Part-time courses in computer studies, accountancy, and business studies flourish and colleges affiliated with foreign universities are emerging.

The Quality of Education

So if the economy has expanded, youth unemployment has declined, and the education system has been democratised, what has been the implication for the quality of the educational experience? In particular, to what extent do examination criteria continue to have a dominant backwash effect on the curriculum?

In the mid 1980s de Silva, Gunawardene, and Rupasinghe (1987) examined students' orientations to learning, including the extent to which students perceived their learning to be influenced by the desire for examination success. Their data suggested that there were differences between and within schools in the degree of "assessment orientation" in attitudes to learning expressed by students. Some students were more likely to feel motivated by examination grades than others. However, as time-series data are not available, comparisons over time between and within schools are impossible.

Compared with twenty years ago a greater proportion of the school-age population participates in examinations. Three hundred thousand school and private candidates sat the GCE "O" level exam in 1977; 526,000 sat in 1991. Forty-eight thousand school and private candidates sat the GCE "A" level exam in 1975; 160,000 sat in 1991.

Perhaps the clearest evidence of the degree of examination-oriented learning comes from studies of participation in private tuition. Private tuition is a common phenomenon in Sri Lanka and is used by students to increase the chances of examination success. Private tuition is followed in organised classes in school and other premises or in one-to-one tutoring in homes. Recent estimates suggest that 75 percent of year 11 students were taking private tuition for the GCE "O" level exam in 1989. This rose to 92 percent among GCE science "A" level students. Comparative figures for 1980–1981 based on smaller and more selective samples suggested percentages of 73 percent and 87 percent for GCE "O" level and "A" level students, respectively, in Jaffna, 60 percent and 84 percent in Colombo city, and 47 percent and 61 percent in Kegalle (de Silva et al. 1991). Since the 1989 data are drawn from across the country (excluding the North and the East) and include representative percentages of rural students, we may infer that the percentages in most areas are increasing.

Students in the 1989 sample spent an average of 9.1 hours per week attending private tuition classes. Not surprisingly, large proportions of children reported that they had little time available for activities other than attending school and private tuition and attending to homework arising from both. Were comparative data available we might find that private tutories are one of the most buoyant components of the open economy and fastest growing elements of the GNP!

RESISTANCE TO EXAMINATION REFORM

The dominant role played by examinations in the allocation of life chances has thwarted its own reform. Earlier in this chapter, reference was made to the NCGE examination reform introduced in the early 1970s as part of a package of educational reforms designed to make the curriculum more relevant to the lives of the majority of children. This reform was shortlived and was overturned in 1977 with the change in government. The examination system returned to the familiar-named GCE "O" and "A" levels. One of the main reasons for this change was the anxiety on the part of vocal middle-class parents about reduced access to further education opportunities outside Sri Lanka (Lewin and Little 1984). Although the GCE "O" and "A" level exams did not guarantee access to overseas universities, it was felt that the chances of access were greater for a student with this title of qualification than for one with the unfamiliar NCGE and Higher National Certificate of Education (HNCE).

In 1987 continuous assessment was introduced as part of the certification of performance at GCE "O" level in selected subjects. But in 1989 continuous assessment was abolished. It was rejected by parents because it required subjective marking on the part of teachers, rejected by some senior educators for being out of line with current international practice, and rejected by members of the insurgent youth party of the extreme left (Janatha Vimukthi Peramuna) for discriminating against the poor rural child.

Overall, then, there is a suggestion that examination success and examination criteria continue to dominate the educational process in Sri Lanka, and perhaps to an even greater degree than earlier. As the Sri Lankan National Task Force on Education noted in 1990:

The education system is currently preoccupied with the interests of those students who will proceed to institutions of higher learning, although less than two percent of the population proceed to University. (9)

The general economic liberalisation of the economy does not appear to have led to any significant reduction in the degree of examination orientation in the education system as suggested by the propositions at the beginning of this chapter. Of course, change in the quality of education is notoriously difficult to assess over time in any education system. Thus it is possible that the influence of exit criteria on the curriculum has indeed reduced but that change in the nature of the influence has been impossible to detect. Alternatively we could accept that the influence has changed little and seek alternative reasons why this may have occurred.

THE LOCATION OF RESTRICTED ACCESS

One possibility is that much of the evidence referred to above refers to segments of the education system where access to further education and economic opportunity has remained restricted in an economy which in general has shown growth. While the highest rate of unemployment among young people in the early 1970s was found among those with GCE "O" level qualifications, the highest rate now is to be found among those with GCE "A" level qualifications. The unemployment rate among those aged 20–24 and with "A" level qualifications nearly doubled between 1970 and 1985, from 27 percent to 52 percent. This represents an increase in absolute numbers of nearly five times, from 9,000 in 1970 to 43,000 in 1985, reflecting the expansion of the education system in the GCE "A" level classes.

An expansion of opportunity in the economy as a whole does not imply an easing of the perception of restriction of access throughout the education system. Indeed, from the point of view of a GCE "A" level candidate the perception of restriction probably increased between the late 1960s and late 1980s. Although opportunities for university education increased during the 1980s with the establishment of university college campuses at Ruhuna and Batticaloa and the establishment of the Open University, the numbers of prospective applicants also increased. Comparisons of numbers of students enroled in "A" level classes in 1963 and 1987 provide illustrative evidence. In 1963 the ratio between numbers enrolled in preuniversity classes and total numbers enrolled in universities was of the order of 2.3:1. In 1987 it was 7.5:1, or 5.5:1 if Open University enrolments are included. Between 1963 and 1987 total enrolment in conventional universities increased from 15,000 to only 20,000. By contrast, preuniversity grade 11 and 12 enrolment increased from 35,000 to 150,000.

ACCESS TO LEVELS VERSUS TYPE OF EDUCATION

A second possible explanation concerns stratification of the perceived quality of education within levels. If the proximity of restriction on access is a key consideration in understanding the effects of examination criteria on quality and if there is *open access* up to year 11, then one must wonder why it is that pressures on primary-school children to succeed in the year 5 scholarship exam seem to have increased when the scholarships themselves carry little or no financial value for the majority of successful students.

Despite the creation of a unified system of education in the 1950s schools remain stratified. Many of the earlier English-medium schools are now the prestigious Sinhala- and Tamil-medium schools. Throughout the 1970s and early 1980s the numbers of scholarships to these schools awarded each year was around 5,000. But the pressures on students became so great that government increased the number of scholarships awarded to just over 20,000 in 1991. Their value in many parents' eyes lies clearly in the access they provide to prestigious schools for secondary education.

In a written submission to the World Conference on Education for All in Jomtien, Thailand, in 1990, the Sri Lanka National Task Force on Education noted that

> more than fifty percent of the children in disadvantaged schools need extra tutoring outside of the school system in order to prepare themselves for the year 5 examination. Nationally, at least twenty five percent of primary school children need such assistance. (Sri Lanka 1990, 9)

This phenomenon underlines the importance of distinguishing *levels* of education from the stratification of *types* of institution within the same level. Democratisation of access to one level of education brings in its wake a differentiation by type or status which ensures that examination criteria retain their influence on curriculum and on learning behaviour.

There is perhaps a third reason for the maintenance of interest on the part of students in examination criteria and their influence on definitions of learning, which reflects broader political change and conflict within Sri Lankan society. This interest arises from political tensions during the 1980s and concerns the affirmation of educational qualifications as legitimate criteria of access to resources.

POLITICAL CONFLICT IN THE 1980S

Since 1977 Sri Lankan society has experienced the fruits of liberal and market-oriented economic policies. This period has also been characterised by armed conflict and increased politicisation of daily life.

The armed conflict has been of two types. The first, and the more intractable from the government's viewpoint, has involved Jaffna Tamil separatists and security forces in the north and east sections of the country. Beginning in the late 1970s it reached a temporary climax in 1983 when members of the civilian Sinhalese population attacked civilian Tamils in towns in several parts of Sri Lanka. The violence subsided but then turned in on itself as Tamil separatist groups competed for supremacy. In 1987, amid opposition from some politicians and sections of society, the Sri Lankan and Indian governments entered into an accord through which India provided military assistance to help implement a peace plan and bring an end to hostilities. The Indian army left the country in 1990, their mission for peace unaccomplished. Conflicts between the Sri Lankan security forces and the Liberation Tigers for Tamil Eelam (LTTE) resumed and continue to date. The assassinations in 1993 of the Sinhalese President Premadasa and that of a powerful Sinhalese opposition leader a week earlier have both been attributed officially to the Tamil Tigers.

The roots of this conflict are complex but can in part be traced to the 1956 Parliamentary Bill to make Sinhala the single official language, in a society where English, but more particularly Tamil, had enjoyed parity with Sinhala hitherto. The communal riots of 1958 were the proximate manifestation of the tensions between the Sinhalese government and the Tamil Federal Party. Despite subsequent concessions to Tamil as a language of government administration in Tamil majority areas and the maintenance of Tamil as a medium of instruction from kindergarten to university, the net result for Tamils in the 1960s was a perception of restricted access to government jobs.

One result of this was an intensification on the part of the Tamil community for participation in higher education and science-stream secondary education. In time this led to resentment among the Sinhala community over the disproportionate representation of Tamils in the prestigious science, engineering, and medical faculties in the university. By the 1970s this imbalance surfaced as an issue and led to several changes in admissions policies to universities, each the subject of intense debate.

The second major conflict in the 1980s involved the security forces and Sinhala rural youth members of the Janatha Vimukthi Peramuna (JVP), or People's Liberation Front. This was a reemergence of the youth movement which had led the insurgency in 1971. The United Front government, a coalition of Sinhala parties of the Left which came to power in 1970, had raised expectations among large numbers of educated unemployed. It demonstrated very soon an inability to meet election promises. The JVP, which drew its support from Sinhala Buddhist educated youth in the 16–25 age group, challenged the leftist United Front, demanding nationalisation of economic assets and an immediate solution to the problems of unemployment.

In April 1971 the JVP armed itself against the government of the Left. The insurrection was shortlived, through lack of mass support in rural and urban areas and the ruthlessness with which it was crushed. The government received military assistance from a range of countries from across the political spectrum including Britain, the United States, India, the Soviet Union, Yugoslavia, and Pakistan (Wilson 1977). It was this movement, under the same leadership, which reemerged in the late 1980s in violent opposition to the government of the Right, which had liberalised the economy and brought economic benefits to some but not all sections of society.

The reemergence of the JVP in the 1980s was not unrelated to the broader ethnic conflict. The peace accord reached between President Jayewardene and Prime Minister Rajiv Ghandi and the arrival of the Indian army in the country in 1987 intensified the cause of Sinhala Buddhist nationalism, which had been growing through the 1980s, and strengthened the chauvinistic aims of the JVP. The response by government was as ruthless as it had been some sixteen years earlier, but the conflict was protracted. No one knows how many died in the worst period of violence between 1988 and 1989. Estimates by government and human rights groups range from 20,000 to 80,000, respectively.

POLITICAL CRITERIA IN JOB ALLOCATION

Although the personal characteristics of the majority of insurgents in the late 1980s were similar to those of 1971—young, Sinhala Buddhist, educated, and unemployed—the profile of grievances included at least one element which differentiated the 1980s from 1971 and which reflected change in the resource allocation system throughout the late 1970s and 1980s. In the late 1970s the "political chit system" became an institutionalised criterion in the allocation of public-sector employment. Although political influence had often been suspected in recruitment decisions for public sector employment during the early 1970s, it had never been sanctioned publicly as a criterion for allocation. In 1977–1978, however, Job Banks for recruitment for all posts in the public sector carrying an initial basic salary of Rs 6790 or less per annum were established. All applicants for registration in the scheme were required to be nominees of the applicant's electoral Member of Parliament (M.P.), or, if the M.P. was in opposition, by a representative of an organisation of the ruling United National Party (UNP). Thus was political patronage institutionalised as a criterion for access to employment resources (Deraniyagala, Dore, and Little 1978). This did not mean that educational qualifications were unimportant. It simply meant that the criteria for jobs had escalated horizontally. Political patronage became important in determining access to jobs and to resources of many kinds (Moore 1985, Perera 1985, Spencer 1990).

When the economy began to surge in the late 1970s and early 1980s, this system worked to the advantage of both the UNP politicians and their supporters. Even opposition supporters might not unreasonably have believed that their turn would come in the not-too-distant future. But important political events in the early 1980s and a slowing of the economy in the mid 1980s were to sow seeds of economic and political discontent.

In 1982 President Jayewardene called a referendum to extend the life of parliament for a further five years, signalling an end to the rhythm of regular and frequent swings in power between the UNP and the opposition which the electorate had come to expect. People just too young to vote in 1977 realised that they were to wait at least a full ten years before exercising their democratic vote for the first time, leading to a growing disaffection with the democratic political process. And in the mid 1980s when the internal defence budget, dominated by the war in the north and the east, diverted expenditure away from other sectors, even some UNP supporters felt that resources available for distribution through political patronage were evaporating. Additional defence expenditures incurred in curbing the JVP violence and the general state of emergency led to a further delay of parliamentary elections until 1989.

The situation facing the new President Premadasa, elected at the end of 1988, was grave. He initiated changes in the criteria for public-sector job recruitment and appointed a commission to report on the problems of youth. The Job Bank, which had registered for public-sector employment educationally qualified youth with recommendations from their M.P. since 1977, was abandoned. Henceforth applicants for all public-sector jobs were to satisfy minimum educational qualifications and sit a competitive examination set by the Department of Examinations. Interviews are held with those selected on these two criteria but they are used solely for the purpose of checking the authenticity of the educational certificates presented and other details such as place of residence and appearance. The final criterion used in the allocation is ethnicity, ethnic quotas for all government jobs having been established in line with the proportional representation of ethnic groups in the population. Political criteria no longer appear to play any role in job recruitment though they continue to influence promotions and transfers of public servants once appointed.

The Youth Commission reported in 1990 and recommended an expansion of the opportunities for tertiary education for Sinhala and Tamil youth. In November 1991 eight provincial university colleges were established. This eased some of the pressure on the government to provide employment for GCE "A" level qualified youth and to provide greater access to the pinnacle of the education system, which, despite some attempts to democratise access in the mid 1980s, had remained severely restricted.

EQUALITY AND QUALITY:
TOWARDS SOME REFINED PROPOSITIONS

This chapter began with a proposition about equality and quality which emphasised the influence of exit rather than entry criteria on the quality of the educational process. I suggested that if access to future education and employment opportunities was democratised, then exit criteria would not dominate the learning process to the same extent as they had done in the past. Despite the picture of economic liberalisation and expansion of educational opportunity at selected points in the system, it was suggested that the overall degree-examination orientation in the system had certainly not diminished and may even have increased. The observation, which ran contrary to the prediction of the initial general proposition, was then examined in three ways.

Firstly it was suggested that access to the apex of the educational system remains sufficiently restricted and valued to generate a strong orientation to examinations and examination criteria. The quality of the learning experience remains determined to a large extent by these access criteria. Although unemployment rates in the labour force as a whole have declined, and particularly so among GCE "O" level qualified persons, the unemployment rate for GCE "A" level qualified persons has increased. It was suggested that the question of access and educational quality must be examined in relation to the perceived proximity of and value attached to the restriction.

Secondly, it was suggested that the access question is not simply an issue of access to subsequent levels of education. It is also a question of access to particular types of institutions within levels. Access to year 11 education in Sri Lanka is open. There are no formal selection hurdles to be crossed in reaching it. Yet the year 5 scholarship exam remains in place and serves to allocate scholarship holders to prestigious schools, which parents believe will enhance their child's chances of success at the GCE "O" level examination. This suggests that discussions of access must distinguish between levels and stratification within levels of education and recognise that, once democratisation of level is achieved, then the value attached to strata within level may be enhanced.

Thirdly it was suggested that the valuation of educational credentials must be understood in terms that go beyond the education and economic system. During the late 1970s and 1980s job allocation had become increasingly politicised in an economy where there were bound to be, over time, losers as well as winners. Participation in the democratic political process had also been severely restricted. Increasing numbers of qualified youth were unable to claim a place in the job queue as they lacked the required political credentials.

The frustration of youth over restricted access to resources and the democratic process which fuelled the JVP movement in the late 1980s and continues to fuel the ethnic conflict has led to a publicly legitimated rejection of political patronage as a legitimate criterion for access to jobs. This has led in turn to an enhancement within the bureaucratic process of the value attached to educational credentials and meritocratic selection exams and, we might predict, to an even greater influence of these on the definition of quality in education.

CONCLUSION

In conclusion, then, the initial proposition which was derived from the diploma-disease thesis may be restated, then extended and refined in the light of experience in Sri Lanka over the past two decades.

The initial proposition and its converse were:

> the more that access to future resources (whether educational or economic) is restricted, the more the quality of the educational process will be determined by the criteria which determine future access.

> the more that access to future resources (whether educational or economic) is democratised, the less the quality of the educational process will be determined by the criteria which determine future access.

This may be refined as follows:

> the more that access to resources in the *immediate* future is democratised, the less will be the influence on the quality of the educational process of criteria which determine access.

This refined proposition is subject to the following caveat:

> if the possibilities for achievement in education at its highest level remain limited, then democratised access at a lower level will lead to an enhanced stratification of institutions at that level and the use of examination criteria to control access to stratified types of institution within that level

Finally,

> the legitimacy of access criteria will be accepted only for as long as people believe that they have some control over attaining them. Loss of a sense of personal control can lead to the social and political rejection of a criterion (e.g., political affiliation). This process of rejection enhances the importance attached to criteria over which one believes there is control (e.g., educational qualifications) and reinforces the influence of these on preceding values and behaviour.

REFERENCES

Alailima, P. (1991) *Labour Force—Current Situation and Future Prospects.* Colombo, Human Resources Development Council/World Bank.

Beeby, C.E. (1966) *The Quality of Education in Developing Countries.* Cambridge, Harvard University Press.

Cleverley, J. (1985) *The Schooling of China.* London, George Allen and Unwin.

Deraniyagala, C.P., Dore, R.P., and Little, A.W. (1978) *Qualifications and Employment in Sri Lanka.* Institute of Development Studies, Education Research Reports Rr 2, Sussex.

de Silva, C.R, and de Silva, D. (1990) *Education in Sri Lanka 1948–1988.* New Delhi, Navrang.

de Silva, W.A., Gunawardene, C., Jayeweera, S., Perera, L., Rupasinghe, S., and Wijetunge, S. (1991) *Extra-school Instruction, Social Equity and Educational Quality in Sri Lanka.* Report to the International Development Research Centre, Singapore.

de Silva, W.A., Gunawardene, C., and Rupasinghe, S. (1987) "The Case of Sri Lanka." In SLOG (ed.), *Why do Students Learn? A Six Country Study of Student Motivation.* Institute of Development Studies Research Reports Rr 17, Sussex.

Dore, R.P. (1976) *The Diploma Disease.* London, George Allen and Unwin.

Gunawardene, G.I.C. (1993) *Equity, External Efficiency and Free Education at Tertiary Level.* Inaugural Professorial Lecture, Open University of Sri Lanka, 19 May.

Hawes, Hugh, and Stephens, D. (1990) *Questions of Quality.* Harlow, Longman.

ILO (1971) *Matching Employment Opportunities and Expectations: A Programme of Action for Ceylon.* Geneva, ILO.

Jayeweera, S. (1989) "Extension of Educational Opportunity—the Unfinished Task." The C.W.W. Kannangara Memorial Lecture, 13 October, National Institute of Education.

Jayeweera, S. (1991) *Equity and Excellence in Education.* The J.E. Jayasuriya Memorial Lecture, 14 February, Colombo.

Lewin K.M. (1984) "Selection and Curriculum Reform." In J.C.P. Oxenham (ed.), *Education versus Qualifications?* London, George Allen and Unwin.

Lewin, K.M., and Little, A.W. (1984) "Examination Reform in Sri Lanka 1972–1982: Modernisation or Dependent Underdevelopment?" In K.M. Watson (ed.), *Dependence and Interdependence in Education.* London, Croom Helm.

Little, A.W. (1992) "The Diploma Disease: A Review of the Literature." In B.R. Clark and G. Neave (eds.), *The Encyclopaedia of Higher Education.* Oxford, Pergamon.

Lockheed, M., and Verspoor, A. (1991) *Improving Primary Education in Developing Countries.* Washington, D.C., World Bank.

Ministry of Education (1972) *Interim Report of the Committee to Inquire into and Report on Public Examinations at Secondary School level in Ceylon.* Colombo, Ministry of Education.

Moore, M.P. (1985) *The State and Peasant Politics in Sri Lanka.* Cambridge, Cambridge University Press.

Nadarajah, T. and Wijemanne, E.L. (1991) *Future Prospects and Employment Abroad.* Colombo, Human Resources Development Council/World Bank.

Nation, The (1971) 30 May.

Perera, J. (1985) *New Dimensions of Social Stratification in Rural Sri Lanka.* Colombo, Lake House.

Ranaweera, M. (1975) "Science at the Junior Secondary Level." *Bulletin of the Curriculum Development Centre no. 1.* Colombo.

Spencer, J. (1990) *A Sinhala Village in a Time of Trouble.* Delhi, Oxford University Press.

Sri Lanka National Task Force on Education (1990) *Education in Sri Lanka: the Past, the Present and the Future.* World Conference on Education for All, Jomtien, Thailand, 5–9 March.

Wijemanne, E.L. (1978) "Educational Reforms in Sri Lanka." *Division of Educational Policy and Planning Reports, Studies Series.* Paris, UNESCO.

Wilson, A.J. (1977) "Politics and Political Development since 1948." In K.M. de Silva (ed.), *Sri Lanka: A Survey.* London, C. Hurst and Co.

CHAPTER 9

The Search for Quality and Equality
The Case of Papua New Guinea

SHELDON G. WEEKS

INTRODUCTION

In this chapter, issues related to the relationship between quality of education and equality in educational opportunity are explored through a case study of educational development in Papua New Guinea. In the Papua New Guinea context "quality" has tended to be equated to "standard," or the outcome of a cycle of education as measured by performance on national examinations. It is interesting that one of the pioneers who focussed attention on issues of quality, C.E. Beeby (1966), was also one of the architects of the Papua New Guinea national education system as a member of the Weeden Commission (Weeden, Beeby, and Gris 1969). Recently the World Bank in its focus on quality has gone beyond mere outcomes to include the training of teachers, the management of the educational system, and a series of strategies designed to improve both what and how children learn (Lockheed and Verspoor 1990).

Equality as a national objective is enshrined in Papua New Guinea's Eight Point Improvement Plan developed in 1972. The second point is:

> More equal distribution of economic benefits, including movement towards equalisation of incomes among people and towards equalisation of services among different areas of the country. (King, Lee, and Warakai 1985, 453)

The five National Goals and Directive Principles developed at independence in 1975 were even more detailed. "Equality and participation" is the second goal, the others being "Integral human development," "National sovereignty and self-reliance," "Natural resources and environment," and "Papua New Guinea ways." The document declared its second goal to be:

> for all citizens to have an equal opportunity to participate in, and benefit from, the development of our country. (King, Lee, and Warakai, 1985, 454)

Internationally a plea that "quality" and "equality" must be viewed together, and strategies developed to achieve both at once, has been made under the slogan "Schooling for All" by Colclough and Lewin (1993). Unfortunately Papua New Guinea remains a long way from achieving these twin or unified objectives.

PAPUA NEW GUINEA

Background

Papua New Guinea lies just north of Australia, its former colonial master. It shares the island of New Guinea, the second largest island in the world after Greenland, with Irian Jaya, a province of Indonesia. Prior to World War I the northern half of Papua New Guinea was administered by Germany. Papua New Guinea achieved its independence in 1975, but remains dependent on Australia in trade and budgetary aid (Commonwealth of Australia 1991). Papua New Guinea has less that four million people spread out over nineteen provinces and the National Capital District (Port Moresby), including six provinces composed of islands, and five highlands provinces with 40 percent of the population. The urban centres are small, with around 150,000 in the National Capital District, 80,000 in Lae and 40,000 in Rabaul, and others scattered through smaller centres in each province, yet 85 percent of the population remains rural. Viewed from the Pacific, Papua New Guinea is a large country, both in area and population. Viewed from Asia, next to neighbouring Indonesia's area and 180 million people, Papua New Guinea is a small country (Turner 1990). (See the map in Figure 9.1.)

Papua New Guinea is one of the most ethnically diverse and fragmented countries in the world, with 850 languages, and 2 *lingua franca* (Melanesian pidgin or Tok Pisin, and Hiri Motu), while the official or national language is English. Most ethnic groups are small, dispersed, and isolated. No one ethnic group has dominated in Papua New Guinea,

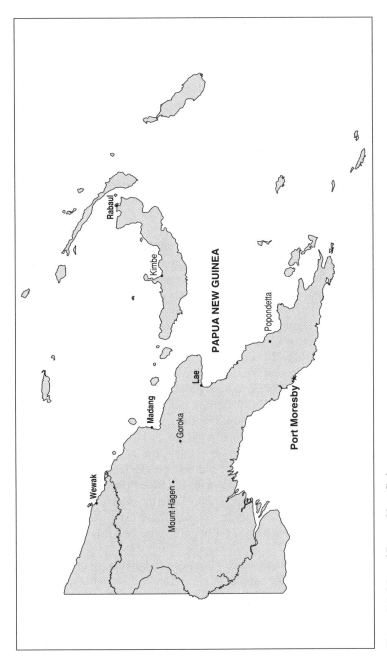

Figure 9.1. Map of Papua New Guinea

though certain groups in Central, Milne Bay, Madang, Morobe, and East New Britain Provinces have benefitted from earlier contact and a head start in formal education. Colonial development from the late 1890s until after World War II was limited to the coastal areas and islands, with many areas in the interior not being opened up until the 1960s. The first schools were opened in 1873 in Port Moresby by the London Missionary Society, 1875 in East New Britain by the Methodists, by the Lutherans in 1890 in Finschhafen, and in 1892 by the Anglicans in Milne Bay (Weeks and Guthrie 1984). Most educational development beyond primary, teacher-training, and trade schools has taken place since 1960. The University of Papua New Guinea in the National Capital District was opened in 1966, while the University of Technology in Lae opened in 1967.

Papua New Guinea remained predominantly an agriculture economy until the opening of Bougainville Copper Limited (BCL) in 1972 following eight years of exploration and construction (Oliver 1991, 121), though there were famous gold mines at Wau and Bulolo in Morobe Province in the 1930s. Coffee and tea were two cash crops in the highlands, and copra and cocoa in the lowlands and islands. Tropical timbers and immense marine resources have only begun to be exploited since independence. During the 1980s copper and gold mines have been developed at Ok Tedi in Western Province, Porgera and Mt. Kare in Enga, and Misima in Milne Bay Province; others are planned on Lihir Island in New Ireland Province, at Wau in Morobe Province, and in other locations. The minerals boom has made Papua New Guinea one of the wealthiest countries in the Third World (Dorney 1990). However, the exploitation of such wealth, mainly developed by foreign multinationals, even when the Papua New Guinea government has shares, has led to environmental degradation and social conflict: for example, the tailings dam at Ok Tedi broke and has never been rebuilt and now the Ok Tedi is a "dead river" and the pollution is spreading down the Fly River. The conflicts in North Solomons Province over who benefits from the mine at Panguna, and demands for compensation for past damage, have led to a disastrous civil war, starting in 1988 and by mid-1993 still unresolved (May and Spriggs 1990, Oliver 1991).

Though Papua New Guinea, because of its thriving export economy, has not experienced the agonies of a Structural Adjustment Programme, it has suffered during the "lost decade" of the 1980s in ways similar to that described for Latin America (Gomes 1992). As in Latin America educational expenditure has decreased, enrolment increased, the status of teachers and their incentives declined. Reforms were superficial and marginal, but "there are financial resources for deep educational change" while issues of equality "and quality were, in general, seriously neglected and postponed" (Gomes 1992, 4, 7). These are some of the issues we will examine in more detail in this chapter.

Education System

The education system in Papua New Guinea has developed in a number of unusual ways. Expansion over the last two decades has been significant, but controlled. During the 1980s the number of new schools and places for students at both the primary and secondary level has hardly kept up with population growth. In 1990 it was estimated that 73 percent of the age group was enrolled at the first level (grades 1 through 6) and 16 percent at the second level (grades 7 through 10). Though enrolments in first-level institutions have grown from 208,419 pupils in 1,557 primary schools in 1970 to 403,000 pupils in 2,510 primary schools in 1990, the attrition rate between grades 1 and 6 has been rising to 45 percent. It is evident that the Gross Enrolment Rate has not improved dramatically over the past decade. (See Figure 9.2.)

Controlled educational expansion has been justified on the grounds that it avoids contributing to social problems: migration and the over-production of unemployed school-leavers, while permitting the maintenance of at least the appearance of quality. The educational system in Papua New Guinea has been kept in check because an explosion based on private schools never occurred as was predicted at independence (Weeks 1975); resources were never allocated to achieve rapid expansion; and a decision was made to employ qualified teachers rather than achieve rapid expansion through hiring unqualified teachers. That a proportion of the national elite can send their children to international schools has not helped this situation, because the elite lack a commitment to the development of a national education system that can deliver both quality and equality (Smith and Bray 1985).

During the "lost decade" of the 1980s Papua New Guinea also suffered a decline in resources allocated to education, with expenditure in real terms dropping as much as 39 percent between 1978 and 1988 (Blyth 1991). Between 1983 and 1991 the expenditure per pupil dropped from K270 to K208, while the expenditure per capita went down from K32 to K26 (National Department of Education 1991, 13). The reason for this decline was not any Structural Adjustment Programme (SAP), but the impact of theories of development on Papua New Guinean planners:

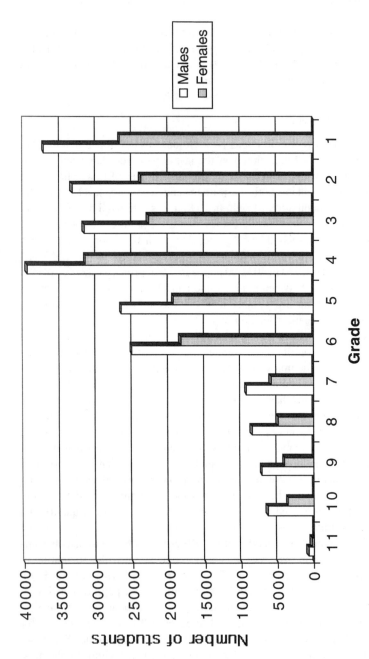

Figure 9.2. Male and Female Participation in the Papua New Guinea School System, First- to Eleventh-Grade Progression

that because of estimated rates of return it would be more efficient to invest in primary education, hold secondary education constant, and reduce tertiary (Psacharopoulos 1981, Gannicott 1987, McGavin and Ross 1988). The tragedy was that the redistribution to primary education never occurred (Weeks 1993). Curtin has also noted that this approach to educational development, boosting primary and curtailing tertiary education, is now being justified on old arguments based on "rates of return" and being followed by the African National Congress (ANC) in the Republic of South Africa (1993):

> [The ANC's advisers' use of educational planning theories] to emphasize only primary schooling, and introduce increased "cost recovery," seems doubly suspect in a country like South Africa. For it is the children of the already highly educated and affluent whites who will monopolize secondary and higher education resources under a cost recovery regime and therefore be enabled to compete most effectively for employment in the new non-racial South Africa (13)

Education in Papua New Guinea was seen as a privilege, not a right, and education was perceived as a luxury (consumption versus investment). What these views ignored was the need for expatriate replacement and the resulting taxes paid by tertiary educated human resources (Curtin 1991). The consequence of restricting the education system is an increased dependence on expatriates and Australia in Papua New Guinea.

Under the Five National Goals and Eight Points or "directive principles" the rhetoric of development in Papua New Guinea was one of equality (Avalos 1993). Equality of educational opportunity, regardless of gender, religion, or place of origin, was "signalled" to the people while the reality fell far short (to borrow a concept from Fuller 1991). Decentralization to the provinces with community support and control with self-reliance through Boards of Management (primary schools) and Boards of Governors (secondary schools) was meant to be the pattern of development. Resource equalisation through redressing inequalities by allowing only a limited number of new high schools in disadvantaged provinces/areas, and with a freeze on new high schools in advantaged provinces/areas, has had the consequence of restricting educational development (Bray 1984b). This happened because insufficient resources have been allocated to support the expansion of second-level schooling.

The most serious bottleneck resulting from restricted educational development over the last twenty years has occurred at the end of grade 10, where students are selected for the elite academic preparatory institutions called national high schools, or, if they qualified, go on for further training in up to sixty "tertiary institutions" which prepare teachers, technicians, nurses, agricultural officers, and so on. At independence there were only two national high schools, and two more were opened soon after independence. The mid-term review of the 1976–1980 educational plan called for the opening of one new national high school every year until there was one in every province (Rogers 1979). Instead, the lid has been kept on, and none built, in spite of the fact that both employers and tertiary institutions would like to recruit after twelve years of education instead of ten.

This bottleneck at the end of grade 10 has been exacerbated by the two universities' phasing out of their preliminary year (equivalent to national high school). One Australian aid project designed to help solve this problem has had the consequence of helping to build up institutions in Australia, while failing to address the problem of capacity and institutional building in Papua New Guinea. The best Papua New Guineans who qualify for national high schools are sent to boarding schools in Australia, and this expenditure of A$8 million is called "aid." Out of this also comes the John Crawford Scholarship scheme, which sends selected Papua New Guineans to do their further studies in Australian universities, another aid project that benefits Australia and does nothing to build institutional capacity in Papua New Guinea. Even the programme to train staff for primary teachers' colleges takes place in Queensland rather than at the University of Papua New Guinea, another example of aid's rebounding to benefit Australia (Commonwealth of Australia 1991, 50–51). These projects may also have serious unintended consequences through the influence of Australian culture and curricula on a future generation of Papua New Guinean elite.

CONSTRAINTS ON EQUALITY AND QUALITY IN EDUCATIONAL DEVELOPMENT

The National Department of Education was the first of the main-line departments (Agriculture, Health, Provincial Affairs, and so on) to devolve powers from the centre, with the establishment of District Education Boards in the 1960s (now Provincial Education Boards), long before formal decentralization in 1978. In spite of decentralization, those that were ahead have stayed ahead, partly because the formulae devised to promote equality through assisting the disadvantaged and constraining the advantaged did not work (Bray 1984b, Weeks 1989). The way in which the Minimum Unconditional Grant (MUG) was set based on 1976 "values" tended to benefit the already advantaged provinces, while the National Fiscal Commission, established to compensate for these inequalities, had its funds scaled down and eventually became defunct (Regan 1985, 136–138). The commitment to face problems of inequalities was present in the rhetoric, but not in the reality (Weeks 1991).

A major review of the educational system in 1991 tried to find a way to achieve expansion through reorganization (National Department of Education 1991). The old 6–4–2 education system, it was decided, should be transformed into a 3–6–4 (2–2) pyramid by adding an "elementary school" at the bottom, extending existing primary schools through grade 8 (taking grades 7 and 8 from the provincial high schools), and making most secondary schools two-year institutions (grades 9 and 10 only), thus doubling enrolments overnight, while allowing at least one high school in each province to take students through grades 11 and 12. The new "elementary school" would begin with at least one year of preparatory classes in vernacular literacy, with a bridging to English as the medium of instruction during the next two years. The elementary schools could be located at existing primary schools or sited separately in the community. In 1993 the National Education Reform was launched in two provinces ("Managing Education Reform . . ." 1993). Whether the provinces have the administrative capacity to implement sweeping reforms constitutes a serious constraint to these plans (Weeks 1989). Is it visionary to plan a new level of teacher training when the existing training of primary school teachers is curtailed and unable to provide the number of teachers required for expansion?

Economic

The resource constraints that education has faced during the 1980s were caused by government policies. The stage was set by the sector reviews under the Michael Somare government in 1984 (Roakeina 1984; see also their justification in Guthrie 1985) and continued by Paias Wingti when he became prime minister following a vote of no confidence in November 1985: except that Wingti now wanted to take from education to develop agriculture! Wingti was returned in a general election in August 1987, but Rabbie Namaliu became prime minister in July 1988 following a successful vote of no confidence. The theoretical basis for past educational policies was questioned by the new advisor on investment policies in the Department of Finance and Planning: it was now deemed sound to invest in education (Curtin 1991). Namaliu was only slowly able to redirect resources to education, but not until 1990. He lost the general election in 1992 and Paias Wingti returned as prime minister.

The development of education in Papua New Guinea is also constrained by serious and expensive communication problems. Much of the country is composed of rural, remote, and isolated communities, with low population densities. There has been a general failure to invest adequately in an infrastructure which would allow for efficient communication (such as two-way radios for remote schools, renewal of provincial government boats, or helicopter visits for inspectors, or ways to distribute materials to these schools). Schools in these locations have trouble attracting and holding teachers, are generally small (level 2 or 3 schools with only a few teachers), and lack the facilities found in larger "station" (patrol posts are mission centres) and urban schools (Gibson 1991). Because of a variety of factors the small schools tend to have the worst results on the primary school-leaving examination, and as a consequence few if any of these children attain entrance to high school, furthering the inequalities between stations and towns and rural and remote areas. These divisions threaten to build a Papua New Guinea which is fragmented between educated urban residents and an undereducated rural mass.

The cost of building provincial high schools has also resulted in a degree of unequal development. For example, new high schools, beginning in 1974, were to be self-help rural day schools (Guthrie 1980). This resulted in anomalies, like students from Pangia in the Southern Highlands Province being allocated to Ialibu High School, and expected to walk up to 50 kilometres to school (Weeks 1987a). During the 1980s most of the original self-help rural day high schools were converted into boarding high schools, but initially the national government refused to pay for this conversion, so it became a provincial responsibility, one that the poorer provinces struggled to achieve.

The supply of teachers has always been a serious constraint. In 1990 there were over 2,130 teachers in provincial high schools of whom 320 were expatriates (mainly volunteers). It is not known how many primary school teachers had been promoted to teach the lower grades in the provincial high schools, but due to shortages the number is probably in the hundreds. The volunteers (who are usually less experienced and, if qualified to teach, were restricted to lower grades) and untrained high school teachers tend to be placed in the rural high schools, thus perpetuating the divisions in quality between rural and urban schools.

The lower grades are overcrowded, but because of the high rate of dropping out, the resulting overall teacher–pupil ratio is deceptive (it was 1:32 in 1990). The inability to plan for and train primary school teachers for a growing school system is the key factor constraining any effort to achieve universal primary education (often a community builds a school, but no teachers are available). The primary teacher training colleges used to produce over 1,000 students a year, but by 1991 this rate had dropped to 800, and only 500 new graduates are expected in 1993 because of a reorganization from two to three years for the course. Will this raise standards or is it another example of "qualification escalation" as described by Dore (1976). Financial constraints and poor planning caused three years to be squeezed into the "space" occupied previously by a two-year programme, causing the marked reduction in the number of graduates. If there had been a genuine commitment to universal primary education it would have begun with a planned expansion of the eight primary teacher training colleges in the 1980s.

Political

Politicians in Papua New Guinea have had a long-term commitment to both universal primary education and free education, passing many resolutions in support of eight years' basic education since independence. But in the game of vote getting and political promise making, free education has taken priority over universal primary education. The links between fee-free primary education and quality and equality are not comprehended or an issue. People are not aware of the contradiction between the different levels of implementation: that the resources directed to enable fee-free education negate universal education is not important. The political platforms have included both universal and fee-free education, while national politicians have tried to introduce only fee-free education since 1980. The steady rise in the rate of dropping out from primary school over the past decade suggests that there is not general grassroots support for universal primary education. Politicians have not been successful in the past in achieving universal primary education because the resources were not available at the scale required, while decentralization and the Organic Law on provincial governments had made fees a provincial function, and therefore provinces could continue to support fees even when the national government wanted education to be free (Bray 1983). The issue of fee-free education became a political football tossed back and forth between different authorities. It was introduced as a "scholarship scheme" that took the form as flat per-student grants to schools under the last Namaliu government at a cost of K2.6 million, but the Wingti government was determined to introduce fee-free education, and in January 1993 released K20.5 million to support the new subsidy scheme (Miria 1993, 3). In reality there is no such thing as free education, as all aspects of education cost something (salaries, materials, equipment, buildings, uniforms, and so on). At a time when only 73 percent of the age group (based on estimates) is in school, an investment in free education means that the government will not be able to provide for the new teachers and support required to extend schools to populations that are still not properly serviced. Free education at this time will only benefit those communities that already have schools, and further disadvantage those who do not (for a detailed study of the problem of unequal distribution of schools see Weeks 1985b). Though fees do not cover more than 25 percent of costs, their removal could also erode current efforts to improve the quality of education.

Language policy can have a key influence on both quality and equality in a Third World school system, a factor that is generally forgotten. For example it is not a significant variable in *Educating All the Children* (Colclough with Lewin 1993), and where it is included, the significance of learning to read and write in the mother tongue for issues of quality and quantity is often ignored (e.g., Messec 1990). In Papua New Guinea, politicians had declared English as the medium of instruction in schools until the policy was altered in 1988. With 850 distinct languages, planners and policymakers could not conceive of any way vernacular could be incorporated into the school system. Efforts following self-government in 1973 to promote mother-tongue instruction were rejected by the government, and the first five-year education plan, finally approved in 1976, made English the official language of instruction (National Department of Education 1976). A research project in North Solomons Province in 1978 sponsored by the Educational Research Unit of the University of Papua New Guinea set the foundation for a new approach, what became known as the Viles Tok Ples Skuls or Tok Ples PreSchools (Ahai 1989, Ahai and Faraclas 1993). By focussing on preschools the policy conflict with the government was avoided, because preschools were not then under the Government's jurisdiction (Delpit and Kemelfield 1985). Vernacular preschools were introduced in Enga and Oro through projects assisted by the Educational Research Unit (Stringer and Faraclas 1987) and have since spread to most provinces, with extensive support from the Summer Institute for Linguistics. The evidence suggests that if children learn to read and write in their own language first, they will then do better in a national language when they continue their schooling as the skills learned in the mother tongue are transferred (Limage 1990). It is also assumed that the increased understanding that results, besides improving academic performance, will help to reduce wastage and to improve the quality of schooling "from the bottom up": vernacular preschools thus should be the foundation of any strategy to improve the quality of education and to promote equality. The 1991 review of education endorsed vernacular preschools and they are now integrated into the new elementary schools, but whether what was a grassroots movement from the bottom up will be properly sustained and supported from the centre and top down is difficult to predict.

Politicians and administrators reveal their commitment to equality through their policies on selection. In Papua New Guinea, after access to school which is now nearly universal and followed by automatic promotion (which is eroded by a 45 percent attrition rate), the critical sorting of students between the "push-outs" and those who can go to high school occurs at the end of grade 6. There have been various efforts to make selection democratic. In the early 1970s it was recognized that primary schools were not of equal quality, that some were more advantaged than others, and therefore a "quota system" in high school selection would promote equality of educational opportunity (McNamara 1971). A brief flirtation with "community selection" in 1973 was followed by a straight "quota," with a transition rate of approximately one-third of the grade 6 students to grade 7 (it varied from province to province—see Guthrie and Kemelfield 1980, Bray 1985b). The implications of various forms of high school selection are considered in the section below on the role of the state.

Social

A number of key "social constraints" are present in Papua New Guinean society that work to block the achievement of equality of educational opportunity and quality in the provision of schooling. The fragmentation of people into many small communities and language groups is in some areas responsible for a low demand for education. This is particularly apparent in areas where the provision of an infrastructure (roads, schools, health centres, etc.) and social and economic development is limited. Consider, for example, the Eastern Highlands Province where the main developments have been along the Highlands Highway with access and coffee cultivation, where the demand for education is not being met; while in more remote areas the supply is greater than the demand and under-enrolment is serious (Weeks 1985a). People in underdeveloped rural and remote areas have difficulty articulating their demands for development; they remain underdeveloped and caught up in a vicious cycle of neglect (particularly true in the less-developed districts scattered throughout Papua New Guinea, like Tapini, Central Province; Pomio, East New Britain Province; Porgera, Enga Province; Wosera, East Sepik Province; Kantiba, Gulf Province; Amanab, West Sepik Province; and so on).

Another serious constraint on developing equality and quality is the high rate of attrition between grades 1 and 6. Dropping-out rates from primary school have been rising steadily. For those starting grade 1 in different years it has been as follows: in 1971 it was 27 percent; 1975, 31 percent; for those starting in 1980 it had risen to 37 percent; and for the 1984 cohort it was 45 percent (Tawaiyole and Gibson 1989). Bray's study (1984a) of dropping out surveys a number of causes, including disillusion with schooling and problems of access to school and the rural infrastructure, through to clan fighting, family factors, nutrition and malnutrition, and the costs of schooling. Between these and other studies there is no shortage of recommendations to deal with attrition. However, the "will" to do something about it on the part of planners, administrators, and politicians has been missing, perhaps because it is seen as a blessing, because wastage during the first cycle reduces the demand for places in secondary schools. It also serves to postpone the attainment of universal primary education and an equitable system well into the next century.

The path to equality of educational opportunity in many education systems can be judged by the proportion of females enroled in primary and secondary school and their transition rate between the two levels. In Papua New Guinea the enrolment of females in schools has improved dramatically since independence (Weeks 1985b). The presence of females in school is constrained in many societies by cultural factors, and Papua New Guinea is no exception. In the matrilineal societies, and some coastal cultural groups with a long history of contact, the enrolment of females in schools is nearly equal to males. In a majority of the patrilineal societies in Papua New Guinea female enrolments lag way behind, and where they have begun to achieve equality at the primary level, they still are a minority in the provincial high schools (Tawaiyole and Weeks 1988). The main vehicle of discrimination against females occurs as by-product of the process of selection of students for high school, which is covered in the next section (Weeks 1987b).

Role of the State

Policymakers, both politicians and administrators in the nineteen provinces and the national government and National Department of Education, have established broad guidelines in relation to educational development in Papua New Guinea. Perhaps the most significant is the Organic Law on decentralization, which divides functions into national, provincial, and concurrent (Bray 1984b). The national government is responsible for standards, particularly the core curriculum, the provision of materials through the Curriculum Development Unit, both in-service and preservice training courses, and the core financing of education. The nineteen provincial governments are responsible for planning and developing the first two levels of education, and have full responsibility for non-formal education (Anderson 1981, Ahai and Weeks 1991). The National Department of Education has been able to maintain formal policies concerning streaming by ability groups and corporal punishment in schools (both forbidden), and control over age of entry, the structure of the education system, and so on.

The national government controlled policies concerning high school selection until challenged by the provinces following decentralization in 1978 and a major study in North Solomons Province (Guthrie and Kemelfield 1980). The provinces then took over high school selection, and by 1980 there were nearly as many different techniques of high school selection as provinces (Bray 1982). Selection plays the role of gate keeping, and a tension exists between equality and quality: if the pendulum is weighted towards equality of educational opportunity, measures are taken to ensure that the same promotion of females is selected to the next level and that there is a fair representation of people from rural and remote areas. Papua New Guinea's National Goals and Directive Principles call for equality of opportunity. Unfortunately systems of affirmative action are complicated to administer and open to accusations of abuse. In the case of high school selection they also result in students' being selected to fill places in high schools who would not have been admitted solely on the criteria of their performance on the primary school-leaving examination, and they take places that might have gone to "better" students (usually urban and male). The urban elite, who are the decision makers, prefer a so-called merit system because it is easier to administer and for the unstated reason that it benefits their children (Urimo 1985, Weeks 1987b). Equality is sacrificed to the expediency of "quality," a decision endorsed by most high school teachers, who prefer not to struggle with students who require remedial teaching (something the education system has failed to provide for).

The Achilles heel of an education system lies in the selection process. It can too easily be manipulated to benefit the children of the privileged. The swing of the pendulum of educational fashion from community-based education and relevance to "standards" at the start of the 1980s in Papua New Guinea was accompanied by a spread of provincial high school selection systems based on so-called merit. The consequence of this policy in many places has been to deny further education to females and to children of poorly educated parents. A study in the Western Province found that many "bright" children in small schools were not being selected for high school, while comparatively "dull" pupils in town schools were, because they have had a better education and other social advantages (Gibson and Weeks 1990). There are three groups that are losing out now and will continue to be deprived in the 1990s: females, children in remote rural areas, and the children of poorly educated parents. These factors combine to present an extreme picture of disadvantage. In some places urban female pupils have ten times the chance of getting into high school as rural females. It has been found that in some rural areas the only children being selected to go on to high school are the children of outsiders: teachers, agricultural officers, health workers, pastors, and so on. Conflict between rural and urban Papua New Guineans will intensify in the future unless something is done to resolve this problem.

Another intervention by the national government, designed to improve both the quality and quantity of formal education, was the introduction in the mid 1970s of provincial educational planning. It did not become official and "take off" until it was made, for 1982, a prerequisite to receive core funding; then only the Western Highlands Province missed out on its grants to primary education (Bray 1984b). The cadre of educational planners have generally lacked a commitment to both universal primary education and quality education. Some provincial governments are not committed to the expansion of first-level education: instead they have focused on expanding high schools to the detriment of primary schools. This is particularly true in a few highlands provinces. There has been a general failure to be committed to the philosophy of "the last first" (Matane 1986). Provincial Divisions of Education have not demonstrated that they have the commitment or concern to implement ways to improve their small rural and remote schools, yet there is no shortage of strategies designed to assist these schools. If they are not acted on, the gap between rural and urban life chances will widen. Even in East New Britain, one of the best managed provinces in Papua New Guinea, educational planning has failed to realize its potential (Weeks 1989).

Educational Innovations

Most but not all educational innovations in Papua New Guinea have been initiated from the "centre" (Bray 1984b, Weeks 1990b). Educational innovations are supported during a time of economic growth and expansion, but shrink during a period of contracting resources. One example of this is the Secondary Schools Community Extension Project (SSCEP), which received considerable attention in the 1980s (Crossley and Vulliamy 1986). Though SSCEP was approved by the Cabinet and endorsed by the Matane Report (1986), it was a casualty of declining resources during the mid 1980s *and* a lack of support from the Curriculum Development Unit where staff turned their attention to other "fashions" in education, such as vernacular literacy (see also Crossley 1994). Declining resources was only one of a number of factors that led to a simplification of the innovation, when what probably was required instead was a system of teacher incentives to ensure the success of the "expansion phase," or the infusion of the innovation through the education system, but this never occurred. SSCEP's unique aspect of integrating between academic or core subjects and practical or nonacademic, noncore subjects (Integrated Teaching Projects or ITPs) was successful as long as it was supported from the centre during the two pilot stages between 1978 and 1985. SSCEP also encouraged the development of "outstations" or school satellites, developed effective in-service training packages, and promoted students, demonstrating what they had learned at school in village live-ins or what was called "community extension." SSCEP was significant in that it reaffirmed the National Department of Education"s policy against streaming by ability groups in provincial high schools and that it developed a unitary approach to integrated learning that benefitted both those students who would go on to the university and those who would go "back to the village." In this respect SSCEP constituted a significant innovation that supported both quality and equality (Crossley and Weeks 1987). Though SSCEP or "curriculum extension," its new name, was endorsed by the 1991 National Education Reform (National Department of Education, 1991, 181–183) it remains "voluntary" and survives in only a few schools.

RELATIONSHIP BETWEEN DEMOCRACY AND DEVELOPMENT

Though the Papua New Guinea experience fits that of dependency theory and supports the model of enclave development (reliance on mining, energy, and timber resources sectors), the pattern of development has also served to intensify inequalities. The elite, as elsewhere in the world, can afford (often with the support of their employers) to educate their children in foreign schools, either overseas or in international schools within Papua New Guinea (Smith and Bray 1985). The civil war in Bougainville, which has dragged on since 1988, has not helped this situation, as tremendous resources have been ploughed into the conflict instead of going to strengthening social services, including education, and infrastructural development.

Two key examples of the lack of commitment to develop equality of educational opportunity and to promote the expansion of quality education are found, first, in the failure to implement nonformal education since it was backed in Education I in 1976 (Anderson 1981, Ahai and Weeks 1991) and second, in the failure to resolve the grade 11 bottleneck (even though some "pseudo" national high schools evolved). The frustrations and grievances of the grade 10 push-outs are perhaps one of the key factors contributing to the escalating law-and-order problems in the country (though preliminary studies show that those who never went to school or who had only primary education predominate in crime statistics, as quoted in Avalos 1993). The "youth anger" is fuelled not only by the blocking of their potential careers because of the limited opportunities for further education after grade 10, but also because wealthy expatriates increase their visibility while hiding behind more and more fortified compounds, the most recent example being that constructed for the Australian High Commission in Port Moresby. Curtin has already pointed out how restricted development of tertiary education has slowed down expatriate replacement (1991).

THE FUTURE

It is one thing to expand the system; it is another to improve its quality. The flight of the children of the educated elite to international schools (a constitutional right) will only be checked when the education offered in the nation's primary schools improves to the point where it becomes unattractive for a family to meet the high cost of international schooling (a problem not unknown, for example, in Australia or the U.K.). Yet will the nation's schools ever improve while the past products of the education system continue to turn against it? Their commitment and leadership to improve the nation's schools is needed if they are to change for the better. It is currently being denied to the local school system.

In the National Capital District, the local primary schools suffer from neglect, overcrowding, and underdevelopment. There are now an average of 45 pupils per teacher (subtracting nonteaching heads) in the National Capital District, while the national average is only 1:32. This overcrowding makes these schools most unattractive to parents who want the best for their children (the ratio is 1:25 in international schools). Add to this a general absence of special facilities (resource centres, libraries, in some schools even staff rooms or canteens), shortage of teachers' houses, the lack of maintenance, and a deteriorating environment (many schools are unable even to control erosion) and the picture is not good. Yet the schools in the National Capital District continue to have the overall best results in the nation. This is not surprising as success, as determined by examinations, is related to factors other than the school situation. Parental support has been found to be a significant variable in the past (Pope and Jones 1974, Tuppen 1981).

How to develop the nation's secondary system will perhaps be the most controversial issue of the 1990s. Papua New Guinea has developed a unique "unitary secondary system of education" (Crossley and Weeks 1987). This will be increasingly under attack during the next decade. There will be calls for a dual system, with elite academic secondary schools for the few and broad, practical community-based institutions for the majority. These second-class high schools may well be rejected by the majority as an inferior system. Yet such rejection does not solve the dilemma of how to expand a unitary high-school system rapidly so that it benefits more than the present 16 percent, or planned 32 percent of the age group. This expansion can only be done by a tremendous injection of resources in both financial and teacher power. The funds may be available for such expansion over the next decade if future governments are willing to make the commitment, but it should not be forgotten that education alone, even technical education, does not create jobs (Foster 1965, Foster 1975). Income-earning opportunities through employment or self-employment result from a vibrant economy and entrepreneurs.

Papua New Guinea, like many other countries, is in a bind that will not be resolved for many decades. Scattered populations in most areas require that second-level institutions provide boarding facilities. Boarding high schools now cost over US$2.5 million to build. The standard expected requires laboratories, practical-skills and home-economics classrooms, libraries, and so on—facilities that are not available at primary schools. The call for "tops" on primary schools, adding grades 7 and 8, is reasonable, but tends to ignore the high costs of facilities required at secondary schools. If tops are added to primary schools the same type of secondary education cannot be provided. These upper primary schools may become inferior and the standards would decline: as a result parents may eventually reject them, even if a province can afford them. In 1978 East New Britain introduced grade 7 in primary schools, only to find that the whole provincial budget would have to go to education if they continued to implement the scheme, so it was then dropped (Weeks 1989).

One might predict that towards the end of the decade a new type of community high school will evolve in those areas with sufficiently high density of population to support day high schools. Day high schools were tried after independence and failed nearly everywhere in rural areas. In the 1990s day high schools will become a concept whose time has arrived. They have already been called for in North Solomons Province (Division of Educational Research 1992).

THE PAPUA NEW GUINEA EDUCATIONAL REFORM OF 1991

The 1991 National Education Reform can be viewed as an attempt to promote equality by restructuring the education system in order to enable rapid expansion: village vernacular feeder schools or "elementary schools" for preparatory classes and grades 1 and 2, extending primary schools from grade 3 through grade 8, doubling of the number of students reaching Grade 10, and increased access to grade 11 (National Department of Education 1991, Tetaga 1992). A variation which was endorsed by the interim government of the North Solomons has not been accepted by the national government. It called for preparatory grades through grade 7, followed by community-based provincial high schools with grades 8 through 12, so that there would be only two levels of teachers (instead of four) and the nineteen provincial governments might then have the administrative capacity to implement the plan (Momis 1991).

Unfortunately, the National Education Reform does not promise to deliver either quality or equality. The planned expansion of the education system is occurring at the same time the output of the primary teacher-training colleges has been reduced, measures which will result in intense shortages of qualified teachers and in the future a dependence on either unqualified teachers or imported expatriates (either volunteers or expensive contract officers). The addition of "tops" on selected primary schools (grades 7 and 8) and provincial high schools (grades 11 and 12) will require the allocation of resources that have yet to be committed to support educational expansion, yet the priority to expanding at the "top" before educational opportunities have been evenly distributed across disadvantaged districts will continue to delay equality of access to primary schooling. An additional danger exists in the cry for "centres of excellence," where university preparatory courses will be available for a minority of students, while the majority will be streamed into inferior vocational courses.

CONCLUSION

Papua New Guinea began the decade of independence, starting in the early 1970s, with a firm commitment to "equal opportunity" and "equalisation of services," objectives enshrined in the Five National Goals and the Eight Point Plan. Since independence in 1976, neither a significant quantitative expansion nor accompanying qualitative initiatives have occurred. Though the economic resources to support an integrated development of both equality of educational opportunity for females, people in rural and remote areas, and other deprived groups exists, the political will and the commitment of the bureaucracy to confront these problems has been missing. Universal primary education (UPE) in Papua New Guinea remains an elusive goal, though the first plan for UPE was announced in 1958. The steps required to promote schooling for all have never been taken: increasing the budget for education, expanding the flow of trained teachers, developing local government capacity to plan and develop new schools, and creating a system of education which wins the commitment of children and their parents so that they will remain in school instead of dropping out. The failure to opt for lower-cost community-based day high schools has meant that the opportunity to reduce cost while raising quality and promoting equality of opportunity has so far been lost. The absence of a commitment to universal education has been fuelled by the four fears: fear of lowering standards; fear of diluting an elite educational system; fear of the high costs of schooling for all; and fear of the consequences of an "overproduction" of educated people. Unfortunately, the education reform of the 1990s has yet to demonstrate that it will help to solve these problems or serve to promote both quality and equality.

REFERENCES

Ahai, Naihuwo (1989) *Report on the Establishment of the North Solomons Tokples Skuls.* Waigani, Language and Literacy Department, University of Papua New Guinea.

Ahai, Naihuwo, and Weeks, Sheldon G. (eds.) (1991) *Non-Formal Education, Working Group 6, Education Sector Study.* Waigani, Division of Educational Research Special Report 5, National Research Institute.

Ahai, Naihuwo, and Faraclas, Nicholas (1993) "Rights and Expectations in an Age of 'Debt Crisis': Literacy and Integral Human Development in Papua New Guinea." In Peter Freebody and A.R. Welch (eds.), *Knowledge, Culture and Power: International Perspectives on Literacy as Policy and Practice.* London, Falmer.

Anderson, Bernard (ed.) (1981) *The Right to Learn: The Neglect of Non-Formal Education in Papua New Guinea.* Waigani, Research Branch, National Department of Education.

Avalos, Beatrice (1993) "Ideology, Policy and Educational Change in Papua New Guinea." *Comparative Education* 29(3): 275–91.

Bacchus, Kazim (1984) *A Review and Analysis of Educational 'Needs' at the Secondary Level in Papua New Guinea.* Waigani, Educational Research Unit Report 48, University of Papua New Guinea.

Beeby, C.E. (1966) *The Quality of Education in Developing Countries.* Cambridge, Harvard University Press.

Blyth, C. (1991) *Government Expenditure in Papua New Guinea: Human Capital Formation.* Port Moresby, Institute of National Affairs.

Bray, Mark (1982) "High School Selection Policies in 1981: The Impact of Decentralisation." *Papua New Guinea Journal of Education* 18(2): 155–67.

Bray, Mark (1983) "The Politics Of Free Education in Papua New Guinea." *International Journal of Educational Development* 2(3): 281–88.

Bray, Mark (1984a) *Dropping Out from Community Schools: The Extent, Causes and Possible Remedies.* Waigani, Educational Research Unit Report 49, University of Papua.

Bray, Mark (1984b) *Educational Planning in a Decentralised System: The Papua New Guinean Experience.* Waigani and Sydney, University of Papua New Guinea Press and Sydney University Press.

Bray, Mark (1985a) "Decentralization and Equality of Educational Opportunity in Papua New Guinea." In Jon Lauglo and Martin McLean (eds.), *The Control of Education: International Perspectives on the Centralization–Decentralization Debate.* London, Heinemann Educational Books.

Bray, Mark (1985b) "High School Selection Policies in Less Developed Countries and the Quest for Equity: Conflicting Objectives and Opposing Pressures. *Comparative Education Review* 29(2): 216–31.

Chapman, David W., and Carrier, Carol A. (1990) "Improving Educational Quality in Developing Countries." In David W. Chapman and Carol A. Carrier (eds.), *Improving Educational Quality: A Global Perspective.* London, Greenwood Press.

Colclough, Christopher, with Lewin, Keith (1991) *Educating All the Children: Strategies for Primary Education in the South.* Oxford, Clarendon Press.

Commonwealth of Australia (1991) *Australia's Relations with Papua New Guinea.* Canberra, Senate Publishing and Printing Unit.

Crossley, Michael (1994) The Organisation and Management of Curriculum Development in Papua New Guinea. *International Review of Education,* forthcoming.

Crossley, Michael, and Vulliamy, Graham (1986) *The Policy of SSCEP: Context and Development.* Waigani, Educational Research Unit Report 54, University of Papua New Guinea.

Crossley, Michael, and Weeks, Sheldon (1987) "Curriculum as an International Commodity: Dilemmas of Relevance and Change." *Directions* 9(1): 42–57. Suva, Fiji, University of the South Pacific.

Cummings, Richard (1982) *A Review of Research on SSCEP: 1978–1981.* Waigani, Educational Research Unit Report 41, University of Papua New Guinea.

Curtin, Timothy (1991) *The Economics of Public Investment in Education in Papua New Guinea.* Waigani, Faculty of Education, Occasional Paper 1, University of Papua New Guinea.

Curtin, Timothy (1993) "The Political Economy of Education in South Africa." *African Affairs* : 3–19.

Delpit, Lisa, and Kemelfield, Graeme (1985) *An Evaluation of the Village Tok Ples Skul Scheme in the North Solomons Province.* Waigani, Educational Research Unit Report 51, University of Papua New Guinea.

Division of Educational Research (1992) *Education and Reconstruction in North Solomons Provinces: Proceedings of the Hutjena Workshop 26 September–*

6 October 1991. Waigani, Division of Educational Research, National Research Institute.

Dore, Ronald (1976) *The Diploma Disease: Education, Qualification and Development.* Berkeley, University of California Press.

Dorney, Sean (1990) *Papua New Guinea: People, Politics and History since 1975.* Sydney, Random House

Foster, Philip (1965) "The Vocational School Fallacy in Development Planning." In C.A Anderson. and M.J. Bowman (eds.), *Education and Economic Development.* Chicago, Aldine Press.

Foster, Philip (1975) "Dilemmas of Education Development: What We Might Learn from the Past." In John Brammall and Ron May (eds.), *Education in Melanesia.* Canberra, Australian National University, 13–38.

Fuller, Bruce (1991) *Growing-Up Modern: The Western State Builds Third-World Schools.* London, Routledge.

Gannicott, K. (1987) *Education in Papua New Guinea: A Study in Wasted Resources.* Canberra, Islands/Australia Working Paper 87/9, Australian National University.

Gibson, Margaret (1991) "Giving Priority to the Nation's Smallest Schools." *Papua New Guinea Journal of Education* 26(1): 53–68.

Gibson, Margaret, and Weeks, Sheldon (1990) *Improving Education in Western Province.* Waigani, Division of Educational Research Report 66, National Research Institute.

Gomes, Candido Alberto (1992) "Education, Democracy and Development in Latin America" Paper. 8th World Congress of Comparative Education, Prague, Czechoslovakia.

Guthrie, Gerard (ed.) (1980) *Day High Schools.* Waigani, Educational Research Unit Report 34, University of Papua New Guinea.

Guthrie, Gerard (1985) "The Role Of The Teacher In National Development." *Papua New Guinea Journal of Education* 21(2): 265–81.

Guthrie, Gerard, and Kemelfield, Graeme (1980) *Standards and Quotas: High School Selection in the North Solomons Province.* Waigani, Educational Research Unit Report 31, University of Papua New Guinea.

Hasluck, Paul (1976) *A Time for Building.* Melbourne, Melbourne University Press.

Hawes, Hugh, and Stephens, David (1990) *Questions of Quality: Primary Education and Development.* London, Longman.

Katak, Roland, Weeks, Sheldon, and Petersen, Kolant (1988) *Report of a Survey of Educational Problems in Tari and Koroba Districts.* Waigani, Division of Educational Research, National Research Institute.

Kenehe, Simon (1981) *In Search of Standards.* Gordons, Hebamo Press.

Khambu, John (1992) *An Evaluation of the Oro Book Flood and Library Project.* Waigani, Division of Educational Research Report 70, National Research Institute.

King, Peter, Lee, Wendy, and Warakai, Vincent (eds.) (1985) *From Rhetoric to Reality: Papua New Guinea's Eight Point Plan and National Goals After a Decade.* Waigani, University of Papua New Guinea Press.

Knox, David (1993) *The Community Schools Agriculture Pilot Project in Papua New Guinea.* Waigani, Division of Educational Research, National Research Institute, forthcoming.

Limage, Leslie J. (1990) "Language and Education." In R. Murray Thomas (ed.), *International Comparative Education: Practices, Issues, and Prospects.* Oxford, Pergamon Press.

Little, Angela (1992) "The Diploma Disease in Sri Lanka 1972–1992: The Attenuating Effects of Ethnicity and Patronage." Paper. Eighth World Congress of Comparative Education, Prague, Czechoslovakia.

Lockheed, M.E., and Verspoor, A. (1990) *Improving Primary Education in Developing Countries: A Review of Policy Options.* Washington, D.C., World Bank.

Matane, Sir Paulias (1986) *A Philosophy of Education for Papua New Guinea.* Waigani, Ministerial Committee Report, National Department of Education.

May, Ron J., and Spriggs, Matthew (eds.) (1990) *The Bougainville Crisis.* Bathurst, Australia, Crawford House Press.

McGavin, P.A., and Ross, M.A. (1988) *Rates of Return to Education in Papua New Guinea.* Port Moresby, Institute of National Affairs.

McNamara, Vin (1971) "High School Selection and the Breakdown of Village Society." *Education Gazette* (November).

Messec, Jerry L. (1990) "Language Issues and National Education Systems: Experience in African Developing Nations." In David W. Chapman and Carol A. Carrier (eds.), *Improving Educational Quality: A Global Perspective.* London, Greenwood Press.

Miria, Clement (1993) "Money Released for School Fees." *Times of Papua New Guinea*, 14 January.

Momis, John (1991) "Education and Reconstruction in North Solomons Province." In *Education and Reconstruction in North Solomons Province.* Waigani, Division of Educational Research, National Research Institute.

National Department of Education (1976) *Papua New Guinea Education Plan 1976–1980.* Port Moresby, Government Printer.

National Department of Education (1985) *Growth of Education Since Independence: 1975–1985.* Waigani, National Department of Education.

National Department of Education (1991) *Education Sector Review: Volume 2, Deliberations and Findings.* Waigani, National Department of Education.

Oliver, Douglas (1991) *Black Islanders: A Personal Perspective on Bougainville 1937–1991.* South Yarra, Melbourne, Hyland Publishing House.

Piniau, Sam (ed.) (1988) *High School Education for All in Manus.* Rabaul, Hanns Seidel Foundation.

Pope, A., and Jones, J. (1974) *Home Background as a Determinant of Success in a Papua New Guinean High School.* Waigani, Educational Research Unit Report 11, University of Papua New Guinea.

Psacharopoulos, G. (1981) "Returns to Education: An Updated International Comparison." In T. King (ed.), *Education and Income.* Washington, D.C., World Bank.

Regan, Tony (1985) "Papua New Guinea: Implementing Provincial Government." In Peter Lamour and Ropate Qalo (eds.), *Decentralisation in the South Pacific.* Suva, Fiji, University of the South Pacific, 119–54.

Roakeina, S.G. (1977) *Standards in Secondary Education in Papua New Guinea.* Waigani, Ministry of Education.

Roakeina, S.G. (1984) *Interim Report of the Education Sector Committee: Medium Term Development Strategy.* Waigani, Ministry of Education.

Rogers, Cyril (1979) *National Education Strategy: Papua New Guinea Education Plan Review and Proposals.* Waigani, Monograph 9, Institute of Applied Social and Economic Research.

Smith, Peter, and Bray, Mark (1985) "Educating an Elite: Papua New Guinean Enrolment in International Schools." In Mark Bray and Peter Smith (eds.), *Education and Social Stratification in Papua New Guinea.* Melbourne, Longman Cheshire.

Stringer, Mary, and Faraclas, Nicholas (1987) *Working Together for Literacy.* Wewak, Christian Books Melanesia.

Tawaiyole, Pani, and Gibson, Margaret (1989) *Survey of Enrolments and Wastage in Papua New Guinea.* Waigani, Division of Educational Research, National Research Institute.

Tawaiyole, Pani, and Weeks, Sheldon G. (1988) "Trends in the Participation of Females in Formal Education in Papua New Guinea." In Eileen Wormald and Ann Crossley (eds.), *Women and Education in Papua New Guinea and the South Pacific.* Waigani, University of Papua New Guinea Press.

Tetaga, Jerry E. (1992) *General Education in Papua New Guinea 1992: The Educational Reform.* Waigani, National Department of Education.

Thomas, E. Barrington (ed.) (1976) *Papua New Guinea Education.* Melbourne, Oxford University Press.

Times of Papua New Guinea (1993) "Managing Education Reform into the Year 2000 and Beyond." *Education Supplement.* Waigani, *Times of Papua New Guinea*, 13 February.

Tuppen, Christopher (1981) *School and Student Differences: Grade Ten Examination and Assessment Results.* Waigani, Educational Research Unit Report 39, University of Papua New Guinea.

Turner, Mark (1990) *Papua New Guinea: The Challenge of Independence.* Victoria, Australia, Penguin.

Urimo, Wilson (1985) "Bridging the Gaps between Selection." *Times of Papua New Guinea.* Port Moresby, 28 April.

Weeden, W.J., Beeby, C.E., and Gris, G.B. (1969) *Report of the Advisory Committee on Education in Papua New Guinea.* Port Moresby, Government Printer.

Weeks, Sheldon G. (1975) *Private Schools in Papua New Guinea.* Waigani, Extension Studies Bulletin 4, University of Papua New Guinea.

Weeks, Sheldon G. (ed.) (1978a) *The "Foster Fallacy" in Educational Planning.* Waigani, Educational Research Unit Occasional Paper 3, University of Papua New Guinea.

Weeks, Sheldon G. (1978b) *Youth in Their Villages.* Waigani, Educational Research Unit Report 24, University of Papua New Guinea.

Weeks, Sheldon G. (1980) "Diploma disease? A Review Essay." *Papua New Guinea Journal of Education* 16(1): 52–62.

Weeks, Sheldon G. (1985a) *Community School Expansion in Eastern Highlands Province.* Waigani, Educational Research Unit Special Report 1, University of Papua New Guinea.

Weeks, Sheldon G. (1985b) "Progress in Promoting Equality of Educational Opportunity for Women." In Peter King, Wendy Lee, and Vincent Warakai (eds.), *From Rhetoric to Reality: Papua New Guinea's Eight Point Plan and National Goals After a Decade.* Waigani, University of Papua New Guinea Press.

Weeks, Sheldon G. (1987a) *Education and Change in Pangia, Southern Highlands Province.* Waigani, Educational Research Unit Report 56, University of Papua New Guinea.

Weeks, Sheldon G. (1987b) "Oro's High School Selection Unfair." *Times of Papua New Guinea*, 12 March: 27.

Weeks, Sheldon G. (1988) "Standards Are Not Falling." *Papua New Guinea Education Gazette* April–May.

Weeks, Sheldon G. (1989) "Problems and Constraints in Educational Planning in Papua New Guinea: A Case Study from East New Britain Province." *Papua New Guinea Journal of Education* 25(1): 57–80.

Weeks, Sheldon G. (1990a) "Educational Research and Educational Change in Papua New Guinea: 1975–1990." Waigani, Division of Educational Research, National Research Institute.

Weeks, Sheldon G. (ed.) (1990b) *Papua New Guinea National Inventory of Educational Innovations.* Waigani, Research Report 52, Second Edition, Division of Educational Research, National Research Institute.

Weeks, Sheldon G. (1991) "Strategies to Achieve UPE." Paper. Waigani Seminar on Population, Health and Development. Waigani, University of Papua New Guinea.

Weeks, Sheldon G. (1993) "Education in Papua New Guinea 1973–1993: The Late Development Effect?" *Comparative Education* 29(3): 261–74.

Weeks, Sheldon G., and Guthrie, Gerard (1984) "Papua New Guinea." In R. Murray Thomas and T. Neville Postlethwaite (eds.), *Schooling in the Pacific Islands: Colonies in Transition.* Oxford, Pergamon.

Weeks, Sheldon G., and Waninara, Joseph (1988) *A Review of Education in East New Britain.* Waigani, Educational Research Unit Report 60, University of Papua New Guinea.

Weeks, Sheldon G., et.al. (1991) *Enga Six-Year Education Plan: 1992–1997.* Waigani, Division of Educational Research, National Research Institute.

Wilson, Michael (1991) *Science Achievement of Grade 12 Students: The Papua New Guinea Perspective.* Waigani, Research Report 63, Second Edition, Division of Educational Research. National Research Institute.

CHAPTER 10

The State, Adult Literacy Policy, and Inequality in Botswana

FRANK YOUNGMAN

Adult literacy programmes in the Third World are widely regarded as promoting equality by extending educational opportunity to sections of the population who have failed to benefit from school education. However, the question of adult literacy in the capitalist countries of the Third World needs to be reconsidered in the context of the relationship of the state to the inequalities in the wider society. In this chapter I suggest that literacy programmes tend to reproduce class, ethnic, and gender inequalities and serve to legitimate the unequal social order, which the state seeks to uphold.

Although the organisations of civil society, such as trade unions, church groups, peasant associations, and community projects, often run literacy activities (some of which counter the hegemony of the state, such as the "popular education" movements in Latin America), most of their work remains on a small scale. In the Third World it is the literacy programmes sponsored and controlled by the state which reach most adults. Analysis of such programmes must therefore be based on a theory of the state and education.

The work of writers such as Apple (1982) and Carnoy and Levin (1985) has helped to clarify the relationship between the state and education from the position of critical theory, and recently Torres (1990) has extended this analysis to adult education. In essence, it is argued that in the class society characteristic of capitalism, the dominant classes exert control over state institutions so that the state's activities such as legislation, public investment, and social policies serve to promote the conditions necessary for maintaining capitalist accumulation and the political power of these classes. However, it is emphasized that this control does not go uncontested and the subordinate classes often exert pressure in their own interests so that the activities of the state become an area of conflict. For example, at times when the working class is strong, it may succeed in getting favourable trade union legislation and social welfare measures passed, or if the alliance of dominant classes requires peasant support, land reforms may be enacted. Thus the contradictions between the classes in society are reflected in the state, and its activities will tend towards the management of these conflicts in order to preserve the capitalist social order, by consent if possible, by coercion if necessary.

Education, as an institution of the state, shares this dual character. To a large extent, public education serves to reproduce the division of labour and the disparities of power within society (between classes, sexes, races, and ethnic groups) and to generate ways of thinking which legitimate the existing social order. Also, given that the capitalist state is controlled by dominant classes within society, education helps to meet the state's own needs to mobilize consensus and to be regarded as legitimate by the population as a whole (Welch 1991). But the provision and expansion of education also represent possibilities of social mobility and political democratisation, and education can provide people with knowledge and skills that will enable them to question the patterns of domination in society.

In the capitalist countries of the Third World, the state has specific characteristics resulting from historical developments which have been explored by writers such as Alavi (1972, 1982) and Thomas (1984) in considering the "postcolonial state" and the state under "peripheral capitalism." Two relevant characteristics can be mentioned here. First, the state "directly appropriates a very large part of the economic surplus and deploys it in bureaucratically directed economic activity in the name of promoting economic development" (Alavi 1972, 42). Thus the state tends towards a relatively high degree of intervention, an interventionism justified by ideologies of "development." Second, there is extensive external involvement in the production systems of these countries, and international capital exerts significant influence on the activities of the state through a variety of means, varying from the use of aid to shape domestic policies to the physical presence of expatriates in the state bureaucracies. Thus educational policy in the Third World is articulated within the discourse of its role in "development" and educational activities are massively influenced by external factors.

The approach to the state and education outlined above assumes that in capitalist society there are different classes with different interests. Based on this assumption, the state is viewed not as a neutral body promoting the "common good" of all citizens, but as a structure through which the dominant classes try to maintain the mode of production and their position in society, often in the face of resistance by the subordinated classes. The educational activities of the state, such as adult literacy programmes, therefore have a class character. It is within this framework that I present in this chapter a critical perspective on the state, adult literacy policy, and inequality in Botswana, focussing particularly on the first ten years of the National Literacy Programme (1980–1989).

THE POLITICAL AND ECONOMIC CONTEXT *

When Botswana became independent from Britain in 1966 it had few apparent resources and was reliant on Britain for grants to cover even its recurrent governmental budget. It was classified as one of the world's twenty-five poorest countries. However, after the discovery of diamonds in the late 1960s the country experienced a long period of uninterrupted economic growth and its annual performance of 11.4 percent growth in the 1980s was exceeded only by Oman. By the end of the 1980s it was categorized by the World Bank (1990) as a "middle-income oil importer" and it was one of the few countries in Africa that had avoided the crisis of economic stagnation and decline. Its economic growth was based mainly on the export of diamonds, but also on exports of beef. Diamond revenues provided capital accumulation for use by the state, while the cattle industry provided possibilities for individual accumulation. Since independence, the capitalist mode of production has become dominant within the social formation of Botswana.

The ruling bloc of dominant classes (namely, the bourgeoisie, petty bourgeoisie, and rich peasantry) improved its own situation significantly in this situation of economic expansion. It used its control of the state to pursue policies which advanced its economic interests, following a development strategy which used state intervention to provide the conditions for private enterprise and foreign investment (Ministry of Finance and Development Planning 1985, 54, 242). But the ruling bloc also used the available surplus to maintain the standard of living of other classes, in

*This section is based on Gaborone, Mutanyatta and Youngman 1988, 359–60.

particular the working class in the formal sector, for whom there was a minimum wage and protection from inflation through regular increases. Of course, not all classes benefited equally from the growth in GNP and the situation of the poor peasants in the rural areas and of the unskilled urban workers deteriorated, so that a government document in 1985 concluded, "It is clear that the majority of Botswana's households are poor" (Ministry of Finance and Development Planning 1985, 21). However, revenues accruing to the state were used to provide social services on a large scale, for example, in the health and education sectors. In particular, the growing immiseration of the rural poor during the drought of 1981 to 1987 was ameliorated by the provision of a safety-net of drought relief and feeding programmes which covered more than half the population (Ministry of Finance and Development Planning 1985, 58, 20). This welfare dimension of the development strategy served to reduce possible social tensions. The main potential area of tension arose from the slow rate of employment creation in the formal sector (the mining industry, for example, is very capital intensive) which led to high levels of unemployment, especially among school-leavers. This problem was exacerbated by the steady decline in the numbers of labour migrants to South Africa.

The ruling bloc sustained its hegemony after 1966 because economic expansion enabled it not only to meet its own class interests but also to maintain the standard of living of other classes. It promulgated an ideology of "social harmony," and class conflict was muted, allowing political stability and the continuance of a pluralist parliamentary system in which, however, the same party held power from 1966. The bloc saw an identity of its own domestic interests in a capitalist social order with those of international capital, and within the geopolitics of Southern Africa Botswana acquired significance to the West as a model of a capitalist, nonracial democracy, attracting high levels of foreign aid as well as investment.

To summarize, it can be said that from 1966 the state acted in the interests of those local and foreign classes which stood to gain from the expansion of the capitalist system of production within Botswana. However, the state claimed legitimation from the population as a whole formally through regular elections and informally through social programmes which took into account the welfare of the peasantry and working class. The resources made available to the state by rapid economic growth enabled it to undertake a variety of legitimation strategies. Thus the essential contradictions inherent in the increasingly class-divided society were ameliorated and a substantial degree of consent to the economic and political order was secured. It is within this context that policies on adult literacy were developed.

THE DEVELOPMENT OF LITERACY POLICY

Adult literacy activities in Botswana since Independence have been dominated by the government and therefore it is appropriate to analyze the development of literacy policy within a framework which focusses on the state and public policy formation (Torres 1990, 109–26). In general terms, as noted above, state intervention in Botswana's political economy since 1966 can be viewed as having been directed towards promoting the conditions for capitalist expansion and also to legitimating the accompanying class relations and social order. In particular, since the mid-1970s the development strategy has been based on mineral-led economic growth, with the mineral revenues being used by the state to create a modern capitalist economy and to improve rural welfare (Parson 1984). The key documents which have presented government policy, in the context of a macro-economic analysis, an articulation of objectives and priorities, and a specification of projects, are the *National Development Plans* produced by the Ministry of Finance and Development Planning at approximately five-year intervals.

The formation of policy on adult literacy has had a number of different dimensions. There have been the technical and political arguments put forward by civil servants in the bureaucracy and by government politicians. The basis of these arguments has largely been shaped by the "modernisation" theory of development, with literacy being viewed as an instrument for the development of a "modern" society and improved productivity. Policy has seldom been a response to expressed demands from the clientele for literacy, but indirectly the significance of the rural population as the basis of the ruling alliance's political support has had weight. Economic determinants have had great significance, particularly with the enormous increase in government resources that became available in the late 1970s (Parson 1984, 81). Finally, an important set of influences, as for most Third World countries, has been foreign donors and organisations, and developments in international policy debates.

When Botswana became independent in 1966, approximately 75 percent of the adult population of 543, 000 was illiterate (Kann and Taylor 1988, 140). However, the legacy of colonial neglect in formal education was so extreme (for example, only four secondary schools offered grade 12) that the dominant concern of educational policy was the expansion of secondary and tertiary education to meet the demands for "skilled manpower" of the public service and the formal sector. The portfolio responsibility for literacy within the government structure lay with the Department of Community Development, but it gave priority to self-help projects for rural construction and, as evidenced in *National Development Plan, 1970–1975* (Ministry of Finance and Development Planning 1970, 117), it regarded literacy as a small-scale activity undertaken by community groups to whom the department would simply supply materials and training assistance.

In 1972, a UNESCO consultant proposed a national work-oriented literacy programme to reach a quarter of a million people in an eight-year period, using the extension staff of various ministries (Brooks 1972). The government rejected the proposal for a variety of reasons. The mass campaign approach was regarded as too ambitious and too demanding of existing extension services. Influential (expatriate) civil servants held negative views of literacy work based on their experience working elsewhere in Africa in the 1960s, in countries such as Kenya. Also there was a change of personnel in the local United Nations Development Programme (UNDP) office which had sponsored the consultancy. Above all, adult literacy lacked priority at a time when government resources were scarce (1972–1973 was the first year in which the recurrent budget was balanced without British grants). This low priority was reflected in the *National Development Plan, 1973–78* (Ministry of Finance and Development Planning 1973, 134), which only expressed the intention of examining the feasibility of functional literacy programmes on a local and national scale.

Thus in the first decade after independence there was no policy commitment by the government to dealing with the problem of adult illiteracy. The only literacy activities were small-scale programmes undertaken by nongovernment bodies such as the University of Botswana, Lesotho, and Swaziland and the Botswana Christian Council. A number of reasons can be advanced for the lack of priority given to adult literacy. These include the preoccupation of educational planners with secondary and tertiary education and the scepticism noted above of civil servants concerned with rural development about the value of literacy, which was reinforced by the failures of UNESCO's Experimental World Literacy Programme, 1965–1975 (UNESCO and UNDP 1976). It can also be postulated that from the perspective of the dominant classes mass adult literacy lacked utility both to the model of economic development followed in the early 1970s and to strategies of hegemony in a period of political quiescence.

In 1975, the government initiated a major review of the education sector, establishing a National Commission on Education which reported in 1977 in a document entitled *Education For Kagisano*. The commission derived its goals for educational development from the government's stated national objectives of democracy, development, self-reliance, and unity, which are synthesized in the "national" philosophy of *Kagisano* (which means *social harmony*). In fact, the notion of "national" values is an ideological one, suggesting interests which transcend the divisions within society, and this is reinforced by the concept of "social harmony," which promotes the idea that there is consensus rather than contradiction between the different classes and other groups in society. *Kagisano* provided a Setswana concept which is consistent with functionalist sociology. This paradigm in sociology (Welch 1985, Alavi 1982) views society as a stable, well-integrated system in which there is a value consensus, such that all members of the society agree on its value system, and the functionalist conception of social development as a unilinear evolutionary process provided the basis for the "modernisation" theory of development which prevailed in Botswana's development planning. Within this theoretical framework, education has a significant role in promoting the value system, including the attitudes and values required to develop a "modern" society. The commission's report, by emphasizing *Kagisano*, gave powerful support to the dominant ideology.

The commission conceived out-of-school education, like school education, as furthering *Kagisano* and stated, "It may be expected to contribute to the individual's development and to the promotion of social welfare" (National Education commission 1977, 165). The commission identified literacy as a priority for out-of-school education:

> A fully literate population is an important long term objective if Botswana's other national objectives are to be met. We do not emphasise literacy as a separate programme, because experience in other countries indicates that literacy should not be pursued in isolation from other development programmes as an end in itself. It is best acquired in the context of efforts to achieve greater productivity, health or control over one's environment; and indeed it will itself contribute to achievement of these objectives. (National Education Commission 1977, 167)

The report gave literacy high priority within out-of-school programmes but its concept, as indicated in the above quotation, was vague. The commission seemed to argue against a literacy programme "as an end in itself" and for some form of functional literacy activities provided in the context of other programmes, such as agricultural extension or health education. Although it appeared to give adult literacy great significance, its rationale was general and it made no operational proposals—indeed, literacy was not included in the extensive list of specific recommendations at the end of the Report.

It is therefore not surprising that the government paper, *National Policy on Education*, which was the government's response to the commission's recommendations, simply stated, "Consideration will be given to literacy programmes" (Republic of Botswana 1977, 12). Senior civil servants and politicians remained lukewarm towards adult literacy programmes, although a group of (mainly expatriate) professionals within the adult education section of the Ministry of Education ran two pilot projects in 1977 and 1978, explicitly to influence policy and demonstrate possible approaches (Botswana Extension College 1977, 5).

In 1978, the Ministry of Education implemented one of the commission's recommendations and established a Department of Non Formal Education. It appointed as Chief Education Officer an expatriate who was a UNESCO expert with a background in adult literacy. He proposed a national approach to the eradication of illiteracy led by the Ministry of Education and he succeeded in convincing influential civil servants (especially in the Ministry of Finance and Development Planning) and the Minister of Education (Townsend Coles 1988). At a speech to a planning meeting to consider the proposal held in early 1979, the Minister referred to the international context of rising illiteracy rates and the World Bank's linkage between illiteracy and other development problems, such as malnutrition and poor living conditions. In respect to Botswana, he articulated the reason for concern with literacy in these terms:

> For the great majority of people, if life in modern society is to be lived to the full, they must be released from the bondage of illiteracy if they are to make their best contribution to their families, their communities and their nation. For them basic literacy, with which numeracy is involved, is an essential requirement. If the lot of ordinary people is to be improved, and the quality of their lives raised, then they must be given the chance of learning to read and write. For these are two of the skills needed to help them play their full part in national development. (Morake 1979, 1)

The rationale for eradicating illiteracy was therefore made in terms of the modernization of society, extended educational opportunity, and the individual's contribution to the nation's development objectives, such as democracy and self-reliance.

The operational strategy for the proposed programme was subsequently presented in September 1979 in an important document entitled *The Eradication of Illiteracy in Botswana: A National Initiative: Consultation Document.* The objective of the programme was very briefly stated despite the fact that this was a document seeking support from politicians and civil servants for a major new policy:

> To enable 250,000 presently illiterate men, women and youths to become literate in Setswana and numerate over the six years 1980–1985. The teaching shall be undertaken in the context of development issues of relevance to the participants and concern to the respective Districts and the nation. The term "literate" shall be interpreted to imply that a person can comprehend those written communications and simple computations which are a part of daily life. (Ministry of Education 1979, 1)

The objective contained an ambitious target of approximately 40 percent of the population over 10 years old (Kann and Taylor 1988, 137) and a limited time frame, so that the proposal was actually similar in scope to the one made by the UNESCO consultant in 1972. The document specifically avoided the concept of a "campaign," which had connotations of literacy work in socialist countries (Townsend Coles 1988, 38–41). It located literacy content in the context of development topics but avoided linking literacy acquisition to other skills because of the lack of success of UNESCO's Experimental World Literacy Programme, which had promoted "functional literacy" as a means to training in productive skills (Jones 1988, 159–211). It therefore took the opposite view to the one suggested by the National commission on Education. Furthermore, the conception of literacy was very narrowly defined and consciously avoided the politicized, Freirean conception which had gained prominence in the mid-1970s, for example, in the Declaration of the International Symposium for Literacy in 1975 (Bataille 1976, 273–76).

The document laid the basis for what became the National Literacy Programme, which has been the largest sustained programme in any area of adult education in Botswana since independence. It began with a pilot programme in 1980, and in mid-1981 it was officially launched as a nationwide programme by the Minister of Education, who once again stressed its modernizing purpose: "If a person is to be able to make their fullest contribution to the modern society we are building here, the ability to read and write are essential skills" (Morake 1981, 1).

The adoption of a nationwide, large-scale literacy programme at the end of the 1970s marks a major policy development (and contrasts with the rejection of a similar programme proposal in 1972). There are a number of micro-level factors, including a persuasive and experienced advocate in a key position as Chief Education Officer, more sympathetic (expatriate) educational planners, receptive donor agencies such as the Swedish International Development Agency (SIDA), and the social demand revealed by the 1977 and 1978 pilot projects. But the more important determinants were the changes in the political economy that had taken place during the 1970s. These changes have been well documented by Parson (1984), who shows the transformations which took place in the economy and the associated processes of class formation, with widening opportunities for wage labour and an expansion of the petite bourgeoisie. The political consequence was that the "class divisions generated during the period of growth began to require much more direct management than formerly" (Parson 1984, 95). The state had expanded resources for addressing this problem: "Botswana's increased ability to generate external aid combined with the country's increased diamonds and customs revenue led to a dramatic increase in available resources" (1984, 81). It can be argued that the provision of social programmes, such as the National Literacy Programme, was now necessary for the "management" of problems implicit in the increased class divisions, while it was also made possible through the state's access to greater resources. The modernization paradigm now underpinning the state's development strategy also provided the ideological basis for the literacy initiative.

Despite its comparatively large scale, the National Literacy Programme was unable to reach its original goal of making 250,000 people literate by 1985. Thus its continuation was included in the *National Development Plan, 1985–1991*. The goal of literacy was restated— "A literate population is essential for the successful implementation of the country's ambitious development programme" (Ministry of Finance and Development Planning 1985, 158)—and a new strategy was proposed with stronger linkages to primary education for young literacy graduates and with a programme of basic education and skills training for income-generating activities for older graduates. This role for literacy was articulated within the wider objectives of nonformal education policy, namely, "to increase educational opportunities and to reduce inequalities in access to education" (Ministry of Finance and Development Planning 1985, 158). The equity dimension of this policy reflected, among other things, the influence of Swedish aid to the education sector and to the National Literacy Programme in particular, while the new emphasis on integrating nonformal and formal education reflected international thinking in bodies such as UNESCO (Jones 1988, 236–38). It marked the beginning of a shift in the discourse about literacy to a broader concern with access to basic education.

This became clear during 1989 and 1990 when policy statements on literacy were framed within the context of the World Conference on Education for All. These statements argued that Botswana's commitment to universal junior secondary education (to grade 9) in conjunction with the National Literacy Programme constituted an existing Education for All policy and programme (Republic of Botswana 1989). Increasingly, literacy was being conceptualized as part of a comprehensive provision of "basic education" within formal and nonformal education, and emphasis shifted to the postliteracy component, as indicated in the Ministry of Education's draft chapter for the *National Development Plan, 1991–1997*:

> A strategy will be developed . . . that will encompass both literacy and post-literacy activities as a continuum with the main focus on the post-literacy component. Emphasis will be on systematic organisation of learning and action programmes geared towards the social, cultural and occupational needs and interests of the newly literate. (1990, 47)

It is likely that future policy development will continue to be influenced by international activity related to the concepts of basic education for all and equity through expanded opportunities.

IMPLEMENTATION OF THE NATIONAL LITERACY PROGRAMME

The policy decision taken in 1979 to undertake a national approach to the eradication of illiteracy was implemented during the 1980s through the National Literacy Programme (NLP) run by the Department of Non Formal Education (DNFE). Just as the process of policy formation described above involved the interplay of different interests, so the process of implementation has involved continued contradictions, particularly over the nature and resourcing of the programme.

The NLP began with an experimental year in five districts in 1980 and moved to national coverage in 1981. It was initially conceived as finite and it was envisaged that it would end in 1986. It was considered as a "development project" rather than an item of recurrent government expenditure, and funding was sought primarily from foreign donors. Expatriate planning personnel in the government had close links with donor agencies and secured commitments from two German government organisations (the German Agency for Technical Cooperation—GTZ— and Credit for Reconstruction), the Swedish and Dutch governments, and UNICEF. The use of donor funds was normal for development expenditure (Parson [1984, 74] notes that 60 percent of development expenditure in 1980–1981 was from external sources) but this dependence certainly had an impact on the programme. For example, the agreement with the German Agency for Technical Cooperation enabled the appointment from 1982 to 1985 of a German as the literacy coordinator, one of the main programme managers in DNFE.

The operational and pedagogical system of the NLP which was established in 1980 remained substantially unchanged during the first ten years of the programme. The country's nine districts were the main unit of administration, with a District Adult Education Officer who was a member of DNFE in charge of the programme. Each district was divided into areas in which a cluster of ten to twenty literacy groups was supervised by a Literacy Assistant, who was a full-time (though temporary) member of DNFE's staff with a minimum of grade 10 schooling. The literacy groups themselves, consisting of approximately fifteen learners, were taught by a Literacy Group Leader. These leaders normally had grade 7 schooling and taught two or three groups. Their work was conceived not as "a salaried appointment, but rather a part-time act of service to the community, for which a small token honorarium is paid" (Townsend Coles 1988, 73). The groups met for an hour or two up to five times a week and undertook a free programme of study based on five primers in Setswana. Reading was taught through the analytic method based on key words, many of which were related to topics on health, agriculture, and other development issues. The key words provided the basis for a syllabic approach to learning how to construct words and sentences. Additional reading material was provided through a monthly broadsheet, and regular broadcasts on the government-controlled radio provided a radio magazine for all involved. An annual cycle of events was established involving the recruitment of Literacy Group Leaders and learners, staff training, materials production and distribution, group instruction and supervision, and reports to the National Literacy Committee.

The scope of the programme during the 1980s is indicated in Table 10.1. The interpretation of this data in Table 10.1 in terms of the NLP's coverage is problematical because the statistics on participants only indicate enrolments and it is not possible to differentiate new enrolments from existing cumulative enrolments (Gaborone, Mutanyatta, and Youngman 1987, 12). However, one estimate based on extrapolation from the sample of learners tested in 1986 suggested that there were 70,000 new learners between 1980 and 1986 (Gaborone, Mutanyatta, and Youngman 1988, 354). It is also not possible to calculate the success rate, that is, the number of learners who can be defined as having become literate in terms of successful completion of the primers. An informed estimate by Kann and Taylor (1988) is that the literacy rate of the population aged 15 and over had increased from 54 percent in 1981 to between 61 and 65 percent in 1987.

Although the overall system changed very little during the 1980s, there were developments relating to the nature and funding of the programme. In 1983 an internal evaluation was undertaken. This evaluation exercise (Ministry of Education 1984) led to some incremental changes within the NLP's operation. In response to pressure from learners, it also focussed attention on the need for postliteracy activities and emphasized the demand for follow-up reading materials and access to skills training for income generation, which it called the "functional component." But above all the report crystallized the view that the programme should be institutionalized as a regular activity of DNFE and a recurrent item of expenditure, with the Literacy Assistants becoming a permanent cadre of "Extension Educators" with wider responsibilities for adult learning.

Table 10.1. Data on the National Literacy Programme, 1980–1989

	1980	1981	1982	1983	1984	1985	1986	1987	1988	1989
Participants	7976	23630	18779	27935	36068	38660	35354	20999	26200	33226
Literacy Groups	696	1779	—	2942	2945	1901	2403	1509	2038	2996
Literacy Group Leaders	—	1427	1188	1559	1633	1480	1221	907	1136	1466
Literacy Assistants	28	105	104	133	133	134	137	143	144	133

Source: Department of Non Formal Education (1990) *Annual Report on the National Literacy Programme: 1989.* (Gaborone: Department of Non Formal Education, p. 9.)

It was clear by 1985 that the initial numerical target of the NLP would not be reached and the Ministry of Education decided to include the continuation of the programme in the forthcoming development plan, for the period 1985–1991. This decision raised issues about the future direction and funding of the programme. These questions were also being raised by the two main donors. GTZ expressed dissatisfaction with the programme's management, its inability to reach its objectives, and its lack of forward planning, and in early 1986 the agency made future funding conditional on an evaluation and a management consultancy. The Swedish International Development Agency in its annual review at the end of 1985 also indicated that it would like to see improvements to the programme and a greater proportion of the costs coming from the Ministry of Education's recurrent budget.

The National Literacy Committee therefore commissioned an evaluation by the University of Botswana, which senior officials in the Ministry of Education viewed as a means for securing continued donor funding and for gaining internal support (particularly in the Ministry of Finance and Development Planning) for a transition to an institutionalized programme. Ministry of Education officials acknowledged that the lack of committed domestic resources indicated a relatively low priority and argued that although politicians saw benefits from the NLP, the public perception of the programme was that it was less significant than, say, the need to expand junior secondary schooling (Youngman 1987). From the perspective of these officials, the main purpose of the evaluation was accountability and policy justification, while its potential to assist in programme improvement was secondary.

The evaluation report submitted in March 1987 provided a comprehensive analysis of the NLP (Gaborone, Mutanyatta, and Youngman 1987). The findings in the report were generally positive. In particular, the results of a literacy and numeracy test administered to a national sample of NLP learners revealed a remarkable level of performance, with 81 percent scoring the equivalent of passing the grade 4 attainment test in the schools. Additionally, by making a series of detailed recommendations, the report suggested that improving the programme was a manageable task in technical terms. The report's overall effect on the donors was positive, and it strengthened the arguments for a transition to a permanent programme going beyond literacy to a comprehensive provision of adult basic education.

The NLP in practice has been an adult education programme which is large scale within the context of Botswana. It has remained a low-key operation without high-level political commitment. For example, the launching in 1981 was done by the Minister of Education rather than the President—and without popular mobilization. It has not met its original target of eradicating illiteracy although it has reached a significant number of adults, and it has promoted very few postliteracy activities. However, because it has had the political advantages of providing a social service to rural adults during a period of long-term drought and the collapse of the rural economy, and because in a period of resource availability it has not competed with other programmes, the NLP has been sustained by the state and donor agencies for a decade at a similar level of operation and resource allocation.

LANGUAGE POLICY AND PRACTICE WITHIN THE NLP

An important aspect of adult literacy policy is the choice of the language of instruction. Decisions on language reflect wider conceptions and ideologies about the nature and purposes of literacy and have an impact on its equity potential. Because the NLP was run by the Ministry of Education, the issue of language was influenced by national language policies. The government's language policy since Independence has been that English is the "official language" (of Parliament and government administration) whilst Setswana, the language of the politically dominant and most numerous ethnic group, is the "national language." Thus English and Setswana are used in the education system (the transition to English as the medium of instruction takes place in grade 5) and in the state-controlled radio and newspaper. The use in formal political, administrative, or educational situations of the mother tongue of minority-language speakers is discouraged by the state although these speakers comprise at least 20 percent of the population. For example, minority languages may not be spoken on the state radio and language-related questions may not be included in the national census data (Nyati 1989, 8). A number of the minority languages (especially in the remote western areas of the country) are not written languages and even in Setswana there is a relative lack of written materials apart from school textbooks and bureaucratic documents. The reasons given for discouraging the formal use of minority languages are that a single national language is a force for national unity against "tribalism" and that the costs of producing materials are prohibitive.

During the planning of the NLP in 1979 there was discussion on the language or languages to be used. It was recognised that choices had to be made in relation to minority languages, Setswana, and English. The professionals involved favoured the use of mother-tongue instruction on pedagogical grounds and also thought that consideration should be given to the use of English, especially in urban areas. However, as the Chief Education Officer of the time records, the decision was taken to provide literacy in Setswana:

> It was at this juncture that political rather than educational or functional considerations carried most weight. To achieve national unity, there had to be the submergence of local, tribal, languages; this was the practice in formal education and this example had likewise to be followed in non-formal education despite the fact that this seemed likely to decrease the motivation of some of the potential learners. (Townsend Coles 1988, 40)

The effects of implementing the Setswana language policy for minority-language speakers have been documented in a number of reports. A progress report on the NLP in mid-1982 drew attention to the problems of teaching Setswana literacy to non-Setswana-speaking groups and recommended that Literacy Group Leaders be given skills in teaching Setswana as a second language (Department of Non Formal Education 1982, 10). DNFE subsequently encouraged the leaders to use translation in the classroom as an aid to learning, but no minority language materials were produced. The 1984 evaluation report included interview data from non-Setswana speakers who were still in literacy groups and those who had dropped out. The data suggested that the problem of having to learn another language created difficulties when also having to learn how to read and write. For example, 50 percent of the drop-outs stated their reasons for leaving related to language. However, the study concluded "The majority of non-Setswana learners actually want to learn Setswana. For many this is the rationale for joining the Literacy Programme" (Ministry of Education 1984, 23). The results of the literacy test recorded in the 1987 evaluation report suggested that for those who manage to remain in the programme and do not drop out, there is very little variation in performance between Setswana speakers and those whose mother tongue is not Setswana (Gaborone, Mutanyatta, and Youngman, 1987, 49–54). There is little evidence of wide-scale pressure from learners to alter the policy of Setswana as the medium of instruction and it seems that for some minority-language groups learning literacy in Setswana is perceived as giving them increased access to the dominant language, thus extending their possibilities for participation in society and the economy.

The issue of access to the English language has been very different because, from the beginning of the NLP, learners have requested English tuition. The field staff of DNFE reported in 1981 and 1982 that the new literates wished to learn English, and learners' letters to the literacy broadsheet reinforced this. A study by a foreign consultant was commissioned in 1982 on the feasibility of a course in English as a second language for new literates. The study confirmed that learners saw English as significant, especially in relation to employment, quoting a group of learners as follows :

> They said they want to learn English because English is the important
> language in the whole world. They say they can't get a better work in
> towns if you don't know how to speak English. (Alley 1982, 5).

The consultant concluded a special course in English was desirable and feasible and produced some materials. However, DNFE's response to the consultant's proposals was slow and although a draft English primer was produced in 1985; it was only used unofficially by a few interested Literacy Group Leaders. Policy statements in 1985 in *National Development Plan, 1985–91* and in 1986 in DNFE documents referred to a nonformal course in English as part of the postliteracy strategy, but in practice nothing was implemented. The survey of literacy learners recorded in the 1987 evaluation report found that two-thirds of the respondents wanted to learn English. The major reasons given for wanting to learn English were "to communicate" (54.4 percent) and "to get employment" (28.5 percent) (Gaborone, Mutanyatta, and Youngman 1987, 81). However, no large-scale English Language tuition was carried out.

The demand for English articulated by the learners represents their realistic perception of its significance as a language for opening up economic opportunities and for giving access to a wider sphere of social, educational, and political participation. This expression of demand was able to influence the policy of the NLP, which from 1985 has had a specific commitment to providing English in the postliteracy phase. However, the pressure from learners was not strong enough to lead to policy implementation. The blockages to the introduction of the English course may be partly attributed to the inherent problems of implementation, such as finding teachers with appropriate language competence. But it can also be postulated that the lack of priority given to introducing English reflects differing conceptions of the purposes of the NLP. For the majority of learners (three-quarters of the respondents to the questionnaire recorded in the 1987 evaluation report), the main reason for joining the NLP was to get employment. Access to English would obviously enhance that possibility. From the viewpoint of the government, although development plans since 1979 stressed employment creation, the expansion of formal-sector jobs could not take place on a scale which could absorb all literacy graduates. Hence while literacy policy was articulated in vague terms of "modernizing" society, its implementation focussed narrowly on reading and writing in Setswana as an end in itself, with some postliteracy assistance to the establishment of income-generating groups. A large-scale demand for employment would have exacerbated problems already being experienced by the pressure from secondary school-leavers.

The demand for English thus exposed an inherent contradiction in the literacy policy, insofar as widespread adult literacy would have raised expectations of further economic participation which could not have been met. The existence of the NLP helped politically to legitimate the state by demonstrating its concern to provide services to the rural and urban poor. But its extension beyond a minimum level would have been dysfunctional in terms of the nature of the economy and the existing labour market: hence the very limited commitment to the NLP in general, and the lack of urgency given to the particular issue of teaching English.

THE NATIONAL LITERACY PROGRAMME AND THE SOCIAL ORDER

The central question here is the extent to which the NLP during the 1980s served to reproduce the existing patterns of inequality in society, thereby reinforcing and legitimating the inequitable social order characteristic of capitalism. The major determinant of the structure of social inequality is arguably that of production, with differences in access to and control over productive resources providing the basis of class divisions. But the disparities derived from the system of production intersect with and reinforce other divisions within society, such as those of ethnicity and gender. The role of the NLP in reproducing these disparities within the social order is underresearched, but it is possible to consider the outcomes of participation in relation to class, ethnicity, and gender.

The period since independence has seen the expansion of the capitalist mode of production within Botswana's social formation. The rapid economic growth that has taken place has been accompanied by growing inequalities in the distribution of wealth and income and by persistent poverty. The processes of class formation have created the class structure typical of capitalist societies in the Third World. There is as yet a very small class of indigenous large capitalists but the petite bourgeoisie has become increasingly strong, using its role in the management of the state to consolidate its class position. Formal-sector employment has expanded and there is a growing working class whose income is derived solely from wage income. An important group remains which is partly dependent on wage labour but which retains involvement in agricultural production, including the migrant mine workers (a group called by Parson, 1984, the "peasantariat" to suggest their dual location). The peasantry, engaged primarily in agricultural production within the household, is internally stratified, with both a proportion of rich and middle peasants and a mass of poor peasants, the last group owning few means of production and often having to work for others. The rural class structure also includes capitalist farmers and rural wage labourers, as well as an underclass of the unemployed and underemployed. There is thus a clear class hierarchy of dominant and subordinate classes, and this is the class context in which the NLP takes place.

There is very little reliable data on the class composition of the NLP participants. The 1984 evaluation report recorded the following information on the occupational background of learners in 1983 (Table 10.2):

The categories are obviously imprecise, as "farmers" gives no idea of location within the stratified peasantry and "housewife" gives no evidence

Table 10.2. Data on the Occupational Background of Sampled Learners, 1983

Housewives	36%
Farmers	21%
Herdsmen	12%
Maids	9%
Drought Relief Programme Participants	5%
Others (mostly skilled workers)	17%

Source: Ministry of Education (1984) *How Can We Succeed?* (n.p.: Department of Non-Formal Education).

of class position. However, it can be deduced from observational evidence and other information on Botswana's social structure that the majority of participants came from the poor peasantry in the rural areas, while in the urban areas unskilled workers and the unemployed predominated. This is substantiated by the perception of most learners that the NLP would help them enter into wage labour in the formal sector—the 1987 evaluation report records three-quarters of the learners questioned giving employment as their main reason for joining the NLP (Gaborone, Mutanyatta, and Youngman 1987, 68). The aspiration of most learners was probably to enter into the working class, with few envisaging a process of greater social mobility. Given the advantages of membership of this class in the period of prolonged economic growth (particularly in relation to the poor peasantry during the drought of the 1980s), this represented a reasonable aspiration, even though the working class was subordinate within the overall class structure. However, although the NLP might have raised this expectation, it did not itself provide employable productive skills, and the restricted growth of the formal sector, coupled with competition from school-leavers, meant the objective likelihood of paid employment for literacy graduates was small. Participants were aware of this: "When we see literacy graduates roaming the streets without a job to do . . . one wonders if one has made the right choice in joining the NLP" (Gaborone, Mutanyatta, and Youngman 1987, 68).

It can be postulated that the social outcome of the NLP in relation to class was that a small proportion of literacy graduates did enter or consolidate their position in the working class. A small proportion of others were enabled to become petty producers on their own or in income-generating groups, while some may have advanced their situation within the strata of the peasantry. But it seems likely that the overall impact of the NLP was to enable very little upward mobility within the existing class structure. The NLP therefore in effect reproduced class divisions, and even the aspirations for advancement of the learners were articulated within the existing class hierarchy. There is no evidence to suggest any activity within the programme (at the level of policy or practice) that called into question the class divisions within the social order. However, it may be that the inability of the NLP to help participants meet their expectation of employment might have begun to generate a consciousness of the inequities in control over the productive resources of society.

One dimension of social inequality which intersects with class is that of ethnicity. At least 20 percent of the population belong to minority ethnic groups, most of which have a subordinate position in society. During the nineteenth century, the numerically dominant Batswana established political and economic control over other ethnic groups in the country. A precolonial class structure emerged in which those groups with the greatest cultural and linguistic distance from the Batswana experienced a degree of economic exploitation and social subordination, akin to serfdom (Datta and Murray 1989, 58–59). While the Kalanga in the northeastern part of the country retained access to land and other means of production and the Ovaherero in the west retained cattle herds, most of the ethnic groups in the west were increasingly dispossessed and drawn into agricultural labour, mainly as cattle herders on the ranches of Boer settlers or for cattle-owning Batswana. Today the dominated ethnic groups of the western areas form a rural underclass which is unemployed or working for irregular payments in cash or kind (Wilmsen 1988).

The political and economic dominance of the Batswana has been accompanied by cultural hegemony, articulated in the postcolonial era in terms of the ideology of nationalism, which regards assertions of cultural identity by ethnic groups as negative expressions of "tribalism" and identifies "the idea of the nation with Tswana culture" (Datta and Murray 1989, 70). Some of the ethnic minorities have written languages but, in the face of official discouragement, they have seldom undertaken adult literacy in these languages. (An exception is the Adult Education Centre run by the Lutheran Church in Sehitwa which taught literacy in the Tjiherero language in 1985–1986). For the majority of the ethnic groups in the western areas, such as those labelled the Basarwa, their languages are unwritten and their literacy levels are very low. One study of households in the western region of the Central District in 1977–1978 found less than 1 percent literacy (Hitchcock 1978, 366).

The information on participation in the NLP by different ethnic groups is sparse, as there are no statistics on the ethnic background of the learners. The 1984 evaluation report (Ministry of Education 1984, 21) recorded the different language groups amongst the non-Setswana speakers interviewed (50 percent spoke Ikalanga) but it gave no indication of the proportion of non-Setswana speakers to Setswana speakers. The 12 percent of learners categorised as "herdsmen" in Table 10.2 certainly included a high proportion of people from ethnic minorities. However, a later study of the remote areas where most ethnic minorities other than the Kalanga reside concluded that:

The National Literacy Programme has not been very successful in [these] settlements. The Literacy Group Leaders find it difficult to recruit learners and even more difficult to keep them in the groups. (Kann, Hitchcock, and Mbere 1990, 94)

The study recommended greater efforts should be made by the NLP to provide literacy skills as these would enable greater political and economic participation (for example, in relation to benefitting from the special government Economic Promotion Fund for these areas).

It is suggested that participation in the NLP had contradictory outcomes for Botswana's subordinated ethnic groups. The acquisition of literacy in Setswana, as noted in the previous section, may have enabled their fuller participation in the mainstream of society. But the terms of that participation were likely to involve reduced cultural identity and greater incorporation into the hegemonic culture. Also, though this literacy may have reduced the extremes of economic exploitation experienced by some ethnic groups, it was likely to provide little advancement within the overall class structure. Thus any transition from marginality to incorporation which was facilitated by literacy would not have significantly altered the pattern of social inequality, and may indeed have served to legitimate it, by reducing the visibility of ethnic discrimination.

In relation to gender, it is important to consider to what extent the NLP reinforced women's inequality in society. The nature of Botswana society is such that women hold a subordinate position in the division of labour and this inequality is buttressed by a strong patriarchal ideology. The majority of women live in the rural areas and are primarily engaged in subsistence agriculture. They represent only a quarter of those in formal-sector employment, where they work mainly in areas such as domestic service, nursing, and teaching. Their participation in significant areas of economic and political decision making is low (for example, only two of the thirty-eight M.P.s are women). In the private sphere, cultural practices and social norms embody male superiority (Mannathoko 1991).

Issues of gender within the NLP have not been adequately researched, apart from some pioneering work by Gaborone (1986, 1989). In order to elucidate the interconnections of knowledge, power, and gender in the context of literacy practice, considerable ethnographic analysis would be required. However, it is possible to make some initial comments based on available information. The starting point must be the fact that almost two-thirds of the learners in the NLP during the 1980s were women—for example, the figure in 1989 was 62.1 percent (Department of Non Formal Education 1990, 8). The reason for this high rate of participation can probably be found in the large numbers of female-headed households (almost 50 percent of those in the rural areas), with women disproportionately represented amongst the poor, unemployed, and unskilled adults who are the potential clientele for literacy. Unfortunately there is no evidence on the comparative drop-out and success rates of women learners in relation to men.

To some extent it is apparent that participation in the NLP served to reinforce women's social position and their place in the sexual division of labour. For example, one purpose of literacy that often appears in official statements is to learn how to read and write letters. The significance of this is that many women in the rural areas are on their own because men have migrated to Botswana's towns and to South Africa for wage labour, so that letters are an important form of communication. In this sense, the NLP may well have reinforced the status quo of migrant labour and women's marginalization. Additionally, a major element of postliteracy provision is home economics, and most of the income-generating groups that DNFE promoted amongst literacy graduates were involved in traditionally female occupations, such as knitting, sewing, weaving, basketry, and baking (Department of Non Formal Education 1990, 3–4). Furthermore, there is some evidence of men being reluctant to allow women to join the programme (Gaborone, Mutanyatta, and Youngman 1987, 68), and of female participants' going to great lengths to conceal their participation from their partners (Gaborone 1986).

However, the implication of emancipatory possibilities suggested by the men's reluctance indicates that, to a certain extent, the acquisition of literacy may be a step for individual women towards exerting greater control over their own situation. Gaborone (1986) quotes one participant as follows:

> My partner used to keep two bank accounts, one for us and the other for girlfriends. And because I was unable to read and make sense of this, he used to leave information lying about. I did not know how much he earned or his wage. But I now know and make him account for every thebe he spends.

Much more research is required on the personal effects of the NLP for women learners, but it is likely that these effects were contradictory.

Participation in a postliteracy sewing project may have given a small cash income that provided material benefits and a greater degree of personal autonomy, while simultaneously entrenching the individual in the lowest levels of the capitalist production system in stereotyped women's work. However, what is certain is that the NLP had no policy commitment to promote forms of consciousness and collective social action that would enable women to free themselves from economic exploitation and patriarchal oppression. Indeed, it is interesting to note that the organisational system of the programme had an important gender dimension. The 1987 evaluation report records that 94.2 percent of the Literacy Group Leaders surveyed and 82.2 percent of the Literacy Assistants who responded were female (Gaborone, Mutanyatta, and Youngman 1987, 102–05). Thus the employment pattern of the programme itself reinforced the situation of women in low-paid, insecure, stereotyped jobs. One can conclude that the NLP in many respects reproduced the gender inequalities in society while at the same time interacting with the latent contradictions in unequal male–female relationships, in ways which have the potential to bring these disparities into question.

CONCLUSION

In this chapter I have sought to provide an analysis of policy development in adult literacy within the specific context of Botswana in the twenty-five years since the country became independent in 1966. I have tried to show how the educational policy of the state in the area of adult literacy relates to the structure of inequality in the wider society. The focus of my discussion has been on public policy formation and on the social outcomes of the National Literacy Programme in its first ten years of operation. I have not considered the NLP in terms of its curriculum, pedagogy, and evaluation. However, I believe an analysis at this level would reveal that its form and content embodied an approach and an ideology which reinforced the status quo. For example, its methods in practice involved authoritarian teachers and passive learners, and its approach was explicitly antagonistic to the notions of empowerment associated with people like Freire. It is recorded that the planners of the NLP in 1979 took note "of the concienstisation approach of Paulo Freire, and . . . the political element in the method was not seen as being appropriate to Botswana" (Townsend Coles 1988, 41). The literacy practices of the NLP supported legitimation and domination rather than transformation and emancipation.

The case study I have presented has centred on adult literacy as a social service provided by the state, and I have looked at the provision of literacy as a means of dominant classes' securing their legitimacy within society rather than as an opportunity for individuals to acquire particular skills. I have done so in order to explore the question of who benefits from literacy in relation to the interests of classes and other groups in society rather than those of the individual. The argument I have made is that the capitalist state promotes a particular kind of literacy (Lankshear and Lawler 1989) for two purposes: first, to legitimate its own role in maintaining the conditions for capitalist accumulation and the political power of the dominant classes; second, to legitimate the existing unequal distribution of power in society between classes, sexes, and ethnic groups. The National Literacy Programme in Botswana in the 1980s can be seen to have served these purposes.

I have focused on the state provision of adult literacy rather than nongovernmental initiatives because I believe analyzing the role of the state is crucial given its dominance over literacy programmes in most Third World countries. However, the particularities of the Botswana case must be borne in mind because of the strength of the state and the weakness of civil society (Molutsi and Holm 1990). The domestic and foreign resources available to the state during the economic boom of the 1980s enabled it to pursue a number of legitimation strategies, including large-scale social expenditure, of which the NLP is an example. In general terms, the latent conflicts within an increasingly class-divided society were successfully managed, and there was little evidence of political or cultural struggles over the state's concept and practice of adult literacy.

Botswana has not yet experienced the economic problems and accompanying crisis of the state which have occurred in many other parts of Africa. However, economic growth in the 1990s has slowed down significantly, and reduced government revenues could lead in the future to a crisis of legitimacy for both the state and the capitalist social order it upholds. This in turn could lead to different policies in the sphere of adult literacy and to different responses from literacy's clientele. However, in the absence of major changes in the economic and political situation, it is likely that the National Literacy Programme would continue to provide a steady incremental increase in the levels of adult literacy whilst contributing to the legitimation of capitalist development and inequality in Botswana.

REFERENCES

Alavi, H. (1972–1979) "The State in Post-Colonial Societies." In H. Goulbourne (ed.), *Politics and the State in the Third World.* London, Macmillan, 38–69.

Alavi, H. (1982) "State and Class under Peripheral Capitalism." In H. Alawi and T. Shanin (eds.), *Introduction to the Sociology of "Developing Societies."* London, Macmillan, 289–307.

Alley, E. (1982) *English as a Second Language—An Investigation into the Feasibility of a Course Suitable for People Who Have Just Learned to Read and Write Setswana.* Gaborone, Department of Non Formal Education.

Apple, M.W. (ed.) (1982) *Cultural and Economic Reproduction in Education.* London, Routledge and Kegan Paul.

Bataille, L. (1976) *A Turning Point for Literacy.* Oxford, Pergamon.

Botswana Extension College. (1977) *Functional Literacy Pilot Project: Draft Plan.* Gaborone, Botswana Extension College.

Brooks, K. (1972) *Proposal for a National Work-Oriented Literacy Programme in Botswana.* Paris, UNESCO.

Carnoy, M., and Levin, H. (1985) *Schooling and Work in the Democratic State.* Stanford, Stanford University Press.

Datta, K., and Murray, A. (1989) "The Rights of Minorities and Subject Peoples in Botswana: A Historical Evaluation." In J. Holm and P. Molutsi (eds.), *Democracy in Botswana.* Gaborone, Macmillan, 58–73.

Department of Non Formal Education. (1982) *How Can We Succeed? Evaluation of the National Literacy Programme: A Progress Report: August 1982.* Gaborone, Department of Non Formal Education.

Department of Non Formal Education. (1990) *Annual Report on the National Literacy Programme: 1989.* Gaborone, Department of Non Formal Education.

Gaborone, S. (1986) Unpublished Notes on Fieldwork Undertaken for the Evaluation of the National Literacy Programme.

Gaborone, S. (1989) *Gender and Literacy: The Case of Botswana.* Paper. Symposium on "Women and Literacy—Yesterday, Today and Tomorrow," Stockholm.

Gaborone, S., Mutanyatta, J., and Youngman, F. (1987) *An Evaluation of the Botswana National Literacy Programme.* Gaborone, Institute of Adult Education.

Gaborone, S., Mutanyatta, J., and Youngman, F. (1988) "The Botswana National Literacy Programme—Progress and Prospects." *Prospects* 18 (3): 352–62.

Hitchcock, R.K. (1978) *Kalahari Cattle Posts.* Gaborone, Republic of Botswana.

Jones, P.W. (1988) *International Policies for Third World Education: UNESCO, Literacy and Development.* London, Routledge.

Kann, U., Hitchcock, R., and Mbere, N. (1990) *Let Them Talk.* Report submitted
to the Ministry of Local Government and Lands and the Norwegian Agency
for Development Cooperation, Gaborone.

Kann, U., and Taylor, D. (1988) "The Adult Literacy Rate in Botswana."
Botswana Notes and Records 20: 135–41.

Lankshear, C., with Lawler, M. (1989) *Literacy, Schooling and Revolution.* New
York, Falmer.

Mannathoko, C. (1991) *Profile of Women and Development in Botswana.* Brussels, EEC–ACP Foundation.

Ministry of Education (1970) *National Development Plan 1970–1975.* Gaborone,
Ministry of Education.

Ministry of Education (1979) *The Eradication of Illiteracy in Botswana: A
National Initiative: Consultation Document.* Gaborone, Ministry of Education.

Ministry of Education (1984) *How Can We Succeed? Summary Report from the
Evaluation of the National Literacy Programme.* N.p., Department of Non
Formal Education.

Ministry of Education (1990) *Draft Chapter 14: Education and Manpower Development.* Gaborone, Ministry of Education.

Ministry of Finance and Development Planning (1970) *National Development
Plan: 1970–75.* Gaborone, Republic of Botswana.

Ministry of Finance and Development Planning (1973) *National Development
Plan: 1973–78.* Gaborone, Republic of Botswana.

Ministry of Finance and Development Planning (1985) *National Development
Plan: 1985–91.* Gaborone, Republic of Botswana.

Molutsi, P.P., and Holm, J.D. (1990) "Developing Democracy When Civil Society Is Weak: The Case of Botswana." *African Affairs* 89 (356): 323–41.

Morake, K.P. (1979–1988) "Speech Delivered at the Opening of the Meeting on
the Eradication of Illiteracy in Botswana." In F. Youngman (ed.), *Documentation on the National Literacy Programme, Vol. 1 1979–1982.* Gaborone,
University of Botswana.

Morake, K.P. (1981–1988) "Draft of Speech by the Hon. Minister of Education
on the Occasion of the Commencement of the Botswana National Literacy
Programme." In F. Youngman (ed), *Documentation on the National Literacy
Programme, Vol. 1 1979–1982.* Gaborone, University of Botswana.

National Commission on Education. (1977) *Education for Kagisano.* Gaborone,
Republic of Botswana.

Nyati, L. (1989) *The National Language and Education for Democracy.* Paper.
Symposium on Educational Research in the SADCC Region—Present and
Future, University of Botswana.

Parson, J. (1984) *Botswana.* Boulder, Co., Westview.

Republic of Botswana. (1977) *National Policy on Education.* Gaborone, Republic of Botswana.

Republic of Botswana. (1989) *Education for All—Meeting Basic Learning Needs. Botswana Country Paper.* Gaborone, Republic of Botswana.

Thomas, C.Y. (1984) *The Rise of the Authoritarian State in Peripheral Societies.* London, Heinemann.

Torres, C.A. (1990) *The Politics of Non Formal Education in Latin America.* New York, Praeger.

Townsend Coles, E.K. (1988) *Let the People Learn.* Manchester, University of Manchester.

UNESCO and UNDP. (1976) *The Experimental World Literacy Programme.* Paris, UNESCO.

Welch, A.R. (1985) "The Functionalist Tradition and Comparative Education." *Comparative Education* 21 (1): 5–19.

Welch, A.R. (1991) "Knowledge, Culture and Power: Educational Knowledge and Legitimation in Comparative Education." In R. Burns and A.R. Welch (eds.), *Contemporary Perspectives in Comparative Education.* New York, Garland.

Wilmsen, E.N. (1988) "The Political History of Minorities and Its Bearing on Current Policy." In A. Datta and K. King (eds.), *Botswana—Education, Culture and Politics.* Edinburgh, University of Edinburgh, 31–52.

World Bank (1990) *World Development Report, 1990.* Oxford, Oxford University Press.

Youngman, F. (1987) Unpublished Notes on Fieldwork Undertaken for the Evaluation of the National Literacy Programme.

CHAPTER 11

The Struggle for Quality and Equality in Iranian Education
Problems, Progress, and Prospects

GHOLAM A. TAVASSOLI, ANTHONY R. WELCH, AND K. HOUSHYAR

INTRODUCTION

This study is an attempt to describe, analyse, and clarify some controversies which arise in attempting to understand quality and equality in Iranian education, and in particular policies in response to problems whose solutions were remote, given the peculiar conditions of Iranian history, culture, and politics. The prospects of achieving a major amelioration, which both enlarged quantity and heightened quality, were vitiated by the formal struggle to expand primary education and extend higher education, struggles which have, on the whole, not been effective. In that sense, it is argued, the explosion of population in recent decades, which shows no sign of abating, prevailed against an increase in either quality or equality of education. Although the growth of population must be considered as one of the decisive factors which inhibited extensions in the quality and equality of education, many other factors also must be taken into consideration, including financial constraints, literacy problems, persistent gender differences, uneven development (especially between rural and urban areas), and war. Equally, the persistence of tensions between the potency of traditional forms of culture and governance, and a desire for some of the material wealth associated with the West (Wallerstein 1978, Mazrui 1980), which are at times held to have led to a renascent nationalism and particularism among Arab nations, are a further feature of the Iranian context, which has since 1979 been grounded upon a "resurrection" (Mazrui 1980, 7) of the Islamic vision.

BACKGROUND AND CONTEXT

The Islamic Republic of Iran is geographically, historically, and culturally distinct from the other countries in the Middle East. Within the region, the country is the second largest in territory (after Saudi Arabia) with an overall size of 1,648,000 square kilometres, making it the sixteenth-largest country in the world. It also has one of the three largest populations in the region (with Turkey and Egypt). The population of Iran has grown from 34 million in 1976, to 49.5 million in 1986, and by 1994 was estimated to have grown to around 59 to 60 million inhabitants. Of this number, approximately 43 percent live in rural areas, and 57 percent in urban settings (*Multicultural* 1994). In 1991, there were 105 men for every 100 women, despite the losses sustained in the recent war with Iraq.

The population consists of various constituents, but Iranians usually employ two main categories:

1. the main component, often refered to as Aryan, who have inhabited this region for some 3,000 years, and
2. the descendants of various invaders and conquerors, largely Arabs, Turks, and Mongols.

As well, there is a significant Kurdish minority (see Hasanpour 1993). This pattern is reflected in the linguistic diversity present in contemporary Iran, as illustrated later in this chapter.

Political geography is also an important part of the context within which Iranian education operates. Iran is bounded in the north by Turkmenistan, Azerbaijan, Nakhjivan, and the Caspian Sea, to the west by Turkey and Iraq, to the south by the Persian Gulf and the Gulf of Oman, and to the east by Pakistan and Afghanistan. Iran has the longest frontier (some 1200 miles) with those Muslim republics (such as Azerbaijan and Kazakhstan) which are currently establishing some independence from Russia.

The national language of the country is Farsi, or Persian, an Indo-European language, although, as is seen below, significant proportions of the population speak other languages.

Some 98.8 percent of the people of Iran are Muslims and 91 percent of them are held to be followers of twelve Imamis Shiat sects, a fact not without significance to the prevailing political and educational ideology (authorities such as Shorish [1988], however, give the proportion of Sunni Muslims as at least 10 percent to 20 percent). The principal religious minorities consist of Christian, Jewish, and Zoroastrian, for whom the Ministry of Education has in recent years commissioned special textbooks, which both combat irreligion and emphasise the commonalities in all four religions. As is illustrated below, the present ruling system in Iran is based firmly on the Constitution of the Islamic Republic of Iran, which came into being after the overthrow of the former Shah by the Islamic Revolution in 1979, under the leadership of Imam Khomeini. The years after the overthrow of the last Shah in 1979 were a period of major change in many aspects of ideology and practice in Iran.

The following sections successively analyse (1) some of the major problems behind the failure to raise the quality of education in Iran, as well as limitations upon the achievement of equal outcomes, (2) some of the successes that have occured, despite the problems, and (3) prospects for the future.

PROBLEMS: OLD AND NEW

There are a number of elements which have conspired to inhibit gains in quality of education in Iran, as also gains in equality. Some of these are historical in origin; others are more contemporary. Of historical factors, mention should be made of the history of colonialism in Iran, as well as the inefficient and inequitable distribution of the country's resources, particularly under the former imperial regime, and the persistence of traditional norms and practices, largely among rural and urban poor. The limitations of finance in the face of a huge increase in both population and demand are also a major factor inhibiting quantitative and qualitative growth.

A historical glance at Iranian education over the last hundred years clearly shows that the change which occurred within educational institutions was generally associated with certain external determinants. Of great relevance here is the process of industrialisation and modernisation of Western Europe, and in particular the growth of imperialist rivalries during the last century. The rivalry of Anglo-Russian governments in Iran during the nineteenth century was of decisive influence in Iran. Missionaries, who had come to Iran from the United States and from other parts of the Christian world, founded the first modern Christian schools, but left a legacy of uneven development. Moreover, the slow pace of change and development was exacerbated by the persistence of some traditional cultural elements in Persian society. The traditional Koranic Schools, or Makhtab, strongly resisted any change, for example, and opposed the building of any modern schools.

A relevant illustration of some of these tensions is contained in the well-known history of the slow progress of "Roshdiah Modern School," established in Iran around the late nineteenth century. Upon his return to Iran from Europe, the then Shah first visited this newly established school in what is currently Azerbaijan, and as a result the school was closed (Roshdiah 1983, 25). In those days, it has been claimed, perhaps somewhat hyperbolically, that "illiterates in Europe numbered only one per hundred; while, in Iran only one per hundred were literate" (Roshdiah 1983, 19). Internal discontinuities and pressures over the spread of education were closely linked to national and international political and economic events. Disharmony was the outcome of both the unsystematic way in which change was introduced and the lack of ultimate common objectives, itself a result of cultural conflict, both internal and imposed by external forces.

Persistent Problems

If the historical development of Iran did not sustain gains in the quality of education, or its spread among all walks of life, there are, in addition, a number of elements which continue to constrain progress. We make mention here of three interactive factors, including the traditional life of the peasantry, high rates of population growth, and the archaic structure of economic life. Beyond this, but clearly also related to limited gains in education, financial limitations are clearly evident, while substantial literacy problems also remain.

Patterns of Life among the Peasantry

The modern schools that were founded in the early nineteenth century and which were extended after the Constitutional Revolution in 1906 continued to grow; but the process of spreading such schools through the countryside was both long and slow. The continuation of traditional (Quranic) schools and geographical conditions, especially a combination of rural poverty and traditional values and practices, have both limited progress in education. In 1954, for example, more than 70 percent of the population still lived in rural areas and there were more than 60,000 villages throughout the country, although urbanisation continues.

There are in addition further traditional ways of life in rural areas, which are generally perceived to have formed a barrier to the spread of modern forms of education, and a more literate culture. For instance, sons who expect to inherit the farm must help their father in their teenage years, while girls in the family would follow their mother in making handicrafts from the age of 5 or 6. The persistence of such patterns of existence has been a serious and longstanding obstacle to the progress of modern education in rural areas (see also Gomes 1992).

In rural areas, peasants and workers are often so economically marginal that they send their children over 6 years old to work, in order to contribute to household income. The persistence of child labour occurs despite the existence of constitutional provisions which mandate eight years of compulsory schooling, for all children between the ages of 5 and 13. In practice, however, the provisions are still frequently ignored, especially in slum areas of cities and in remoter rural areas, which are both out of range of government measures to enforce compulsory provision. Frequently, children work in agriculture or make handicrafts in rural areas, while street children in towns and cities may be engaged in selling. Earnings for such activities are very low, while their working conditions are not regulated. This situation, together with the extent of illiteracy among parents and the high rate of population growth, has created a critical situation for extending a generalised program of quality schooling in rural areas and among the urban poor.

Family, Work, and the War Against Literacy

Contemporary accounts of literacy stress its complex and multifaceted construction and are much less willing to resort to simple, quantitative measures which had more often been used in the past, and which often obscure the different realities associated with differing literacy experiences (Freebody and Welch 1993, Luke 1988, Lankshear and Lawler 1987). Nonetheless, by any measure, literacy problems in Iran are profound. While substantial efforts to eradicate illiteracy have been made since the Islamic revolution in 1979, these have met with only partial success, and differences between rural and urban dwellers, and males and females (Hendessi 1991, Haeri 1990), still exist throughout society, including in education. Despite a major national campaign entitled "War against Illiteracy" which was awarded a United Nations prize in recent years, and the wider availability of night school, the extent of adult illiteracy is also still too high, most notably in rural areas and among those who have left the countryside, dislocated by war or in search of a better life.

Of 9.7 million families living in Iran in 1986, some 16.8 percent (1.63 million families) were judged to have no literate member. Significant disparities existed between different sectors of the population: for urban families, for example, the proportion was said to be 12.6 percent, while for rural families it was judged to be 25.6 percent. Experience, however, showed that one single member of a family could change the situation: he (or less frequently she) could help the other members to overcome literacy problems. Militating against this prospect, however, is the fact that within many poor families, especially in rural areas, young people are obliged to work to enable the subsistence of the family. If and when the oldest sibling is working, and earning enough income, younger family members may be enabled to attend school, alhough (as indicated above) this attendance may still be irregular at best. It is still the case that many married couples are illiterate, as are many workers, a situation which inhibits the rate of economic development and reduces productivity. Moreover, the human and social costs are high: illiteracy both reduces the quality of life for those individuals, and exacerbates existing inequalities.

In Iran, the census of 1986 indicated that 52.9 percent of married women and 32 percent of married men did not know how to read or write. For rural areas, gender differentials in literacy attainments are even starker, and proportions of illiterates among both genders are even higher—69.9 percent for women and 44.8 percent for men. The effects of illiteracy are not confined merely to those individuals, however: many of these same men are the heads of their family, and thus their decisions have great effects on the decision of the other members. Equally, mothers with literacy problems are unable to assist their children in the crucial preschool years.

A recent census judged that more than 40 percent of the working population aged 6 and over were illiterate, a statistic which, as indicated above, reflects the persistence of child labour in spite of compulsory education provisions. In addition, some 37 percent of women, were deemed illiterate, and 31.5 percent of unemployed workers were judged unable to read or write. These together comprise a high proportion of the economically active individuals in Iranian society. Too many, particularly in the rural areas which make up such an important sector of economy, as well as significant numbers of urban and dispossessed poor, continue to be illiterate. An examination of the two last censuses in Iran reveals that the population aged 6 and over increased from 27.1 million in 1976 to 38.8 million in 1986 (an increase of 44.1 percent in ten years); over the same period, however, the rate of illiteracy decreased from 52.5 percent to 39.3 percent among that population. Nonetheless, the number of illiterate people increased in absolute terms (from nearly 14 million to nearly 15

Table 11.1. Growth in Urbanisation and Population (aged 6 years or over) in Iran (1976–1986)

Region	Census 1976	Census 1986	Percent Increase	Numerical Increase
Urban Area	13,182,568	21,327,338	61.8	8,144,770
Rural Area	13,930,276	17,545,061	25.9	3,614,785
Total	27,112,844	38,872,399	43.4	11,759,555

Source: General Census of 1976 and 1986.

million). Tables 11.1 through 11.4 reveal how the increase of population inhibited the struggle against illiteracy in Iran.

Tables 11.1 through 11.4 show that improvements have been made despite the many difficulties which beset Iran during the decade 1976–1986, both in quantitative terms as well as in terms of narrowing the gap between rural and urban areas, and between genders. Clearly, significant inequalities persist, however. The most important of these revealed by this study are gender differences, some of which are enshrined in religious education classes in schools (Haeri 1990, Hendessi 1991), and differences between rural and urban dwellers. We see that gender and rurality function as a double barrier: women rural dwellers remain the most disadvantaged group, and remain the most illiterate subgroup in the country. As argued before, although overall illiteracy rates have decreased over the last three decades, absolute numbers of illiterates have increased at the same time, due to substantial increases in the population. Age differences account for both these trends, to some degree:

TABLE 11.2. Increases in Percent Rates of Literacy, by Sex (1976–1986)

Sex	1976	1986	Increase in 10 Years
Male	58.9	71.1	12.2
Female	35.5	51.7	16.2
Total	47.5	61.7	14.2

Table 11.3. Urban and Rural Literacy Rates (1976–1986)

Year	Sex	Urban	Rural	Urban–Rural Difference
	Male	74.5	43.6	30.9
1976	Female	54.6	17.3	38.3
	Both	65.5	30.5	35.0
	Male	80.6	60.1	20.4
1986	Female	65.2	36.0	29.2
	Both	73.1	48.2	24.9

while the proportion of illiterates under the age of 10 is less than 10 percent, that for the cohort aged 50 years and over is 90 percent. There is still
a significant problem among children of school age, however. In 1986,
over 15 percent of this cohort was illiterate, despite the fact that primary
and lower secondary schooling is compulsory. Here again, gender plays a
role, as 21.4 percent of girls among this subpopulation are deemed illiterate, and 9.7 percent of boys.

One of the explanations for such differences, as noted above, may be
the differing occupations of young people in rural areas, which often
conspire to prevent their regular attendance at school. Internal migration,
which sees such individuals often migrating to urban centres, can be
another problem. As well, other variables may be significant, such as differential rates of birth and death, which affect the population numbers in
different age groups and in different regions. Of relevance here also is the
effect of continuing illiteracy on the consciousness and lifestyle of peasant

**Table 11.4. Increase in Literacy Rates by Gender and Geography
(1976–1986)**

Sex	Urban	Rural	Rural–Urban Difference
Male	6.1	16.5	—
Female	10.6	18.7	—
Both	7.6	17.7	—

families, for example with respect to issues such as birth control and principles of health and hygiene.

Financial Factors

Financial factors are a further important dimension of the contemporary equality and quality problematic in Iranian education. Although Iran is not underendowed with natural resources, notably oil, depressed world prices for its staple commodity are responsible for genuine financial constraints. The poor utilization of the resources of the country, however, notably including fuel resources, further inhibit more equal development. Moreover, inflation has exacerbated this problem in recent decades: whereas in 1978 the exchange rate between the U.S. dollar and the Iranian rial was approximately 1:78, by 1994 this had deteriorated to approximately 1:1,600. Salaries have on the whole failed to keep pace with inflation. For example, the salary of a university professor has increased by some 1,500 percent over the last fifteen years, while prices of items such as automobiles have increased some 5,000 percent over the same period.

In addition, for many years financial gains were restricted to a relatively small, Westernised elite surrounding the imperial family. The patrimonial and feudal structures of traditional society, and the unequal distribution of the resource wealth which was generated, generally inhibited development. The former (prerevolutionary) Pahlavi imperial regime was surrounded by an often Western-oriented upper class, including a small number of intellectuals, who absorbed much of the wealth generated by oil resources, and fostered the unequal distribution of the nation's wealth. This for some time delayed the spread of more modern forms of education, despite repeated avowals by the former imperial regime, as well as delaying the equalisation of provision for all Iranians. In particular, the universalising of education, and the elimination of illiteracy throughout the country, together with a more scientific and technological orientation and commensurate high levels of scientific qualification, has still not been achieved, especially for rural dwellers and women.

The recent war against Iraq (1980–1988), which resulted in heavy loss of life and substantial disruption to significant sections of the population, also consumed a large amount of the overall Iranian budget during those years, creating further strains on limited budgets for education, just as with other areas of social activity. In total, the huge amount expended on the war in these years is estimated to have represented a substantial diversion of funds from education, despite the strong desire to enhance quality and access.

There are three further reflections of the problem of financing expansion, in an era of rapid growth in demand. One is seen in the bifurcation of education into vocational and professional strands at the upper secondary level in Iran. Due to the higher expenses which are involved in vocational education compared with the professional strand, and despite the increasing need for education which is related to work, vocational education has developed slowly. Thus during the decade 1980 to 1990, the percentage of pupils in vocational schools at the upper secondary levels decreased from 21.8 percent to 12.7 percent.

The second consequence has been the increasing privatisation of education, in response to the government's manifest inability to expand finances to keep pace with demand. As a response, the private sector has mushroomed at all levels in education over the 1990s, a development which has been assented to by government, which provides licenses for these institutions. Private educational institutions have become popular and are regarded also as a lucrative form of business investment.

Thirdly, the insufficiency of financial resources and difficulties involved in preparing comprehensive, good-quality textbooks has limited the quality of education. This was a major problem after the Islamic revolution, when, as in other instances involving the replacment of one regime with another, texts needed to be substantially revised in the light of the newly prevailing ideology. The process of rewriting textbooks at all levels involved nothing less than legitimating a change in the knowledge-stock (Welch 1991) to reflect the change in the sociopolitical system, and in values. Naturally, this took some time and was paralleled by a large upswing in demand for materials occasioned by a substantial demographic increase, one which continues to place strains on the financing and production of materials.

Shorish's brief (1988) account of the textbooks employed at various levels and in several areas in the postrevolutionary era provides a sketch of the model Iranian citizen: "a thoroughly commited individual to one God" (Shorish 1988, 59). Textbooks, like other agencies of socialisation, present Islam as a response to what was seen as the preexisting oppression, secularism, and corruption of earlier periods of Iranian history. School texts, however, are seen as a particularly important vehicle to inculcate the spirit of Islam, with its values of bravery, love of God, and commitment to the weak. Indeed Shorish points out the priority of ideological training, commitment, and purification in such Iranian values of Islamic virtue over all other activities in which an individual might engage, a view which gives considerable importance to education and to teachers, including religious leaders and the family. The virtues over other forms of society, of the new Islamic form of government, and its emphasis on the rule of God, as explained in the teachings of the Prophet, are now expounded in school social science texts (Mohsenpour 1988, 82). Martyrdom is also praised, especially of those who, to support the Iranian revolution, gave their lives in the fight against the Shah.

As is evident from the above, the measure of quality in education is seen to be closely related to the values of Islam, as exemplified in the life of the Prophet, and the Imam Khomeini (Mohsenpour 1988). The importance of conformity between the ideals of Shi'i Islam and the actions of religious leaders and the government is stressed within school texts, and school practices and organisation. These ideals are argued to be universal and potentially to embrace all individuals irrespective of ethnic or religious affiliation. Thus equality is also enshrined in Iranian education—through an emphasis on the universal qualities of humankind, and through a stress on the brotherhood of Islam. The unity of mankind, and of the Islamic community, is taught as a cardinal value, as is solidarity with oppressed peoples, especially Islamic brethren such as Palestinians (Shorish 1988, Mohsenpour 1988). The protection of the weak from oppression *(dhulm)* and the search for justice (key elements in the curricula, and in textbooks) are, however, defined in opposition to other political ideologies, notably capitalism, nationalism, and socialism, none of which are seen as capable of fostering a revolution from *within* individuals. The fostering of capitalism is now seen to be associated with the earlier prerevolutionary era, when students were instructed in notions such as usury in school texts (Mohsenpour 1988, 80). Marxism, too, is now argued to be have been influential in prerevolutionary era school texts (Mohsenpour 1988, 78), especially in spreading atheism, and explaining social customs.

The Islamic revolution in Iran has been argued to consist of two dimensions :

> for social justice and against oppression, discrimination, racism, colonialism and imperialism, on the one hand, and a revolution against self-ignorance and *(waswas)* mischief that reside within individuals on the other. (Shorish 1988, 69)

There is, therefore, explicit recognition of the inherently political dimensions of being Islamic, especially in terms of support for oppressed peoples, the poor and dispossessed: "one of the aims . . . was to instill justice and invite all of humanity to join this struggle for Allah's way" (Shorish 1988, 69).

Nonetheless, despite the emphasis on quality and equality contained in Iranian texts, achieving an increase in the quality of education has been a mammoth task under the conditions outlined above, as also has been success in reducing the inequalities which exist between males and females, urban and rural areas, or ethnic groups or regions. The major, if not the only, concern of authorities was to attempt to respond to all these competing demands, which at the same time largely prevented them from addressing questions of quality and equality in the education system as a whole. Indeed the major effort has been to respond to quantitative pressures, thus delaying any substantial improvements in both quality and equality.

In addition to financial constraints, democratic institutions and constitutional practices have not yet developed sufficiently or been spread widely enough to guarantee long-term political stability; hence residual social and political tensions lie unresolved. In relation to this issue, we may mention a general and persistent traditionalism, which has meant that, even after the constitutional revolution in 1979, many poorer parents continued to resist modern forms of schooling and, for example, did not allow their daughters to attend the new schools. This feature, as was seen above, is not new in the educational history of Iran.

PROGRESS

Nonetheless, there has been some significant progress in education, albeit largely in quantitative terms. Despite the legacy of colonialism and uneven development, undemocratic governance and unequal distribution of wealth, the losses and dislocations imposed by war, and the dramatic rise in the Iranian population from 34 million in 1976 to around 60 million in the early 1990s, the rate of literacy has been measured as increasing from 47 percent to 60.7 percent over this same period.

This was accomplished by a sustained effort involving national literacy efforts, which were not merely directed at children. Night schools were established and an intensive campaign developed in the area of adult literacy, including the founding of a new government department entitled

"War against Illiteracy." During the period 1976–1986 the number of pupils enroled in primary and secondary schools also grew significantly: from 7.08 to 10.18 million (a relative increase of 53 percent). Despite these sustained efforts, however, the rate of illiteracy among the whole population aged 6 and over is still 38.3 percent, due at least in part to the high proportions of adult illiteracy, as described above.

It is recognised of course, as underlined by recent scholarship, that it is no simple matter to define the notion of literacy, which is at the least no longer able to be understood as a merely technical process, apart from prevailing ideologies and practices in society (Freebody and Welch 1993, Luke 1988, Lankshear and Lawler 1987). Equally, it is clear that the context for literacy action in a Third World country such as Iran may well be very different from that which obtains in advanced industrial states, and that, unless more national and international resources are devoted to dealing with Third World illiteracy, it is likely that the gap between First and Third World states will widen rather than narrow (Limage 1993).

Traditionally, however, in Iran what has been accounted as minimum literacy was the ability to read and write in a basic manner the Iranian writings. In practice, this was at least equivalent to two classes of schooling in a normal school.

Expansion of School Education

Despite the major problems with persistent illiteracy listed above, there has been demonstrable growth in education over the 1970s and 1980s. The formal school education structure in Iran is as follows :

primary stage of 5 years (ages 6–10),

lower-secondary stage of 3 years (ages 11–13), and finally

an upper-secondary level of 4 years (ages 14–17).

At the end of each cycle, pupils complete a set of uniform final examinations.

The major trends in expansion of school education during the period 1976–1986 are evident in Table 11.5. The greatest increase occurred at lower-secondary education (a relative increase of 70 percent) compared with increases at primary level of 52 percent and at the upper-secondary education level of 36 percent. During this period, the number of pupils enrolled in regular education grew from 7.08 million to 10.81 million, an

Table 11.5. Growth of Enrolments by Sex and Level of Education (1976 = 100)

Education Level	Year	Enrollment (000)			Enrollment Growth (1976 = 100)		
		Boys	Girls	Both	Boys	Girls	Both
	1976	2,940	1,829	4,769	100	100	100
Primary	1981	3,170	2,113	5,283	108	116	111
	1986	4,059	3,174	7,233	138	173	152
Lower Secondary	1976	876	493	1,369	100	100	100
	1981	1,079	671	1,750	123	136	128
	1986	1,406	893	2,299	160	181	170
Upper Secondary	1976	609	333	942	100	100	100
	1981	672	414	1,086	110	124	115
	1980	768	510	1,278	126	153	136
	1976	4,425	2,655	7,080	100	100	100
Total	1981	4,921	3,198	8,119	111	120	115
Increase	1986	6,233	4,577	10,810	141	172	153

increase of 53 percent. As may be seen in Table 11.5, girls' enrolments increased at a higher rate than those of boys.

Table 11.6 indicates the changes in class sizes over the same decade, revealing at the same time some improvements at all levels, offset, however, by the intractability of problems of quality over this decade.

As may be seen in Table 11.6, the pupil–teacher ratio was 35:1 at the elementary level of education in 1976. During the period 1976–1981, a marked improvement in the pupil–teacher ratio was effected, while during the period 1981–1986, this ratio tended to worsen once more. The lower- and upper-secondary levels of education also exhibited a much improved ratio during the period 1976–1981, but a much slighter improvement during the period 1981–1986 (during which the war with Iraq was at its height). The pupil–staff ratios (which also includes staff other than teachers) in 1986 were 27.9:1, 19.1:1, and 17.0:1, respectively, for primary, lower-, and upper-secondary levels of education.

Table 11.6. Changes in Class Sizes During the Period 1976–1986

Educational Level	Average Class Size (1976)	Average Class Size (1981)	Average Class Size (1986)
Primary	35	27	30
Lower Secondary	41	32	31
Upper Secondary	42	34	32

THE CONSTITUTIONAL SITUATION

The "disruption of the normative order" (Ajami 1992, 7) resulting from the overthrow of the monarchy in 1979 was followed by promulgation of the the new Islamic Constitution, under which all colours, and races, and men and women were proclaimed to have formal equality. The Islamic foundations of the new constitution are clearly and widely reflected in educational ideology, with traditional exhortations displayed promininently in signs throughout the country: "Education, like prayer, is necessary for all men and women," and "Seek knowledge from cradle to grave."

The Islamic and constitutional form of government is held to guarantee the integrity of a strong nation-state while providing some formal guarantees to ethnic minorities, of whom there are several. One of the issues that Iran confronts in its attempt to construct a modern nation state is the implications of its complex ethnic and linguistic composition: nearly 66 percent of the Iranian people are of Persian origin and speak Farsi (Persian), while 25 percent speak Turkish, some 5 percent speak Kurdish, and 4 percent speak an Arab language.

A number of constitutional provisions relate to equal provision for ethnic and other groups in Iran. Constitutional provisions such as Article 2, paragraph C; Article 3, paragraphs 3, 9, and 14; Article 15; and Articles 19, 20, 21, and 30 are of specific importance in this regard. For example Article 19 of the constitution proclaims: "The Iranian people, of any ethnic groups or tribes, have equal rights, and, colour, race and language may not lead to any special privilege for any groups," while Article 20 likewise proclaims: "All individuals, men or women, are equal and under the protection of law and enjoy all economical political social and cultural rights under Islamic law." Article 3 also relates to formal equality of educational provision: "General education and physical education must be free and gratis for all people, and at all levels," while Article 15 addresses the specific issue of ethnic equality under the law: "The official and common language and writing of Iranian people is Persian; the documents, official correspondence, and textbooks must be written in this language. Nevertheless, the use of local and ethnic languages in the press and in mass media (Radio—Television, etc.) and teaching of their literature at the school parallel to the Persian language is permitted."

As pointed out in the introduction to this chapter, scholars of the Arab world have pointed to general cultural tensions between tradition and reform: between the authority of traditional forms of power and social structure in the Arab world, and the desire to attain some of the fruits of modernisation (Ajami 1992, 7), especially in the period after the beginning of the "oil crisis" in 1973. Such accounts may help to explain why implementation of equality of education is somewhat more complex than the formal guarantees within the Iranian constitution suggest.

In addition to the gender differences which are alluded to above, and the persistent rural–urban differentials, a recent structural example which reveals the difficulties of attaining that equality referred to in the constitution is the development of a three-tiered system of provision within higher education, which undermines the formal equality of access guaranteed by the constitution. The topmost rung of insititutions is the government universities, which are also the most competitive in terms of entry requirements. Each year perhaps a million or more applicants compete for the 100,000 available places at these institutions, which are best equipped and attract the most highly qualified staff. Unsuccessful applicants tend to gain entry to either of the other two types of higher educational institution. The first of these is the open university, which has lower entrance requirements, while the third broad type provides access through distance education. Although the second- and third-mentioned forms of education provide much greater access than would be the case if they did not exist, there is a clear hierarchy of prestige among these three tiers, which vitiates the formal parity guaranteed under the constitution.

PROSPECTS

The problem of ensuring "Quality and Equality of Education" in a Third World country is generally connected with its relative situation of development. In turn this raises issues of its relations with other nations, and regions in the world. Third World countries generally reveal an educational "gap," both qualitative and quantitative, when compared with a developed country—a situation which is often due, not only to particular internal factors, but also to some external factors (Carnoy 1974, Altbach and Kelly 1981).

To study the relationship between the quality and equality in education in a less developed context implies an overview of the structure of education at four levels: primary, secondary, higher, and adult education. Each of these levels has its particular and special effects on the achievement of equality and on those qualities needed for the harmonious development of the nation. Certainly, as has been argued before, both the kind and degree of education alone may reflect much of the quality of life and degree of development in a country.

In a developing country such as Iran, the level of education achieved is connected to one's whole life-chance: for different classes, ethnic minorities, peasants, and women. Equally, the question of unemployment and rising qualification levels expected by government and employers (Dore 1976, Welch and Freebody 1993, Little 1992) has disorienting effects, including lower morale, for school children, and upon the organisation of education as a whole.

When we examine the problem of schooling and that of the limited availability of school places, we are immediately made conscious of serious quality problems in education, when what is wanted is to increase quality for all and to slow the increase in pupil numbers, which will shortly reach 15 million. Given this explosion in numbers, and limited economic resources, it has proved necessary to increase pupil–class ratios, particularly in lower- and upper-secondary levels of education, and utilize school buildings more intensively by resorting to double-shift or even triple-shift schools. Public primary schools, which cater to the middle class in Teheran and other larger cities, often have two shifts, the first from 8.00 A.M. to 11.30 and the second from 12.00 to 4.00 P.M. Schools in poorer urban and rural areas, serving areas of unskilled workers and peasants, often operate three shifts: 7.00 to 10.30, 10.30 to 2.30, and 3 to 5.30 (Sabbaghian 1992). Despite multiple shifts, classes are often as large as 50 students. A continuation of current population trends, combined with ongoing financial constraints, may well mean that both quantity and quality will be further compromised (Gomes 1992).

The general situation described above, which demonstrates persistent inequalites in education between men and women, between urban centres and rural areas, and between those poorer groups in society and those with more material resources, inhibits economic development and may also be a factor in inhibiting swifter progress towards democracy. Indeed, the persistence of these inequalities, together with the tensions described above between a desire for certain aspects of Western technology and economic affluence and traditional values and structures of authority within Iran, may be conceived as an instrument for exploitation, and a guarantee of a poor quality of life, for significant numbers of the population.

International comparisons are complex and delicate exercises, demanding cross-cultural knowledge and sensitivity, a variety of data, and, often, a command of several different disciplines. Nonetheless, even simple statistical comparisons between the rates of population growth, illiteracy, and economic development indicate a clear distinction between the developed and less-developed countries—that is, those in which high rates of illiteracy are accompanied by very high rates of population growth, and where the nation's level of economic wealth is low. Simple examples suffice to reveal something of the disparities which persist between wealthier nations and those in the Third World. A comparison, using the case of Pakistan, for instance, illustrates the substantial differences involved, and the difficulties involved in addressing structural problems.

Table 11.7. Illiteracy and Population in Selected Countries

Countries	Population (in Millions)	Rate of Population Increase	Illiteracy Rate: (Men)	Illiteracy Rate: (Women)
Pakistan (1980)	82.14	3.1%	61%	82%
Iran (1980)	40.24	3.0	45	70
Iraq (1980)	13.24	3.6	32	68
Turkey (1980)	44.92	2.3	17	47
Afghanistan (1980)	15.95	?	67	94
USSR (1982)	270.02	0.9	—	—
USA (1979)	227.74	1.1	—	(0.5%?)
Israel (1980)	3.87	2.3	9.0	4.0
Spain (1980)	37.43	1.0	4.0	1.0
Italy (1981)	57.20	0.4	4.0	5.0

Source: Selected statistics of the world, 1984, 1986, UNESCO.

The rate of increase of population in Pakistan in 1980, for example, was 3.1 percent per year, while the rate of illiteracy for men and women was 61 percent and 82 percent, respectively; but the rate of economic growth was very low. A comparison with the United States of America at much the same time reveals that the rate of population growth in United States was 1.1 percent per year, and the proportion of illiteracy was relatively low, while the rate of economic growth was high. Table 11.7 serves to illustrate some of the relevant differences, although, as indicated above, the question of measuring illiteracy is rather more complex than is shown in Table 11.7.

Internal Efficiency

Table 11.8 provides an idea of promotion, repetition, and drop-out rates by grade and sex for different levels of education in 1986–1987. The data in Table 11.8 reveal that promotion and repetition rates for girls at all levels of education are, respectively, higher and lower than those for boys, but the level of drop-out for girls in primary education is higher

Table 11.8. Promotion, Repetition, and Drop-out Rates (1986–1987)

Grade	Boys				Girls			
	P	R	D	Total	P	R	D	Total
1	79.8	15.2	5.0	100	82.1	12.3	5.6	100
2	88.0	10.1	1.9	100	91.1	6.6	2.3	100
3	92.1	7.2	0.7	100	93.0	4.6	2.4	100
4	84.3	12.9	2.8	100	86.2	9.7	4.1	100
5	72.3	17.8	9.0	100	70.2	12.7	17.1	100
6	64.6	22.2	9.0	100	71.0	17.0	12.0	100
7	75.3	15.9	13.2	100	80.7	11.6	7.7	100
8	71.6	17.7	10.7	100	72.5	13.2	14.3	100
9	70.9	15.8	13.3	100	82.0	9.4	8.6	100
10	78.6	12.4	9.0	100	83.7	8.1	8.2	100
11	86.4	10.2	3.4	100	87.0	6.3	6.7	100
12	55.6	3.0	41.4	100	67.0	0.5	32.5	100

Note: P = promotion rate; r = repetition rate; D = drop-out rate.

Table 11.9. Percentage Survival Rates, by Level (1986)

Grade	Boys	Girls	Difference
2	94	93	1
3	92	91	1
4	91	89	2
5	88	85	3
6	76	68	8
7	60	56	4
8	53	51	2
9	44	42	2
10	36	37	−1
11	32	34	−2
12	31	31	0

than that for the boys, while in secondary education it is lower. In general this means that the girls are more likely to be promoted than the boys, but for those girls who are not promoted in primary education, the probability of dropping out is higher than that for the boys.

If the rates observed in 1986–1987 remain constant, the capacity to address questions of both quality and equality is likely to remain low.

Table 11.9 reveals that the difference shown between survival rates for boys and girls increases over time, most particularly around the transition from primary to secondary school. Due to higher drop-out rates for boys at upper-secondary education, however, the gender difference tends to decrease after grade 6, and finally the survival rate in year 12 is the same for each group. Comparisons with other developing countries indicate that the Iranian survival rate to grade 4, which is 91 percent for boys and 89 percent for girls, compares favourably with equivalent figures which average around 75 percent (Aziz Zadeh 1989, 12).

Higher Expenditure Levels: Lower Quality of Education

Developing countries often struggle to maintain the quality of educational provision in the face of rising aspirations and rising population. Iran has been subject to just these pressures, and although its response has been considerable, the prospects of a continuation of these twin demands may well militate against increases in the quality of education, as well the success of efforts to extend equality among rural and urban groups, and between genders.

Educational expenditure (including higher education) increased as a percentage of government expenditure from 15.7 percent to 19.5 percent during the period 1980–1985. Over the same period, the proportion of recurrent expenditure in education to the total sum expended in education has increased from 88.4 percent to 92.9 percent. This latter rise reflects the increasing difficulty in providing the needed growth in capital expenditures to fund the substantial increases in population over this period.

All areas of education are likely to continue to suffer from financial constraints. Higher education, which is sometimes argued to have a greater impact upon the economic development of a country, only developed very slightly during the period 1975–1986: the gross enrolment ratio in higher education increased only marginally over this period—from 4.9 percent to 5.1 percent. This modest increase however, probably reflects in large part the profound reorientation in most areas of Iranian society which followed the overthrow of the Shah. In the years after 1979, for example, women were made to conform to stricter interpretations of Islamic practice, including the covering of their faces, while *mut'a* (a system of temporary marriage) was reintroduced and reinforced, including being taught in schools (Haeri 1990, Hendessi 1991). Men, too, were made to adopt more modest dress, while all bars which served alcohol were summarily closed. As part of this national resurrection of Islamic values, all universities in Iran were closed for a four-year period immediately after the Islamic revolution (1979–1983, a period which also included the first few years of the war with Iraq), in order to review and reorder their purpose and values.

It should be noted that, on this account, there are two areas which seem less well developed, relative to school education levels—higher education, and the "War against Illiteracy." The somewhat slower development of higher education is to be compared with progress within the other levels of education. Equally, the high numbers of illiterates in the country—Iran is one of the twelve countries of the world which have more than ten million illiterates—may lead to the conclusion that a reduction in the share of resources available, in order to respond to the demands of school education, does not seem to be appropriate. Yet, ultimately, the question of levels of educational expenditures, especially in a context of severely limited financial resources, is a matter of overall priorities within that society. Is it more important to strengthen further the existing substantial national efforts to extend literacy throughout Iranian society? How might this compare with the considerable costs, and the benefits, involved in extending the system of higher education, which as argued above is already subject to increasing privatisation?

In brief, it appears that, during the last ten years, due to the rapid expansion of schooling, high rates of increase of the young population, high rates of fertility, and rapid development of urbanization, and despite increasing generalization of primary and secondary education for all social classes, educational quality has fallen. This occurred despite the regular increase of the governmental budget of education, which includes the fact that, for example, the annual education budget in 1990–1991 reached almost 24 percent of the total governmental budget. This figure, which seems extraordinarly high, is made to appear more reasonable when it is recognised that more than 70 percent of the civil service are employed in education. Given that educational personnel form the greatest proportion of the total civil service, education necessarily absorbs the greatest proportion of the state budget. The number of employees (teachers, administrators, and office personnel) has now risen above 1 million, a rise which is a consequence of both demographic growth and the horizontal and vertical growth of educational insitututions and organisations. No other area of society over the last twenty years has experienced such dramatic effects of demographic increase as education. Percentage increases in expenses for the two areas of education, and hygiene and health, of which education consumes the greater part, illustrate this growth. In 1976, the collective total percentage of the state budget from the two areas was 19 percent. This had more than doubled (to 40 percent) by 1986, and had risen further to (43.1 percent) by 1992, thus explaining the apparently high figure, alluded to above, of more than 20 percent of overall government budget's being devoted to education.

Nonetheless, per capita pupil expenditure decreased by nearly one-third in the decade from the early 1980s to the early 1990s. Larger class sizes, lower amounts of space per pupil, double shifts at schools, privatisation of all sectors of education, and higher pupil–teacher ratios are all indexes of lower quality in education; thus, despite the greater availability of education and the quantitative expansion of the education system, the quality of education can be said to have decreased over the period studied. In respect to equality some progress has been shown, with a gradual narrowing of the traditional gap between the genders in terms of participation and retention, yet significant differences remain between the genders and between urban and rural dwellers. The persistence of child labour among rural peasantry and the dispossessed urban poor also prevents gains in equality being extended to some of the neediest groups in society.

In practical terms, then, although Iranian education has been witness to some progress during the past three decades, and although there has been some progress towards democratisation and actualization of educational opportunities, it must nevertheless be concluded that the quantitative expansion of education in the country and the qualitative improvements in education have both been outstripped by a combination of rising demand and, particularly, demographic increase. The perpetuation of such a discrepancy between the pressures for educational expansion, and the desire for qualitative enhancements in education, and equalisation of educational outcomes, are likely to continue to constrain the development of the whole educational system of the country and in some measure to inhibit the equalisation of opportunity in society.

CONCLUSION

Improvements in the quality of education in Iran, as also the equalisation of educational opportunities, are beset by a matrix of problems familiar in the Third World (Gomes 1992). A continuation of past trends would imply a need for the rapid quantitative expansion of education, which would necessitate a higher allocation of resources to most areas of education. It should be noted that, although enrolments are projected to increase substantially over the next few years, expenditures would need to increase at a higher rate. Demographic projections indicate that upper-secondary education—which is more costly than several of the other levels of education—may need to expand at a higher rate. Moreover, any increase in promotion rates or decrease in repetition rates in primary and lower secondary levels of education—both of which are considered to be necessary to achieve universal basic education—would imply a higher increase in upper secondary education, and as a result a higher rate of demand for higher education. This phenomenon—if the transition rate to upper-secondary education is not to decrease—will necessitate rapid increases in educational expenditure levels. A possible consequence is that, if finances are not sufficient to cope with this projected expansion of enrolment, a further lowering of quality in education could ensue.

Thus, as mentioned above, the underdeveloped situation of Iran and the general conditions of the country (despite the existence of major national resources, in particular, fuel), has limited changes, as much as they were desired. The problems of the quality and inequality of education remained similar to other less-developed nations in Asia, Africa, and Latin America. Nevertheless, recent trends may show some progress on this issue, and Iran is attempting to take further steps in its general education.

This similarity of Iran's situation with that of other Third World states is revealed in the quote by Joseph Kotsokoane, former Minister of Education of Lesotho, who once proclaimed:

> What our people need today is basic education such as literacy and vocational training to enable them to know themselves and be open to ideas that will contribute to their personal and collective self improvement. (1976, 76)

For Iran, this challenge remains one of the most insistent and intractable ones for the promotion of national development.

REFERENCES

Ajami, F. (1992) *The Arab Predicament: Arab Political Thought and Practice since 1967.* Cambridge, Cambridge University Press.

Altbach, P., and Kelly, G. (1981) *Education and the Colonial Experience.* New York, Longmans.

Aziz-Zadeh, H. (1989) *Educational Development in the Islamic Republic of Iran: Past , Present, and Future Perspectives* (1971–2001). Paris, International Institute for Educational Planning (IIEP).

Behravan, H. (1991) *Survey on Social and Economic Situation and Job Tendency among the Students of Ferdowsi.* Mashad, University of Mashad.

Carnoy, M. (1974) *Education and Cultural Imperialism.* New York, D. Mackay.

Constitution of Islamic Republic of Iran (1979) (Iranian text). Tehran, Majlis (Parliament).

Dore, R., (ed.) (1976) *The Diploma Disease.* London, Allen and Unwin

Evaluation of Literacy in Iran (1987) Tehran, Iranian Center for Statistic and Census (ICSC).

Freebody, P., and Welch, A. (1993) *Knowledge, Culture and Power: International Perspectives on Literacy as Policy and Practice.* London, Falmer.

General Census of 1976 (1978) Tehran, Iranian Center for Statistics and Census (ISCS) (in Persian).

General Census of 1986 (1988) Tehran, Iranian Center for Statistic and Census (ISCS) (in Persian).

Gomes, C. (1992) "Education, Democracy and Development in Latin America." Paper. *Eighth World Congress of Comparative Education*. Charles University, Prague, July.

Haeri, S. (1990) *Law of Desire: Temporary Marriage in Iran*. London, IB Taurus.

Hasanpour, A. (1993) "The Pen and the Sword." In P. Freebody and A. Welch (eds.), *Knowledge, Culture and Power: International Perspectives on Literacy as Policy and Practice*. London, Falmer.

Hendessi, M. (1991) "Review Article: Law of Desire: Temporary Marriage in Iran." *Feminist Review* 38 (Summer): 71–78.

Kotsokoane, J. (1976) "African Identity and the New Order." *Culture* 3 (4): 76–82.

Lankshear, C., and Lawler, M. (1987) *Literacy, Schooling and Revolution*. Sussex, Falmer.

Le Thanh Khoi (1981) *Education Comparée*. Paris, Armond Collin.

Limage, L. (1993) "Literacy Strategies: A View from the International Literacy Year Secretariat Of Unesco." In P. Freebody and A. Welch (eds.), *Knowledge, Culture and Power: International Perspectives on Literacy as Policy and Practice*. London, Falmer.

Little, A. (1992) "The Diploma Disease in Sri Lanka (1972–1992): The Attenuating Effects of Ethnicity and Political Patronage." Paper. *Eighth World Congress of Comparative Education*. Charles University, Prague, July.

Luke, A. (1988) *Literacy Textbooks and Ideology: Postwar Literacy Instruction and the Mythology of Dick and Jane*. Sussex, Falmer.

Mazrui, A. (1980) *The African Condition*. London, Cambridge University Press.

Mohsenpour, B. (1988) "Philosophy of Education in Post Revolutionary Iran." *Comparative Education Review* 32 (1): 76–86.

Multicultural Australasian Moslem Times. (1994) 17 February.

Reza, N. (1989) "Culture and Development." Paper. International Experts Meeting, "Cultural Sensitisation of Decision-makers in Development," Budapest, November. *Hungarian National Commission for UNESCO*, and Center for Cultural Training and Innovation.

Roshdiah, S. (1983) *Savanehe-Omre* (*The Events of My Age*). Tehran, Nashre Tarikh Iran (in Persian).

Sabbaghian, Z., et al. (1992) "Kindergarten and Primary School Education in Iran." In G. Woodhill, J. Bernhard, and L. Prochner (eds.), *International Handbook of Early Childhood Education*. New York, Garland.

Shorish, M. (1988) "The Islamic Revolution and Education in Iran." *Comparative Education Review* 32 (1): 58–75.

Tavassoli, G. (1972) "Amouzesh-Savad Tawam-Ba-Herfa" (*Work- oriented Literacy in Iran*). Tehran, Institute for Social Study and Research, University of Tehran.

Tavassoli, G. (1987) "Problems of Quantity and Quality of Education in Iran."
    Paper. *Fifth World Congress of Comparative Education*, Rio de Janeiro,
    Brazil, 6–10 July.
UNESCO (1984) *Participer au Developpement*. Paris, UNESCO Office of Sta-
    tistics.
UNESCO (1986) *Annuaire Statistique*. Paris, UNESCO Office of Statistics.
UNESCO (1990) *Compendium of Statistics on Illiteracy*. Paris, UNESCO Office
    of Statistics.
UNESCO (1991) *Statistical Yearbook*. Paris, UNESCO Office of Statistics.
Wallerstein, I. (1978) "Civilization and the Modes of Production." *Theory and
    Society* 5.
Welch, A. (1991) "Knowledge and Legitimation in Comparative Education."
    Comparative Education Review 35 (3): 508–32.
Welch, A., and Freebody, P. (1993) "Introduction: Explanations of the Current
    International 'Literacy Crises.'" In Freebody, P., and Welch, A. *Knowledge,
    Culture and Power: International Perspectives on Literacy as Policy and
    Practice*. London, Falmer.

BIOGRAPHIES

Anthony R. Welch works in the Faculty of Education at the University of Sydney, Australia, and has published widely on international policies and practices in education, as well as nonmethodological issues in comparative research. Much of his current work is devoted to international issues in higher education, and the academic profession. His most recent books include his 1996 *Australian Education: Reform or Crisis?* (published *as Class Culture and the State in Australian Education*, by Peter Lang in 1997), and *Tradition, Modernity and Postmodernity in Comparative Education* (with V. Masemann), published by Kluwer in 1997. He is currently completing a book on the impact of structural adjustment programs on education in Asia, and another book on the academic profession.

Robert F. Arnove works in Comparative Education at the School of Education at Indiana University, USA, and has published widely, including on theory and method of comparative education, the impact of philanthropic agencies on education, issues of neo-liberalism in education, education in Latin America, and comparative literacy campaigns. His latest book, with C.A. Torres, is *Reframing Comparative Education: The Dialectic of the Global and Local.* Pittsburgh, Rowman and Littlefield, 1999.

Ibtisam Abu-Duhou lectures in the Faculty of Education at the University of Melbourne, Australia, and works in the fields of economics of education, and comparative education. She has acted as adviser to the Palestinian Authority on educational matters.

Ronald Price was for many years Senior Lecturer in Comparative Education, School of Education, La Trobe University, Melbourne, Australia. He has published widely on Chinese education, as well as on issues of theory and method, including science education. His first degree was in botany and zoology (London University). He has taught science in England and Bulgaria and English language in China and helped train science teachers in Ghana, and in Melbourne. E-mail address: rfprice @c031.aone.net.au

Irving Epstein is Associate Professor in the Department of Educational Studies at Illinois Wesleyan University. His research interests include the study of Chinese education, children's rights, the education of street children, and comparative theory and methodology. From 1988–1998 he was an associate editor of the *Comparative Education Review*.

Jane Orton is a Senior Lecturer in the Faculty of Education at the University of Melbourne. She co-ordinates studies in modern languages education and runs a professional practicum in Beijing for students in the Faculty. Her research interests are in intercultural communication issues between Australians and Chinese in workplace settings. Recent publications include contributions to both Anthony Milner (ed.), *Australia in Asia. Comparing Cultures.* Melbourne: Oxford University Press, 1996; and *Intercultural Learning in a Short-term Program: Selected papers from the SIETAR 96 Congress*, Munich. Sietar Europa, Munich, 1998.

Anne Hickling-Hudson is a Senior Lecturer in Education and Deputy Director of the Centre for Policy and Leadership Studies in Education at the Queensland University of Technology, Australia. Born and raised in Jamaica, she took degrees in history, education and media in the West Indies, Hong Kong, and Australia. Her academic focus is on cross-cultural and international studies in education, and she is interested in developing a postcolonial framework to inform teaching and research.

Angela Little is Professor of Education (Developing Countries) at the Institute of Education, University of London, and Head of the Education and International Development group. She has undertaken educational research on Sri Lanka for more than twenty years, and is a former President of the British Comparative and International Education Society.

Sheldon G. Weeks is Professor of Education and Head of Graduate Studies in the Faculty of Education at the University of Botswana, Gaborone,

Botswana, and has also taught and researched for many years at the University of Papua New Guinea. He has published widely on issues of development education, including issues of youth, equality of access and provision, women's education, and educational planning

Frank Youngman joined the University of Botswana in 1975. He has been Director of the Institute of Adult Education and Dean of the Faculty of Education and he is currently Head of the Department of Adult Education. He has published extensively on many aspects of adult education, including the books *Adult Education and Socialist Pedagogy* (Croom Helm, 1986); with S. Seisa, *Education for All in Botswana* (Macmillan, 1993); and with P. Wangoola, *Towards a Transformative Political Economy of Adult Education* (Northern Illinois University, 1996). He was a member of the National Commission on Education which reviewed Botswana's educational system in 1992–93.

Gholam Abbas Tavassoli is a member of the Faculty of Social Sciences at the University of Tehran, Tehran, Iran. **Houshyar Ghahremanlou Kheirollah** is Associate Professor in the Department of Mathematics and Applied Statistics at the University of Oroumieh, Ourimieh, Iran, and is currently finalising his Ph.D at the University of Sydney. **Anthony Welch** is listed above.

Index

REFERENCE BOOKS IN INTERNATIONAL EDUCATION

EDWARD R. BEAUCHAMP, Series Editor